CRIME, JUSTICE AND COVID-19

Edited by
Christopher Kay and Stephen Case

BRISTOL
UNIVERSITY
PRESS

First published in Great Britain in 2024 by

Policy Press, an imprint of
Bristol University Press
University of Bristol
1-9 Old Park Hill
Bristol
BS2 8BB
UK
t: +44 (0)117 374 6645
e: bup-info@bristol.ac.uk

Details of international sales and distribution partners are available at
policy.bristoluniversitypress.co.uk

© Bristol University Press 2024

British Library Cataloguing in Publication Data
A catalogue record for this book is available from the British Library

ISBN 978-1-4473-6315-6 hardcover
ISBN 978-1-4473-6316-3 paperback
ISBN 978-1-4473-6317-0 ePub
ISBN 978-1-4473-6318-7 ePdf

The right of Christopher Kay and Stephen Case to be identified as editors of this work has been asserted by them in accordance with the Copyright, Designs and Patents Act 1988.

All rights reserved: no part of this publication may be reproduced, stored in a retrieval system, or transmitted in any form or by any means, electronic, mechanical, photocopying, recording, or otherwise without the prior permission of Bristol University Press.

Every reasonable effort has been made to obtain permission to reproduce copyrighted material. If, however, anyone knows of an oversight, please contact the publisher.

The statements and opinions contained within this publication are solely those of the editors and contributors and not of the University of Bristol or Bristol University Press. The University of Bristol and Bristol University Press disclaim responsibility for any injury to persons or property resulting from any material published in this publication.

Bristol University Press and Policy Press work to counter discrimination on
grounds of gender, race, disability, age and sexuality.

Cover design: Hayes Design and Advertising
Front cover image: freepik/rawpixel-com

Contents

List of Figures and Tables v
Notes on Contributors vii

1   Introduction: Understanding and Responding to Pandemics   1
    in Criminal Justice
    Christopher Kay and Stephen Case

PART I COVID-19 and the Criminal Justice System   9
2   Emergence and Maturity in Policing COVID-19   11
    Peter Kawalek, John Coxhead and Lisa Jackson
3   Reimagining the Open Court in the Time of   31
    Pandemic: Towards 'Portal Justice' and 'Broadcast Justice'
    Sarah Moore
4   COVID-19 and Community Sanctions   50
    Sam Ainslie, Andrew Fowler, Jake Phillips and Chalen Westaby
5   COVID-19 in Custody: Responding to Pandemics in   76
    Prisons in England and Wales
    Christopher Kay
6   Youth Justice and COVID-19: Courts, Community   107
    and Custody
    Kathy Hampson and Stephen Case

PART II Crime, Justice and COVID-19: Critical Issues   135
7   Racism, Policing and the Pandemic   137
    Scarlet Harris, Remi Joseph-Salisbury, Patrick Williams
    and Lisa White
8   Crisis within a Crisis: Sex Workers, Emergency Response 150
    and Creative Service Provision
    Rachel Fowler, Abbie Haines and Teela Sanders
9   COVID-19 and Drug Trends   166
    Mark Monaghan and Ian Hamilton
10 Professional Qualification in Probation and COVID-19   190
    Andrew Fowler, Laura Martin, Aileen Watson and Tom Brown

PART III	**The View from the Inside**	**217**
11	The Box Project at HMP Parc *Introduction by Phil Forder*	219
12	Write Inside Sessions at HMP Manchester *Introduction by Maureen Carnighan*	242
13	Conclusion: The Lessons – Recovery and Pandemic Preparedness *Christopher Kay and Stephen Case*	254
Index		264

List of Figures and Tables

Figures

5.1	Shipping containers used as temporary prison accommodation	87
9.1	Percentage of adults aged 16 to 59 and 16 to 24 reporting use of any drug in the last year and last month, 1995 to 2020	170
9.2	Percentage of adults aged 16 to 59 and 16 to 24 reporting use of any drug in the last year, by frequency of use, 2020	171
9.3	Percentage reporting use of any drug in the last year, by age group, 1995 to 2020	174
11.1	A box of art supplies	220
11.2	Box 1, outside	221
11.3	Box 2, outside and inside	222
11.4	Box 3, outside	223
11.5	Box 4, outside	224
11.6	Box 5, outside	225
11.7	Box 6, outside	226
11.8a	Box 7, inside	227
11.8b	Box 7, outside	228
11.9	Box 8, outside	228
11.10	Box 9, outside	229
11.11	Box 10, outside	229
11.12	Box 11, outside	230
11.13	Box 12, inside lid	230
11.14a	Box 13, letter	231
11.14b	Box 13, outside	232
11.14c	Box 13, inside	233
11.15a	Box 14, outside	233
11.15b	Box 14, inside	234
11.15c	Box 14, inside lid	234
11.16	Box 15, outside	235
11.17a	Box 16, outside	235
11.17b	Box 16, letter	236
11.18a	Box 17, outside	236

11.18b	Box 17, letter	237
11.19a	Box 18, outside	237
11.19b	Box 18, inside	238
11.19c	Box 18, inside lid	239
11.19d	Box 18, manual	239
11.20	Box 19, outside	240
11.21a	Box 20, inside lid	241
11.21b	Box 20, inside	241

Tables

5.1	Cohorting units	84
6.1	The four tenets of Child First justice	110

Note on Chapter 11 figures

To view colour versions of the figures in Chapter 11, please visit https://policy.bristoluniversitypress.co.uk/crime-justice-and-covid-19.

Notes on Contributors

Sam Ainslie is Senior Lecturer in criminology at Sheffield Hallam University. She is part of the Community Justice Learning Team and teaches undergraduate criminology and on the Professional Qualification in Probation. She joined Sheffield Hallam University in 2019, having previously worked as a probation practitioner and manager for 17 years. Her research interests relate to desistance, probation practice and probation training. She is currently involved with other members of the Department of Law and Criminology in research relating to professional curiosity, emotional labour and burnout within the context of probation practice. She is also working towards the Professional Doctorate in Education. Her research relates to pedagogical approaches to enhancing critically reflective practice in probation practitioners.

Tom Brown is Senior Lecturer in community justice at Sheffield Hallam University. He spent ten years as an operational probation officer in Sheffield, specializing in work with the 'Prolific and Priority Offending' team. He also worked with individuals on drug rehabilitation requirements of community orders. For his last five years in probation, he was a practice tutor assessor, mentoring and assessing probation trainees on the vocational aspect of the Professional Qualification in Probation (PQiP). His research interests are diverse and growing, with work in 'Probation in Objects', probation in the pandemic, barriers to probation as a career, and promotion of wider access to probation services.

Maureen Carnighan is the distance learning coordinator for HMP Manchester. She worked alongside colleagues at MK College and the Prisoners' Education Trust to produce the book *Write Inside at HMP Manchester*.

Stephen Case is Professor of criminology at Loughborough University. Previously an associate professor and director of undergraduate studies at Swansea University, his primary research interests are youth justice, youth crime prevention and social justice, particularly the promotion of positive, children first ways of working with children embroiled in the youth justice system. He is a member of the Youth Justice Board's Academic Advisory Panel and sits on the steering group of The Association of Panel Members.

John Coxhead is a British policing educationalist and a professor of policing innovation and learning at Loughborough University and an honorary professor of practice at Keele University. He is also twice winner of the Queen's Award for Innovation in Policing Learning and Development. His is currently the regional research partnerships manager for the East Midlands Policing Academic Collaboration, covering forces in Derbyshire, Nottinghamshire, Lincolnshire, Leicestershire, Northamptonshire, the East Midlands Special Operations Unit, and the universities of Loughborough, Nottingham, Leicester, Nottingham Trent, Lincoln, Derby, De Montfort and Northampton.

Phil Forder is the executive coach and mentor for the Ruskin Mill Trust. Prior to this, he served for 20 years as a community engagement manager at HMP Parc. In 2021, Phil was named a Stonewall Cymru role model.

Andrew Fowler is Senior Lecturer in criminology at Sheffield Hallam University. Prior to working in probation, he worked in an educational charity, teaching adults, during which time he completed a Postgraduate Certificate in Education. In probation, he started as an employment, training and education advisor, moving into group programmes and then qualifying as a probation officer. This involved completing the Diploma in Probation Studies, which included a community justice degree at Sheffield Hallam University. He qualified as a probation officer working in the magistrates' court and Crown Court, community offices and prisons. His specialist areas of interest are emotional labour, community sentences and teaching in higher education.

Rachel Fowler is a service manager/specialist independent domestic sexual violence advisor at Changing Lives, working in the Red Umbrella Project, which supports people involved in sex work, selling sex and/or experiencing sexual exploitation to combat instances of violence and crimes against them and bring perpetrators to justice.

Abbie Haines is a specialist women's outreach worker and independent sexual violence advisor at The Magdalene Project. The Magdalene Project, founded in 1999, is a Christian charity offering an independent counselling service covering East Lancashire. It specializes in sexual trauma and abuse but covers many other areas of need. It works with all ages, genders, ethnicities, religions and social backgrounds, irrespective of their ability to pay.

Ian Hamilton is Honorary Fellow (Associate Professor) in addiction at the Department of Health Sciences, University of York. Prior to joining the university in 2004, Ian provided clinical help to people who have problems with drugs and mental health. Ian engages with a range of media outlets, providing expert commentary on topical news stories related to drugs and alcohol as well as working with producers on investigative stories and documentaries. He writes a weekly column for *The Independent* and contributes regularly to *The British Medical Journal* and *The Conversation*.

Kathy Hampson is Lecturer in criminology at Aberystwyth University. Her research focuses on children and young people who offend, youth justice and Child First justice. She is currently researching the use of youth custody in Wales and children's perceptions of their capacity for meaningful collaboration in youth justice decision-making processes and understandings of effectiveness.

Scarlet Harris is Postdoctoral Fellow in sociology at the University of Manchester and a teaching associate at the University of Cambridge. She received her BA in Sociology from the University of Edinburgh and her MRes and PhD in Sociology from the University of Glasgow. Dr Harris has held various research posts at the University of Manchester, including within the Centre on the Dynamics of Ethnicity. She is currently writing a book based on her doctoral research (to be titled *Islamophobia, Anti-racism and the British Left*), which will be published by Manchester University Press.

Lisa Jackson is Professor of risk and reliability at Loughborough University. Her main interests lie in reliability of engineering systems, system safety and enhanced service provision. She is currently undertaking research on the development and application of reliability methods for enhanced reliability performance, fault diagnostics and prognosis, and safety provision. Lisa has worked with a number of different companies across a variety of sectors, including the Ministry of Defence, Rolls-Royce, BAE Systems, Urenco, Intelligent Energy and Leicestershire Police.

Remi Joseph-Salisbury is Presidential Fellow in ethnicity and inequalities at the University of Manchester, with particular interests in racism and antiracism in the contexts of education and policing. He is co-author of *Anti-Racist Scholar-Activism* (2021). He won the British Sociological Association's Philip Abrams Memorial Prize in 2019.

Peter Kawalek is Professor of information management and director of the Centre for Information Management at Loughborough University. He is interested by the digital economy and the effects of digitization on business and then society. He is developing a research stream related to the attention economy, building on prior work in media and social media. This accompanies his existing work on information and communications technology and its large-scale and long-term effects on organizations. Peter has led or co-investigated research projects to a value of around £2 million, via sources including the Engineering and Physical Sciences Research Council, UK central government and local councils. He is the author of numerous academic papers related to information systems, social media, organizational change and technological impact on strategy.

Christopher Kay is Senior Lecturer in criminology at Loughborough University. His research focuses on how people with convictions experience criminal justice and how this experience shapes their desistance and rehabilitation efforts on release. He has recently started focusing on the role of sport and physical activity in supporting early desistance efforts for people with convictions. He sits on His Majesty's Prison and Probation Service's Effective Practice Sports Panel.

Laura Martin is Senior Lecturer in law and criminology at Sheffield Hallam University. Laura worked in the Probation Service for 14 years in a variety of roles, including accredited programmes tutor, treatment manager, probation officer and senior probation officer. During the latter stages of her probation career, she also began to teach on the Probation Qualification Framework, on a variety of modules. She left the Probation Service in January 2016 and spent a short time teaching on a foundation degree in criminology in the University Centre at Blackburn College before joining Sheffield Hallam University in September 2016.

Mark Monaghan is Reader in criminology at Loughborough University. The issue of illicit drugs has been central to Mark's ongoing research programme and has served as an introduction into various areas of interest. Influenced by realist methodology, his research straddles the disciplines of criminology, social policy, public policy, sociology and political science. It contains three main strands: the impact of recent welfare reform for drug users as well as changing patterns of drug consumption and treatment responses; the scientific and political battles in drug policy making in the United Kingdom, with a particular focus on the use of evidence and expertise in policy; and the links between the international drug trade and elite and state criminality.

Sarah Moore is Senior Lecturer in sociology at the University of Bath. Her research interests range across the sociology of crime and justice and the sociology of health, with a particular interest in how blame, responsibility and accountability work. Her current research falls into three categories – the place and role of the public in the courtroom and, in twenty-first-century public policy more broadly, gender and risk, and the effects of the retrenchment of legal aid.

Jake Phillips is Reader in criminology at Sheffield Hallam University. He has worked in various roles in the criminal justice system. These roles have all involved working with offenders in the community and have, at different times, focused on employment, training and education; drug-using offenders; and housing support. His research centres on the intersection of policy and practice in the field of probation and community sanctions. He is currently engaged in research on emotional labour in probation; the impact of inspection on probation; and the deaths of offenders in the community, with a focus on self-inflicted deaths and access to justice.

Teela Sanders is Professor in criminology at the University of Leicester. Her research sits on the borders of criminology and sociology, exploring the interrelationship between sexuality and socio-legal structures. The COVID-19 outbreak and the policies put into place to manage it are creating severe, life-threatening challenges for marginalized communities around the world. Professor Sanders is exploring the impact of the virus and its management on female sex workers in Kenya. She is researching these changes and developing ways to deliver healthcare to sex workers during the restrictions. She is exploring new and enhanced technological ways to deliver these services while adhering to COVID-19 restrictions.

Aileen Watson is Senior Lecturer in criminology at Sheffield Hallam University.

Chalen Westaby is Senior Lecturer in law at Sheffield Hallam University. Her current research centres on the empirical analysis of aspects of emotional labour. She has completed a study of immigration solicitors and the production of emotional labour in their everyday work. More recently, she received funding from the Legal Education Research Network to complete a study of the impact of law clinics on law students' perceptions of emotional labour.

Lisa White is Senior Lecturer in criminology at Liverpool John Moores University. Her current research is concerned with deaths in detention and custody, while previous work has explored the motivation, significance and consequences of narrating state torture in relation to Northern Ireland. She is particularly interested in the lived impact of official discourse around state violence and how this is experienced by the most marginalized.

Patrick Williams is Senior Lecturer in criminology at Manchester Metropolitan University. He undertakes research and publishes in the area of 'race' and ethnicity, with a particular focus on racial disparity, disproportionality and differential treatment within the criminal justice system. Having previously worked as a research and evaluation officer for the Greater Manchester Probation Trust, he continues to advise and support the development of interventions premised on the principles of empowerment for a number of local and regional statutory and voluntary and community sector organizations. In conjunction with colleagues in the Policy Evaluation and Research Unit at Manchester Metropolitan University, he was involved in the evaluation of short-term prisoner resettlement projects delivered by HMP Manchester and HMP Preston.

1

Introduction: Understanding and Responding to Pandemics in Criminal Justice

Christopher Kay and Stephen Case

On 31 December 2019, an outbreak of an unknown respiratory disease, later known to be coronavirus disease 19 (COVID-19), caused by severe acute respiratory syndrome coronavirus 2 (SARS-CoV-2) was reported in Wuhan, China. The disease rapidly spread through China and, eventually, the rest of the world, resulting in the World Health Organization (WHO) characterizing COVID-19 as a pandemic on 11 March 2020 (WHO, 2020a). At the time of writing, some two years after the initial cases of COVID-19 were reported in Wuhan, there have been 526 million reported cases and nearly 6.2 million deaths worldwide.

The disease appears to be transmitted through 'droplets and fomites during close unprotected contact' between infected and uninfected individuals (WHO, 2020b: 8). Research shows that the severity of symptoms among COVID-19 patients can be quite broad, 'encompassing asymptomatic infection, mild upper respiratory tract illness, and severe viral pneumonia with respiratory failure' which can prove fatal (Zhou et al, 2020: 1054). Research also shows that severity of disease is dependent on such things as the presence of pre-existing health conditions (Guan et al, 2020) and patient age (Coker, 2020) as well as location and intensity of transmission (WHO, 2020b).

The first cases of COVID-19 in the United Kingdom (UK) were reported on 29 January 2020. In March 2020, in response to the threat posed by the virus, the UK government introduced a range of measures to reduce incidents of community transmission. Central to these recommendations were the implementation of stringent social distancing measures (involving the closure of schools, recommendations to avoid nonessential travel and the suspension of all public events) along with recommendations for anyone with at least one of two common symptoms of COVID-19 (a persistent cough or a fever) to self-isolate for a minimum of seven days. Self-isolation was also recommended for those most at risk of developing severe disease.

While life as most of us knew it paused, or even ground to a halt, for a range of public services it became more a case of business as *unusual*, and the criminal justice system in England and Wales was no exception. 'Crimes continued to be committed, reported and investigated; cases were charged and progressed; detainees remained in the adult and youth secure estates; and those under the care of youth offending and probation services remained so' (Criminal Justice Joint Inspection, 2021: 5).

In order to remain operational, the system as a whole had to respond rapidly after the emergence of COVID-19. Provisions for digital working needed to be developed, and ever-changing COVID-19 policies were introduced and subsequently implemented alongside significant testing infrastructures which could be utilized to reduce transmission of the virus across the system. This was happening against a backdrop of considerable uncertainty 'in which predictions of infection levels among staff were frequently high, and changes to lockdown restrictions swift and often with little notice' (Criminal Justice Joint Inspection, 2021: 8).

The pandemic also emerged at a time of considerable political and social unrest in England and Wales. There were a number of high-profile significant protests in the UK in 2020 in the form of the Black Lives Matter movement's response to police violence and the public vigil after the murder of Sarah Everard by police officer Wayne Couzens, as well as the Extinction Rebellion protests, anti-'lockdown' protests and the fallout from the UK's withdrawal from the European Union. At the same time, increased restrictions were placed on the right to protest under the Police, Crime, Sentencing and Courts Bill 2021, which itself resulted in further protests. Such unrest was taking place at a time when the criminal justice system was already under considerable pressure. A prolonged period of budget cuts, staff shortages and failed privatization attempts meant that even before the pandemic, the system lacked the resilience required to deal with the pressures it was facing. While the emergence of COVID-19 was bound to introduce new problems of its own, it was also extremely likely this would exacerbate those that already existed within the system. All of these factors must be remembered when attempting to understand the impact of the pandemic on issues of crime and justice.

The need for a holistic approach

The impact of the pandemic on the justice system (and its response to it) was swift. The police, criminal courts, prison service, probation service and youth justice system were all required to respond to a range of concerns arising throughout the pandemic, and, understandably, each agency focused on its own needs in its own time. Also, as one might imagine, a hive of research activity and academic publishing was undertaken with the aim of understanding the initial impact of the pandemic on the justice system and the experience of criminal justice for practitioners and service users alike (Kay, 2020; Godfrey et al, 2021; Phillips et al, 2021; Hampson et al, 2022). Much of this work is highly commendable and provided a rapid and detailed insight into issues around crime and justice during the pandemic. Yet while the knowledge gained during this early period was considerable, there were areas that remained underexplored. One such area was the broad issue of the impact of the pandemic on the criminal justice system in England and Wales *as a whole*. This is understandable given the necessary preoccupation of each organization with their own responsibilities during this time, even within the context of academic research. We argue here, however, that there is just as much learning to be taken from the impact of the pandemic on connections *between* these agencies as there is from the impact on these agencies separately, both in relation to the realities of delivering (and experiencing) criminal justice during the COVID-19 pandemic itself and the long-term planning around recovery and future pandemic preparedness. Adopting a holistic approach allows for a more detailed exploration of the ways in which the COVID-19 pandemic impacted not just the *individual* criminal justice agencies but also the system *as a whole*. It also allows for an investigation of the ways these interconnections were utilized effectively while also highlighting areas for concern.

Perhaps an analogy will help to elucidate. Let's perceive the criminal justice system as a body of water formed of all of its component agencies (police, criminal courts, prison system, probation service, youth justice service and so on), turbulent yet part of a connected whole. If a stone is dropped into that body of water at any location, it sends out ripples across the remainder of that body, with more severe impact in some places than in others. In order to understand the full impact of the stone dropping, we need to examine not just where it landed, but how far (and in what direction and shape) the ripples went. In turn, our preparation for the next stone will be based on the knowledge we gained from the examination of the first one. COVID-19, to continue this analogy, could perhaps be thought of as multiple stones, sending multiple ripples across our body of water, which was already shallow owing to the number of previous stones lying at the bottom.

Examples are found in the current collection: The introduction of COVID-19 exacerbated an existing backlog of cases going through the criminal courts (see Chapter 3). As a result of this, the prison system was able to reduce its population, allowing for single cell occupancy and increased social distancing across the prison estate (see Chapter 5). While this helped to reduce transmission of the virus in the immediate sense, it also extended the length of time individuals would spend on remand, disproportionately impacting on residents from minority ethnic communities. The initial proposal for a prisoner early release scheme relied on the additional arm of community supervision by the Probation Service, but this would have increased the burden on this already underfunded and overstretched agency (see Chapter 4). It is only by observing the impact of the COVID-19 pandemic at a system level that we can see how far the ripples of impact travel. A more holistic approach, therefore, could also be utilized to develop pandemic recovery and preparedness strategies to reduce, or at least minimize, the long-term impact of pandemics in the future.

Before we begin to outline what such an approach looks like, it is important to note that we are not suggesting this approach should apply to the study of criminal justice universally. Indeed, there are significant debates which suggest that certain aspects of criminal justice should be annexed from this umbrella altogether, particularly in the field of youth justice, where it is argued that more emphasis should be placed on seeing young people as 'children first' (see Case, 2021) and that we should avoid the assumption that children who offend possess levels of cognitive, moral and emotional development equivalent to adults in the criminal justice system. Consequently, children (aged 10–17 years) who offend should be treated as a 'child first', with increasing emphasis placed on promoting their positive identity development and diversion from the criminogenic and iatrogenic processes of the formal youth justice system (Youth Justice Board, 2021).

When examining the impact of the COVID-19 pandemic, and recovery from it, on issues of crime and justice, it is suggested that a holistic approach which sees the connections between criminal justice agencies would allow for a more detailed exploration. It is from this position that the present collection takes its departure.

Crime, justice and COVID-19: an overview

In order to demonstrate the need to assess the impact of the pandemic across the system as a whole, and in line with the call for a more holistic understanding of criminal justice whereby a change in one component of a system requires an understanding of the impact of this change across the entire system, this collection is divided into three parts.

Part I of the collection considers the individual agencies involved in the delivery of criminal justice. In Chapter 2, Kawalek, Coxhead and Jackson discuss the policing response to the pandemic. Utilizing a case study from a single police force in England and Wales, the authors discuss the themes of 'emergence', which is understood as the manifestation of new levels of complexity in a dynamic situation, and 'maturity', or the capacity for systematic responses that are appropriate and effective, in order to understand how this force responded to the pressures of the pandemic on the personal and professional lives of frontline police staff.

Acceleration, as a result of the pandemic, of the development of a digital infrastructure to facilitate online management of cases and virtual hearings is discussed by Moore in Chapter 3. With roughly half of court buildings in England and Wales closed during the peak of the pandemic, and face-to-face hearings reserved for priority cases and remote hearings held wherever possible, the chapter aims to answer a number of questions: How have emergency court measures dealt with the demands of visibility and timeliness? What lessons might we draw concerning the opportunities and challenges of remote hearings? And what might post-pandemic justice look like in the criminal court? Moore also identifies distinctive forms of emerging justice that are taking the place of the open court: 'portal justice' and 'broadcast justice'.

In Chapter 4, Ainslie, Fowler, Phillips and Westaby explore how probation providers in England and Wales adapted to the pandemic, considering what this meant for providers, probation staff and people on probation. Drawing on primary evidence collected during the pandemic and on criminal justice policy, the chapter considers how the pandemic shaped the way the service met official aims and objectives and the impact on people under probation supervision and staff. The chapter evidences positive developments as well as tensions (some previously hidden) being exposed in ways that starkly illustrate the pressures service users and staff have been facing for many years.

Chapter 5 provides a detailed discussion of the policies and practices introduced to try and reduce the transmission of COVID-19 across the prison estate in England and Wales. In the chapter, Kay examines epidemiological evidence along with design and implementation of prison COVID-19 policy, the Exceptional Regime Management Plan, population management and cohorting strategies, and the imposition of the COVID-19 National Framework for Prison Regimes and Services, and explores the implications of stringent public health initiatives within a prison environment. Kay also provides a discussion of the knock-on effects of such initiatives for prison life, for both staff and residents. The chapter examines the ways prison COVID-19 policy was (and, in some cases, was not) used, and it makes suggestions regarding tensions between public health-focused prison policy and populist politics. It concludes with recommendations for how the prison service can recover from the COVID-19 pandemic and better deal with any future pandemics.

The impact of the pandemic on engagement in youth justice (both practitioners and system engagement with children and vice versa) is discussed in Chapter 6 through the dual lenses of children's rights and Child First as the guiding principle for a youth justice system which (at least in rhetoric) sees children as children rather than offenders. In this chapter, Hampson and Case argue that this engagement has been adversely affected (pains) throughout all levels of involvement from prevention work to custody and resettlement, damaging support to vulnerable children, foregrounding them as offenders and eroding their vital rights as children. It also considers, however, where there have been gains through rapidly developing practice and innovation. The chapter utilizes an examination of policy and legislative changes affecting youth justice in England and Wales, inspections of practice which took place at various stages of the pandemic lockdowns, and informal conversations held with youth justice practitioners and managers to gain insight into how this was being felt at the coalface when working with justice-involved children.

Part II of the collection draws on a range of critical issues across the themes of crime and justice, drawing from the perspectives of those working in criminal justice and those subject to it. Chapter 7 looks at the theme of racism and policing in the pandemic. In this chapter, Harris, Joseph-Salisbury, Williams and White utilize the accounts of research participants to offer insight into the ways in which policing in the pandemic has been experienced by those most subject to it. It addresses how lockdown conditions, in combination with new police powers, built on and further enabled long-standing patterns of racialized policing, before moving on to consider police contact amid the dangers of virus transmission and the associated trauma arising from such encounters. Finally, the chapter highlights how those subject to policing navigate and manage police encounters in an attempt to mitigate the risk of police violence and criminalization.

Chapter 8 draws on research commentary, practitioner engagement and lived experience of the authors to reflect on the pressing issues for sex workers during the crisis of COVID-19 in 2020–21. In this chapter, Fowler, Haines and Sanders chart the effects of lockdown for a population already marginalized through working in the informal economy, which is partly criminalized and therefore cut off from the safety net of government social protection programmes. They highlight how experiences of social isolation and marginalization have compounded stigma and associated discriminations against sex workers. At the same time, support services were faced with changing the nature of their business with immediate effect as they became frontline emergency services, violence intervention workers, housing workers and the first point of contact for many people living in complete isolation with no food or money. The authors review the immediate experiences of the lockdown, how 'doing sex work' has been affected and how service provision has used creative ways to respond to those in crisis.

In Chapter 9, Monaghan and Hamilton explore the impact of COVID-19 on drug trends and drug markets in the UK. First, they consider the impact of the pandemic on supply, focusing on changes in drug availability, before moving on to consider how drug distribution has been impacted by the responses to the pandemic (as well as specific responses to the drug issue).

Next, it examines the impact of the pandemic on alcohol, noting some overlaps with the issues around other drugs. The chapter also includes a consideration of the impact of the pandemic on drug harms.

The last chapter in this part, Chapter 10, examines the experience of students on the Professional Qualification in Probation (PQiP) during the COVID-19 pandemic. While the impact of the pandemic on probation has been documented by the House of Commons Justice Committee (2020) in their report *Coronavirus (COVID-19): The impact on probation systems*, there was no mention of PQiP students in the report. Fowler, Martin, Watson and Brown address this omission by drawing on empirical data collected from students in a range of PQiP cohorts at various stages of the qualification when the pandemic occurred. The chapter offers a range of reflections on the implications and nature of probation education moving forward.

Part III takes a different approach to that of the first two. The aim of this part, titled 'The View from the Inside', is to provide a platform for those who were subject to incarceration during the early stages of the pandemic – those who experienced the first and second lockdowns from behind the door of a prison cell. It does so by presenting the artistic creations from residents who took part in arts-based interventions in two prisons in England and Wales during the first two lockdowns. These capture a moment in time, reflecting life on the inside. Chapter 11 highlights work produced by 19 residents involved in the Box Project at HMP Parc, and has an introduction by Phil Forder, who was a key facilitator in the project. Chapter 12 includes creative writing (letters and poems) by five residents of HMP Manchester who were involved in the Write Inside Sessions, along with a foreword by Maureen Carnighan, who ran the project. The work published in this chapter is provided without academic commentary or comment. It is the intention that the work stands for itself, reflecting the experience of incarceration during the pandemic without being diluted by external influence or input. The collection concludes in Chapter 13 with a summary of the key lessons learnt from these contributions alongside some policy recommendations around future pandemic preparedness

This collection pieces together an understanding of the ways COVID-19 shaped both the function and experience of criminal justice during the pandemic and offers lessons we can take from COVID-19 into any future pandemics. But perhaps more important, it demonstrates why successful pandemic preparation and recovery must be based on a holistic understanding of criminal justice, recognizing that the system as a whole is more than just the sum of its parts.

References

Case, S. (2021) *Youth Justice: A Critical Introduction* (2nd edn), London: Routledge.

Coker, R. (2020) *Expert Report: Covid-19 and Prisons in England and Wales*, Howard League for Penal Reform, [online] Available from: https://howardleague.org/wp-content/uploads/2020/04/2020_04_01_COKER_Report_HL_PRT.pdf

Criminal Justice Joint Inspection (2021) *Impact of the Pandemic on the Criminal Justice System: A Joint View of the Criminal Justice Chief Inspectors on the Criminal Justice System's Response to Covid-19*, [online] Available from: www.justiceinspectorates.gov.uk/hmicfrs/wp-content/uploads/2021-01-13-State-of-nation.pdf

Godfrey, B., Richardson, J.C. and Walklate, S. (2021) 'The crisis in the courts: before and beyond Covid', *The British Journal of Criminology*, 62(4): 1036–53.

Guan, W., Ni, Z., Hu, Y., Liang, W., Ou, C., and He, J., et al (2020) 'Clinical characteristics of coronavirus disease 2019 in China', *The New England Journal of Medicine*, 382: 1708–20.

Hampson, K., Case, S. and Little, R. (2022) 'The pains and gains of COVID-19 –challenges to Child First justice in the pandemic', *Youth Justice*. doi: 10.1177/14732254221075209.

House of Commons Justice Committee (2020) *Coronavirus (COVID-19): The Impact on Probation Systems*, Third Report of Session 2019–21, HC 461, [online] Available from: https://committees.parliament.uk/publications/1944/documents/18919/default/

Kay, C. (2020) 'COVID-19 in custody: responding to pandemics in prisons in England and Wales', *British Journal of Community Justice*, [online] Available from: https://mmuperu.co.uk/bjcj/articles/covid-19-in-custody-responding-to-pandemics-in-prisons-in-england-and-wales/

Phillips, J., Westaby, C., Ainslie, S. and Fowler, A. (2021) '"I don't like this job in my front room": practising probation in the COVID-19 pandemic', *Probation Journal*, 68(4): 426–43.

WHO (World Health Organization) (2020a) 'Coronavirus disease (COVID-19) pandemic', *World Health Organization*, [online] Available from: https://www.who.int/europe/emergencies/situations/covid-19

WHO (2020b) *Report of the WHO-China Joint Mission on Coronavirus Disease 2019 (COVID-19)*, [online] Available from: www.who.int/docs/default-source/coronaviruse/who-china-joint-mission-on-covid-19-final-report.pdf

Youth Justice Board (2021) *Youth Justice Board for England and Wales: Strategic Plan 2021–2024*, London: YJB.

Zhou, F., Yu, T., Du, R., Fan, G., Liu, Y., Liu, Z., Xiang, J. et al (2020) 'Clinical course and risk factors for mortality of adult inpatients with COVID-19 in Wuhan, China: a retrospective cohort study', *The Lancet*, 395(10229): 1054–62.

PART I

COVID-19 and the Criminal Justice System

2

Emergence and Maturity in Policing COVID-19

Peter Kawalek, John Coxhead and Lisa Jackson

Introduction

The early decades of the 21st century have provided many dramatic examples of the police's role in managing the emergent risks of society. This drama of policing is more evident today, perhaps because of the prevalence of crime but certainly because of the pervasiveness of social media. Through this recent form of media, people become acquainted with the day-to-day risks of police work as officers attend to street incidents, assaults, car crashes and the like. Common incidents such as these are captured on the smartphone cameras of passers-by and posted to global platforms. Through this process, in some rudimentary way, the public becomes increasingly well versed in the difficulties and decisions that confront every frontline police worker. Alongside day-to-day incidents, there are also less common but history-making traumas of flood, fire and terrorism. Again, the smartphone camera is usually in the vicinity of the ordeal and so the public quickly come to witness the diverse and difficult decisions that police officers must make in the face of some emergent actuality that they cannot yet comprehend.

At its front line, the police service is a kind of risk management service, whether working in response mode to some dangerous event or proactively urging caution on populations of drivers, clubbers, drug users, gangs or some other segment. Society has its activities, these activities carry risks, and when these risks threaten to overwhelm, the police are called to action.

That the police act as a kind of risk response and management service is not a new idea. Arguably, policing is society's public service of last resort. Risk is intrinsic to police work. The types of risk encountered when attending incidents are very diverse. Consider anew undertaking a routine traffic stop, marshalling cars through a busy junction, finding a lost dementia sufferer, taking care of children after an incident of domestic violence, attending to an ill person on the street or giving chase to criminals in a car. Such situations are dealt with using special knowledge, special training and bespoke risk management procedures.

Yet not all risks are known and can be foreknown. Nor can everything about a known risk be prepared for in advance. It is in the character of work on the front line that new situations will unfold. There is always an element of the unpredictable. This can be explained in theoretical terms through the concept of 'emergence' (Checkland, 1994). This term is used to describe outcomes of a system that are characterized by different properties and engender a new level of concern. Emergence, then, is not 'outcome' nor 'unintended outcome'. It is a new level of complexity possessing different qualitative properties. In policing, it is likely to be a visceral encounter, perhaps requiring a shift in the level and nature of concern. Where the system of concern is highly dynamic, emergence might seem spontaneous, and it might be highly dangerous.

The early decades of the 21st century have witnessed sharp shocks from climate change and terrorism. The global COVID-19 pandemic brought another shock in 2019. The scientific community knows a great amount about viruses. Pandemics are foreseen problems. Yet, no doubt, for every police unit in the world, this global pandemic has been a test of its preparation, methods, resources and know-how. It has been a test of the ability of police to deal with emergence. The case presented here is of a single force in the United Kingdom (UK) and its responses during the pandemic. With society ushered into a state of lockdown and isolation, the arena for policing changed very profoundly. As one officer put it:

'999 calls dropped massively ... But priority calls went up.'

This chapter reviews the issues presented by this force through an inductive, grounded theory study incorporating interviews. In order to develop a theoretical account that is of value for future learning and practical preparation, the idea of emergence is developed alongside a second concept, 'maturity'. While emergence can be understood in terms of the manifestation of new levels of complexity in a dynamic situation, maturity can be understood as the capacity for systematic responses that are appropriate and effective. A highly mature organization is able to deploy a greater range of systematic responses towards the solution or containment of some risk. A less mature organization relies more immediately and more often on the heroic actions and in situ improvisation of its staff, in this case police frontline workers. The concepts of emergence and maturity, therefore, serve as counterpoints. Emergence threatens to overwhelm; maturity seeks to contain.

Maturity

Typically, maturity models describe progress between organizational forms that rely on chaotic, ad hoc and heroic action (low maturity) through to those that that are systematic, coordinated and learning focused (high maturity). Different variants of these maturity models are applied to different problems and sectors. Each contains a set of observations, prescriptions and measures that serves as a kind of manual for organizations that seek to develop higher maturity. The intention is to use the model to help such organizations develop processes and practices that promote effectiveness, resilience and efficiency, moving away from erratic, risky and inefficient work. One common observation made about organizations with low maturity is that they rely on individuals who work 'over and above'. Such organizations exceed fair demand in order that they are able to extemporize and fix poor-quality practices. It follows that low maturity is associated with greater risks, both short term and long term. Such risks include providing services or products that are defective.

Maturity models originated in the process of software development. The most prominent was the Capability Maturity Model (CMM) (Paulk et al, 1993) developed by the Software Engineering Institute of Carnegie Mellon University. The CMM was created to address poor quality in the software industry in the late 20th century. It describes five steps from a basic 'initial' level to a sophisticated 'optimizing' level of maturity:

1. Initial – processes are ad hoc and potentially chaotic. Few processes are usefully defined, and the success of the organization depends on individual effort and heroics.
2. Repeatable – basic project management processes are established. These repeatable processes track cost, schedule and completion of functionality. It follows that the organization at this level has developed the capability to repeat earlier successes in projects with similar characteristics.
3. Defined – the process for both management and engineering activities is documented, standardized and fully integrated. All projects use approved processes.
4. Managed – detailed measures of process and product quality are collected and utilized. There are effective controls that allow the organization to respond to issues identified through data emanating from the processes.
5. Optimizing – continuous process improvement is embedded into the organization and enabled by quantitative feedback from the process. As a consequence, the organization is able to systematically innovate in its processes, services and products.

Latterly, the Capability Maturity Model Integration (CMMI) (CMMI Product Team, 2010) has replaced the CMM. The new model contains the same five steps but allows for a more integrated measurement of outcomes based on results in practice. This additional feedback loop means that the model is structured in a way that should promote fundamental innovation, responding to the effects of software in the real world. In theoretical terms, the system becomes responsive and adaptive to its environment, or, alternatively, it gains a 'meta-process' (Snowdon and Kawalek, 2003).

Maturity models are not limited to the software industry but have also been developed to guide government institutions through their development of electronic services (e-government) and to address general problem areas, including the management of risk (CMMI Product Team, 2010) and effective project management. The concept of process maturity is also fundamental to the generic discipline of business process management, which in turn draws on ideas in the literature on quality as well as information systems, business process re-engineering (Hammer and Champy, 1993) and firm practices.

Maturity therefore provides a conceptual way of thinking about how organizations in general cope with their reality. Is an organization systematically progressing and learning, or is it stretched and dependent on the heroic and 'over and above' actions of employees? There are similarities between the ideas of maturity and 'dynamic capabilities' (Teece et al, 1997). The latter concept refers to the capabilities that firms develop, normally as a response to tests of market competition. It extends the classic 'resource-based view' that is fundamental in literature on firms and firm strategy (for example, Wernerfelt, 1984). The resource-based view holds that a firm, or any organization, is as valuable as its resources (its technology, orders, people, physical assets and so on). The idea of dynamic capabilities extends this by focusing on management practices as part of that resource base. In other words, it asks: What has this firm learned to do well? This learning, this capability or maturity, is a distinctive asset that characterizes a firm. The practices so developed determine how firms do things, with what technology and with what knowledge. This package of experience and know-how goes a long way to distinguishing good firms from bad. Empirically, dynamic capabilities have value. Under Teece's framework, dynamic capabilities are classically structured into three parts: sensing, seizing and transforming (Teece et al, 1997). Firms sense opportunities, seize what is there and transform when meeting challenges. Translated to a policing environment, a police service might sense the threats to community, seize the incidents and events to which the service can contribute and transform itself in the face of new challenges. Given that risk is central to policing, as evidenced every day by the smartphones and social media of the public, we might expect that services have highly developed capabilities with regard to transformation.

Risk implies transformation.

Emergence

The root of the word 'emergence' is the Latin *emergere*, to bring to light, the common root also of 'emergency'. An emergency service is then, necessarily, one that deals with emergence, or what is brought to light by dynamic interactions in the situation being managed.

Emergence is a significant concept utilized to describe the behaviour of complex systems.[1] The term describes the evolving patterns of interaction between different agents or components of a system, and how such interactions can produce innovations (for example, Patel et al, 2010; Jones and Corner, 2012). Emergence should be understood as a new layer of complexity that requires a different mode of description (Checkland, 1979; Beer, 1985; Tsoukas and Hatch, 2001). Checkland describes it as follows: 'Emergent properties are meaningless in the language appropriate to the lower level' (1994: 78). He further writes that emergence is 'the principle that entities exhibit properties which are meaningful only when attributed to the whole, not to its parts' (Checkland, 1999: 314).

This theoretical explanation is manifest in policing when a situation transcends the operation of a normal management protocol, necessitating some response from police that is innovative. Such innovation might take place in a dynamic operational setting – for example: The unexpected arrival of the woman's son at her home transformed the situation from one of routine fact-finding to one of threat and immediate danger.

Policing during COVID-19 in one UK force

The arrival of the COVID-19 pandemic has proven to be momentous, changing life in many ways. As with all emergency services, policing needed to adapt to the new situation. The account given here is developed from a diverse group of basic command unit (BCU) personnel within one police force in England. BCUs are the standard operational organizational structure for police forces in England and Wales. There are 228 BCUs in the UK.

The approach here been conducted according to inductive ethnographical principles, specifically grounded theory (Strauss and Corbin, 1997; Glaser and Strauss, 2017). The anonymized interviews, with a variety of ranks and roles, do not to seek to claim representativeness or replicability but do identify apparent themes that offer insights and lessons.

Themes relating to emergence

Five themes were identified in relation to the concept of emergence. Each represents a new level of concern, beyond the normal functioning of the system. Each, then, constitutes a new area of culture and concern for policing. The themes are discussed in the sections that follow.

Family life and tensions

A theme of emergence concerned how, first and foremost, police personnel had to react and adjust their family responsibilities to the pandemic. The domestic pressures around family and children were acute, and some reported feeling they had a difficult choice to make between home or work. Fundamentally, there was a fear of going outside the house and of bringing the pandemic home:

> 'My kids were asking why can't you work from home like other parents? I don't think I was alone in saying it caused some "crossroads" thinking – can I do this?'

> 'At first this was a challenge like no other. It felt like I was having to choose my job over my family. I was so worried about going out and bringing back the infection into our home.'

One respondent provided a focused assessment of the tension in terms of family life:

> 'I think it was a gear change that wasn't thought about, because it was new-enough about the psychological pressure about having to bring this into your family, who haven't signed up for emergency work.'

The tensions show that policing had a low level of maturity in terms of its preparedness for the pandemic. It became dependent on the decisions of workers vis-à-vis family and policing tensions, where the best source of information was often public media:

> 'We were having to work quite unprofessionally and that was a stress on us – we would get the update on the 5 pm briefing on the telly, and from that we're supposed to work out, there and then, what to tell the public. There may have been working out in the background, but we weren't part of that – everything was coming as a surprise in a way.'

> 'One of the reactions was being scared. There was the issue of family and kids to look after, then the issue of not being sure what we'd be doing

and how dangerous it was. There was a lot of talk about making sure the NHS wasn't overrun, but there wasn't anything about looking after the police. In fact, in a short space of time we ended up the baddies to some people. In reality, we were in the middle of trying to work out what we were being asked to do with, at first, very little guidance or equipment.'

'If this had been an operational issue, years ago we might have been billeted, but we don't do that for over a long period – we might do it for a short burst like a G7. Policing is now about your home situation – can't not be.'

Families had to debate their willingness to support the actions of policing, and this happened on a nightly basis. In this sense, the service was dependent on the heroic support of families who, to keep policing active, were prepared to make decisions that would potentially compromise their own safety:

'Lockdown was a meltdown. Everyone was watching the same news and there was a growing sense of panic and dread. Most of the information was coming off the news, for all of us I think.'

'We're emergency service workers and that's about risk. Having said that, the nature of a pandemic is not something we'd probably thought about. For example, you can't leave it at work when you leave, as you can bring it home with you.'

Such tensions and difficulties led many of those interviewed towards some significant introspection over their job:

'People might forget that we were juggling all the same things they were around home-schooling, and it was hard for everyone, including us, juggling things. But then we had to go to work patrolling the streets and people were looking to us for guidance. At times, we were the only visible service out there.'

'It made me feel about how we were valued by society. We started to get equipment like hand sanitizer, but then I thought, given the job we do, that is something we should have always had. We make do so much in policing – I really don't think the public get that.'

There were also insights into how the service learned from these tensions:

'Although things at work were slow to respond, I think, to what was happening, support did kick in and [we] got amazing support eventually.

I was offered a lot more flexibility over my shifts, and lots of meetings went online, which was great when we got access to equipment.'

The collective in sensemaking

The training of police officers equips them with standard procedures that help in the management of defined activities. Such formalized practices enable officers to enact procedure when questioning people, stopping traffic, attending domestic violence incidents and other regular interventions with society at large. With this standard and formal set of procedures comes a predominately top-down mode of leadership. This is carried out and enforced throughout the police ranks, from the chief constable through the deputy chief constable, assistant chief constables and so forth.

The term 'sensemaking' is used to describe how communities and institutions come to agreement over the nature and justification for action. Sensemaking is a process that translates a flow of circumstance into agreed codes and ways of action. Language, conversation and writing are key to this cultural production, which is necessarily retrospective as it is a response to what is happening (Weick, 1995).

The novelty and all-pervasiveness of the COVID-19 crisis meant that the processes of sensemaking were shared widely across the collective of police officers and other staff. In essence, the normal top-down structures were overtaken by the flow of new information coming into the organization. The more senior officers often had no more information than their more junior colleagues. The hierarchy was levelled out in some ways. From this, officers reported that a new collective culture came forth:

> 'People for quite a while were talking about is this real? We'd watch the news and try and make sense of it.'

> 'In a way, we were seen as Boris's little army. That's how closely people associated us with the daily TV briefings. But they didn't get we were watching those same briefings trying to keep up too.'

This collective culture of sensemaking was oriented around a need to find practical solutions to everyday issues and to share these solutions back at base. This came about because staff faced practical challenges in carrying out what had hitherto been standard and routine procedures:

> 'I remember, as things started to change, there were two sets of PPE in the sergeant's office. What good was that? There wasn't enough to go around. And were you supposed to go back and fetch it if you came across a COVID case?'

'Things changed in stages. Response got PPE first. I remember some started working from home, like CID [Criminal Investigation Department]. Neighbourhoods were out there facing people but didn't get the equipment soon enough. There was a difference between PCs [police constables] and PCSOs [police community support officers] when you look at it.'

Such issues with PPE (personal protective equipment) revealed very clearly a service that had become reliant on the heroic action of its personnel. Respondents reported that they had to find new ways of coping and then of improving the service. Innovations followed at the front line:

'We started to find ways to adapt with our contact with young people and schools and how we policed in a way. Local teams were responsible for ASB [antisocial behaviour] and initially COVID matters got counted as ASB, so we had spikes of being very busy. Sometimes it was about trying to persuade people who didn't see the sense in the COVID restrictions.'

'We worked out we needed to change how we engaged with the public. There were lots of new approaches, using different languages, that we could use for outreach to support the COVID messages. That was a good thing.'

Throughout, there was a need to make sense of an event that was literally unfolding every day. Police personnel did not know its significance, nor its likely duration:

'Back then, we were hearing different stories about what was unfolding, I think. I was hearing we'd be facing a long-term change. Others might have thought this was "a blink and it'll be gone". I think initially, overall, COVID just wasn't treated seriously.'

'I think we were slow to realize what was happening. It was surreal. Even when things were getting worse out there, we'd go back into the police station and it was business as usual.'

Tensions persisted, and front-line personnel had to engage with very difficult scenarios with the added risk of infection, while other staff faced less immediate risk:

'There was a difference on roles. I had colleagues who were given laptops and who could work flexibly. If you were on uniform response, there was none of that obviously. In a way, it's like different police have been through a different COVID experience depending on their role.'

'I'd say uniform response was basically cannon fodder.'

Curtailing normal life

A common view expressed by police staff is that in their normal function, they serve the public by facilitating normal life. The daily operations of police serve to make everyday life more liveable for the people of their community. COVID-19 challenged and changed this. For long periods, the role of the police altered from being facilitators of normal life to being responsible for curtailing that life. It was noted that the public, faced with this reality and the intrusion into their normal freedoms, exhibited notable differences in acceptance and support of the police between the first lockdown (March 2020) and the second (October 2020):

'The lockdowns were really different when you look back. In the first lockdown, there was a genuine fear. There was much more of a real lockdown feel. But then things changed. It didn't seem so real, so serious any more, in how the public were acting. Things that weren't questioned in lockdown 1 were questioned in later lockdowns more and more.'

'In lockdown 2, there were far more pushbacks when we tried to intervene. Kids at the park would say it makes no sense, we've been together all day but we can't meet after school. People working in factories would say the same – we've been together all day at work so why can't [we] stand on [the] street together after.'

There was uncertainty, and police had to make sense of rules and guidance on behalf of the whole community:

'The police were, in the middle of the lockdowns, trying to enforce what they had been told and advise where it was guidance. People perhaps don't realize there was a complicated mixture of law and guidance in what the government were broadcasting. It was not the law to socially distance – it was guidance. But we'd get called a lot about that, and the confusion would all get put on our shoulders.'

'I remember in the second lockdown, where that had been the messages about getting back to work, I'd be trying ... had to encourage social distancing at a bus stop and then a work bus would turn up and everyone would turn up and everyone would pile in on top of each other. I'd think just what is the point?'

Again, such improvisation was symptomatic of a service that was reliant on its front line to make decisions rapidly in new and changing circumstances. Public attitudes remained dynamic. There were marked differences between the lockdowns:

'In the first lockdown, when we did see people, most were very thankful for us being there and things were very positive. We'd get thank you notes and packets of biscuits left for us.'

'The public would discuss the death rate – it was on the telly every night. In the first lockdown, there was a that fear in those numbers. But as things eased, the attitudes changed and [we] started thinking we're nearly through this now. It's all over.'

'Part of the kickback to us policing the second lockdown was people coming back at us saying there were mixed messages and the rules were silly. We'd just try our best to persuade. Many would know we were just trying to do our job, but some would think we've made these rules and would be challenging us about them.'

A new demand topology

In normal circumstances, police personnel are knowledgeable about the patterns of demand that will typically present themselves at different times and in different geographies. With the abnormality of the pandemic, patterns changed and a new demand topology emerged. As public behaviour changed, police staff reported on the new patterns that emerged:

'We saw a change in demand, and I think that was because of the fall in night-time economy, [which] tends to draw other types of crime. The roads were also quieter and that affected travelling crime – slowed it down. But while that was coming down, the COVID demand was going up. Overall, it probably added up to about the same demand. Same but different.'

'Most people complied in the first lockdown. In some ways, it allowed us to see some types of crime easier. You could see people moving about for drugs easier, for example. That had been hidden in plain sight before as the streets were so busy.'

With many people spending more time at home, domestic incidents seemed to become more prevalent and a greater part of the overall level of demand encountered by the policing service:

> 'I think, though street crime went down, my perception is that domestic abuse went up [and] that we're only starting to get [it] reported now.'

Enforcement of the COVID-19 regulations were themselves a major driver of the demand and were encountered together with the sickness and precautionary isolation that accompanied the pandemic:

> 'I suppose it's linked to demand, but when we weren't ready for COVID, then it hit us with sickness [and] it left a period when for those who were left at work, their demand was through the roof, picking up reallocated crime reports.'

> 'Policing COVID breaches was more complex than people might realize, [which] added to the demand. There was the law and guidance issue, the media representation and a complexity around a number of exemptions, and things kept shifting so it was hard to stay on top of the latest direction and to take the public with you.'

The extended duration of the COVID-19 pandemic was a new challenge for policing. The service is used to emergencies of a short-term duration, such as major traffic incidents or terrorism. There was no precedent for an emergency of such extended duration. One respondent noted that the service was well used to preparing for sprint events but had no prior experience of something that could be likened to a marathon:

> 'It did take a long time to get some basics in place, like cleaning and masks. That means probably we recognized but weren't able to follow it through like we normally would do. In normal emergencies, we would operate as a form of sprint [but] we were not used to a marathon. That's not happened before. Marathon emergencies mean you can't postpone, and that caused learning and realization that we needed to do the two things at once, even though people will ask what gives? We prepare for sprinting – we don't prepare for marathons.'

The situation was described as one where normal work is carried out alongside an extended, ongoing emergency:

> 'If that had been a major flood or something like that, I think we would have mobilized better, because we would have been used to the

logistics – this was different. With a flood that['s] the focus, we identify and contain, we prioritize and stop normal business as such, as it's an emergency. COVID was like an ongoing emergency [along] with normal business over a long period of time – quite unprecedented.'

Some lessons were learned that have potential implications for good practice in the longer term, beyond the achievement of a post-pandemic society:

'I think that during COVID we got better at saying no and asking more questions before sending off a response. I think we can learn from that long term.'

'I think, in terms of demand, we sorted out some of our internal demand better. Being online more saved a lot of travelling and tasks were done a lot quicker. Initially, several meetings stopped altogether, and nobody missed them.'

Cohesion in policing and working with partners

One aspect of sensemaking was working out how relations with partner agencies would be enacted in the circumstance of COVID-19. Other agencies, having different degrees of risk preparedness, were able to justify a retreat from normal working into new modes of online or reduced provision. This exposed the police's identity as a public service of last resort alongside healthcare workers, such as nurses, doctors and domestic staff:

'Partner agencies seemed to disappear overnight. They were really quick to move to online working. We just didn't have the equipment and were really behind then.'

'Partners locked down in the first one and virtually closed down, and that affected our joint work in safeguarding a lot. They perhaps took it too seriously and retreated, and we in police were slow to change to be more cautious.'

'The way some partner agencies just disappeared was amazing. We were like the last people going out on the streets. And they'd ask us to do tasks for them. I think it exposed just how we are the first and last service when it boils down to it.'

During this time, public appreciation of healthcare workers was widespread, including weekly doorstep clapping, posters displayed in cars and houses and even spontaneous graffiti on streets. There was no similar appreciation shown for police who had remained at work:

> 'I think a lot of us feel like the forgotten professionals.'

> 'We got a medal for the Queen's jubilee, but I doubt we'll be getting one for policing COVID.'

As central government prepared the budgetary response to the COVID-19 pandemic, there were newspapers articles that speculated on the possibility of pay rises to express appreciation towards frontline workers across the public sector. In the event, pay awards were below the inflation rate:

> 'After all we've been through, to get the news of cuts and no pay increase was a slap in the face. People off work had got paid, and there was Universal Credit for the unemployed. We had to police all the way through this at the front end with very little recognition. After lockdown 1, policing became pretty much a thankless job.'

Frames for understanding the police response during the pandemic

How can a critical service enact a mature response to unexpected circumstances? In more stark terms, what happens when normally mature levels of operation are blown apart by circumstances?

The evidence reported here can be developed as three complementary frames for understanding the policing response to the fundamental and prolonged challenge of COVID-19: a transition achieved; an immaturity exposed; and building back better: a case for maturity perspectives in policing.

A transition achieved

This is a case study of organizational survival. Faced with major challenge, the service survived and its rank structure remained intact, and the service was beneficial to its community. In the years ahead, there will be arguments about how much this all cost and in what form the cost was paid (such as through early severance, unpoliced crime or financial expenditure), but nonetheless this intermediary evidence can be interpreted as a transition achieved.

The themes relating to emergence represent new qualitative realities for policing. In each theme, adjustment was made. Police and their families were able to find ways of carrying on with work life and carrying on with family life even as one threatened to bring disease to the other. Policing has always depended on its families but here was a new poignancy. Faced with a fast-moving situation, collective concern and learning was given more emphasis. Everybody, no matter the rank, was watching the same television briefings, and these sources of information relied on collective interpretation. What is more, the front line took on an additional importance in the sensemaking: those police personnel who spent most time dealing with the problems of the pandemic in communities had to solve issues in situ, report and share. Police personnel had to confront a new identity whereby they constrained the freedoms of people, rather than being responsible for facilitation and enablement of everyday life. This in turn required additional sensitivity to how policing was perceived by the community, and how their implementation of lockdown restrictions was being perceived. This additional sensitivity was again a collectively shared concern. A common justification given by police to the difficult interventions that they might have to carry out is: We have our jobs to do; but here there was an additional and new: Are we doing our jobs? The demand topology was new. Some criminal activity was exposed more clearly than ever before – for example, drug deliveries were more conspicuous in lockdown. Alongside this, some other areas of crime became still more deeply entrenched and volatile. Police were called to heated and difficult domestic violence cases, but how can a police officer separate family members in a lockdown? Moreover, how can police bring partners into complex problem-solving situations when those partners are working from home? The issue of changed relations with partner agencies was a fundamental and unexpected shift for police. The service has spent years cultivating sophisticated partner relations so that issues (for example, domestic violence, drug dependency, mental health, homelessness, dementia) receive the sophisticated responses that they merit. Suddenly, while most other front-line staff were at home offering services by video, email and phone, police officers needed to manufacture ways of handling complex cases without the same levels of support from other agencies.

The transition was achieved and COVID-19 was policed. Within this, positive points of learning were found, which might hold for a long period:

> 'The changes we made to communicate with communities were good, and that now helps us do more of that, working in different languages more. We made those changes quickly as well, so I think we can be proud of that.'

There were also successes within the organization. As noted earlier, although it took time, staff did receive support and more flexibility in terms of shifts along with being held meetings. However, there are also questions which might persist for some time:

> 'I think there is an opportunity now to discuss with our partners how policing was left carrying everything and how that was unacceptable, so that it doesn't happen again.'

It is significant to note that the police service was stretched during this transition and that it depended on heroic action. This leads to the question of maturity.

An immaturity exposed

One argument is that a pandemic is a rare and far-reaching event of great consequence. It is ultimately unforeseeable, its character unknowable. Under this argument, it might be implied or expressed that COVID-19 is something for which preparation would always have been inadequate. Rare as pandemics are, it should be expected that they will throw public agencies into a state of stretch, most of all the front lines of policing and healthcare services. By this argument, heroism is always native to policing when a pandemic starts; it simply becomes the norm.

Yet pandemics are known about and planned for. Even a coronavirus pandemic is a known possibility[2] within the strategic gamut of public agencies. Moreover, policing is centrally concerned with risk. It is the public service of last resort. Its organizational design is centrally concerned with risk. Where an event can be foreseen, the procedures of policing diminish the complexity of operations, and its ranks and structures learn quickly about whatever is emergent or brought to light.

Yet, as one participant said:

> 'I think we exist on just enough – too often not quite enough, actually – and that level of resilience means the only way we survive is our people manage to pull us through.'

If heroism is the norm, then the organization is immature. Even in a pandemic, if an organization is not successfully working to diminish its dependency on heroism, then it exposes its immaturity at that level of threat. System-level change is not easy, but to transform is an organizational capability recognized in the dynamic capabilities model (Teece et al, 1997). Firms do it in their own circumstances of greatest threat – for example, strategic transformation or corporate turnaround. Therefore, there is an argument that a greater degree of systemic response should have been possible during COVID-19 and that a public service centrally concerned with risk should have had a set of mature responses readily available to it – for example, new information-sharing protocols, new team configurations, ready vulnerability assessments for staff and their families, immediate rollout of training to respond to new patterns of demand, preplanned protocols for working with partners and enough PPE already in stock. At its best, such capability would integrate the service into its environment, no matter the stress and flex exhibited by that environment. Instead, as we have heard, uniform police were thought of as "cannon fodder".

Building back better: a case for maturity perspectives in policing

To return to the interviews, an obvious question was whether a stressed service might build back better after the pandemic. Are there feedback loops that will enable the service to learn from its experience? Might a greater level of resilience and capability follow from the problems and adaptations that have been encountered? The responses were not unequivocal. There are some areas in which positive outcomes are likely, such as the wider use of languages to engage with different communities, cited earlier. Additionally, there are lessons that personnel want to take onwards:

> 'For me, COVID has highlighted the importance of neighbourhood policing. There have been cuts there in the past. We've got the uplift but it's barely filling the gaps form the previous cuts. I think neighbourhoods, to take the public with us, needs more investment learning from all this.'

> 'The technology showed us some opportunities for change – I don't think we'll go back [to] pre COVID in that. That's a positive. That use of technology will make us more efficient. It can mean policing can be delivered in different ways.'

> 'The call filtering with telephone ringback and the use of online meetings have saved thousands of hours, which we can keep going now. That frees up a lot of our time to do things more proactively.'

This was further developed in the sense of what might be learned:

> 'We could learn a lot about how we deploy resources. We're a bit too hierarchical and HQ-centric. It's all based on a centralized command centre. There's more lessons in this … than flexible homeworking. That could open us to do more transformational change.'

> 'The process is the start of a reflective challenge to identify learning, which may point to some disconnect with strategic vision and operational practice play out. COVID represented change at every level, and the opportunity here is to learn from it. Reflecting on resistance to change in normal circumstances is perhaps worthy of consideration given the accelerated change that was proven to occur during the pandemic. In other words, can we volunteer for change

more, rather than [having] to comply with ... it without the impetus coming from a sense of crisis?'

There are also concerns that meaningful lessons will not be learned and that there will be an element of the service continuing to lurch onwards in a make-do fashion:

'I think, like we always do, we made do. We're like that, aren't we, in policing. We just get on with it. I think that will always be the same. I don't think we'll be getting any investment any time soon.'

Finance is part of this picture. Police personnel are sceptical of government intentions around financing:

'The biggest problem now looks like the funding, as it sounds like we're going back to austerity. We've had lots of cuts over time, and the recent uplift investment was a catch up. Now the cuts are maybe going to start again. It's more surviving that bounce back.'

Yet, beyond this, there is also concern about the intrinsic ability of the service to learn successfully:

'I don't think we will. We'd like to. It would be great to capture all the learning. Policing has a form of resilience, like a balloon that expands and then contracts to where it was before.'

'I think we'll take some of the opportunities, but I don't believe we will change as much as we could.'

Indeed, the resilience of the police service was a common topic of enquiry before the pandemic. Policing was commonly perceived as too often 'just coping' and reliant on personnel who sought to find solutions through their own personal heroic action. In such light, the consolation of various tactical advancements achieved under COVID-19 could be embraced as foundational capabilities of policing and as elements of a new maturity model for policing. Even from the limited evidence presented earlier, it is possible to distill some key areas of innovation where change might be systematized. One prospective area of advancement might be labelled as 'future working approaches'. Take as an example the new shift patterns made available to support families. Additionally, the use of online services have quickly become more familiar and acceptable to the public. In the right areas, there might follow a series of long-term efficiencies. Reflections on demand and partner relations also feed new ideas into future working approaches. The pandemic prompted thinking about why the police were responsive to so many calls and issues, especially as it became clear that other agencies were not. A service based on risk has to be good at risk assessment. It follows, then, not that the police might do less, but that the service might mature its ability to better assess risk before it deploys resources into the community. There are other ways to make life more liveable for communities than relying on sending a response to multiple issues on a precautionary basis.

Conclusion

The cameras of social media show us police cars in pursuit, assaults, bungled drug drop-offs interrupted by chance and cops jumping barriers at stations in pursuit of lithe thieves. Risk is intrinsic in police work. Heroism never really stops, even when a police officer operates within a framework protocol that is designed to contain unpredictability. Adrenaline too is part of the job. Officers complain of the contrast between the interaction and action of the street and the relative mundanity of putting names and addresses and other call-out details into the police computer.

Take the example of police officers who stop a car in order to question its occupants. There is a protocol around this that is part of the training of the officers who execute it. This is essential. Should there be a sudden escalation – let us say that an occupant in the car has a knife – then there is an escalation procedure. A different set of responses is called on. For example, backup is called and the police at the scene move into a mode where a direct threat is involved.

Maturity is just this, but at the organizational level. The organization carries out its daily operations and embeds itself in feedback so that the degree to which it is able to satisfy public values becomes established and known. It seeks to systematize. The organization is mature. Given a crisis, the mature organization escalates its responses. Within this, it tries to lower the risks and harm encountered by its employees, to diminish the necessity of meeting emergence with heroism. A different set of protocols might be deployed; different capabilities might become relevant. Ultimately, given an enduring and potentially transformative crisis, it invokes a further set of responses. At this transformational level, the organization seeks its own institutional innovation in a way that means it learns about the new emergent reality through systematic processes of discovery, sharing and innovation. Against the adrenaline of everyday encounters on the street, designing this set of capabilities might not seem to be the highest priority. Yet such dynamic capabilities are the means by which policing might stay closest to its values, protect its employees and serve its community in the seeming new normal of challenges brought about by change.

Notes

1. The lineage of the concept is in systems theory, and it features in that literature and overlapping literatures concerning complexity theory and cybernetics.
2. Nassim Nicholas Taleb, author of the widely cited book *The Black Swan* (2007), publicly acknowledges COVID-19 as a 'white swan' – that is, something anticipated in advance. Despite this, many commentators carried on calling it a 'black swan'.

References

Beer, S. (1985) *Diagnosing the System for Organizations*, Chichester: Wiley.
Checkland, P. (1994) 'Systems theory and management thinking', *American Behavioral Scientist*, 38(1): 75–91.
Checkland, P. (1999) 'Systems thinking', in W.L. Currie and B. Galliers (eds) *Rethinking Management Information Systems*, Oxford: Oxford University Press, pp 45–56.
CMMI Product Team (2010) *CMMI® for Services, Version 1.3*, CMU/SEI-2010-TR-034, Pittsburgh, PA: Software Engineering Institute, Carnegie Mellon University.
Glaser, B.G. and Strauss, A.L. (2017) *The Discovery of Grounded Theory: Strategies for Qualitative Research*, London: Routledge.
Hammer, M. and Champy, J. (1993) *Reengineering the Corporation: A Manifesto for Business Revolution*, London: Nicholas Brealey.
Jones, R. and Corner, J. (2012) 'Seeing the forest and the trees: a complex adaptive systems lens for mentoring', *Human Relations*, 65(3): 391–411.
Patel, N.V., Eldabi, T. and Khan, T.M. (2010) 'Theory of deferred action: agent-based simulation model for designing complex adaptive systems', *Journal of Enterprise Information Management*, 23(4): 521–37.
Paulk, M.C., Curtis, B., Chrissis, M.B. and Weber, C.V. (1993) 'Capability Maturity Model, version 1.1', *IEEE Software*, 10(4): 18–27.
Snowdon, B. and Kawalek, P. (2003) 'Active meta-process models: a conceptual exposition', *Information and Software Technology*, 45(15): 1021–9.
Strauss, A.L. and Corbin, J.M. (1997) *Grounded Theory in Practice*, Thousand Oaks, CA: Sage.
Taleb, N.N. (2007) *The Black Swan: The Impact of the Highly Improbable*, London: Penguin.
Teece, D.J., Pisano, G. and Shuen, A. (1997) 'Dynamic capabilities and strategic management', *Strategic Management Journal*, 18(7): 509–33.
Tsoukas, H. and Hatch, M.J. (2001) 'Complex thinking, complex practice: the case for a narrative approach to organizational complexity', *Human Relations*, 54(8): 979–1013.
Weick, K.E. (1995) *Sensemaking in Organizations*, Thousand Oaks, CA: Sage.
Wernerfelt, B. (1984) 'A resource-based view of the firm', *Strategic Management Journal*, 5(2): 171–80.

3

Reimagining the Open Court in the Time of Pandemic: Towards 'Portal Justice' and 'Broadcast Justice'

Sarah Moore

Introduction

As spaces for public gatherings, courts have long had to manage the risk of disease spread. When London's sessions house – more popularly known as the Old Bailey – was redesigned in the 1770s, like many early dedicated court buildings, it was built with avoidance of disease transmission in mind. Jackson (1978) notes the keen awareness among court officials, justices and members of the public of the risk of contracting typhus in the courthouse (this was so common an ailment among prisoners that it was known as 'gaol fever'). They had good reason to be concerned. In 1750, the disease had 'killed two judges; the Lord Mayor, several aldermen and some fifty members of the public, including jurymen and spectators' (Jackson, 1978: 29). Architecturally, the response to the risks posed by physical co-presence in the courtroom was to make these spaces more open and better ventilated, however uncomfortable that made court proceedings in practice.

In striking contrast, the global response to COVID-19 involved the mass closure of criminal courts. Roughly half of the court buildings in England and Wales were closed during Spring 2020 – the start of the first wave of the pandemic in the United Kingdom (UK) – with face-to-face hearings reserved for priority cases and remote hearings held wherever possible (Criminal Justice Joint Inspection, 2021: 8). Even in hearings held face to face, normal service was significantly disrupted, with the public barred from access to proceedings due to the government's 'stay at home' order.

This chapter outlines the immediate effect of the COVID-19 pandemic on criminal courts in England and Wales and considers the longer-term opportunities offered by digital transformation of justice processes as well as the challenges in implementing wholesale change. Before that, and by way of introduction, I want to make two preliminary observations that in turn provide the point of departure for this chapter. First, when we look across the various parts of the criminal justice system and their response to the COVID-19 pandemic, it is reasonable to suggest that criminal courts fared especially badly – in the context of England and Wales, at least. This is true, in the first instance, in terms of the agility of the organizational response. Godfrey et al (2021) convincingly argue that the criminal courts were the least innovative and responsive part of the criminal justice system when it came to managing the crisis. The role of longer-term problems – for example, increases in caseload and insufficient resourcing – in constraining the management of criminal courts during the pandemic are outlined in the next section. This is to think of the official response to the public health crisis in purely operational terms and to make comparisons on that basis. It is also possible to think of the pandemic's impact on criminal courts as different in kind to its impact on other parts of the criminal justice system. While the pandemic led to a series of measures that *intensified* the work of the police and the prison service – by extending police powers and, in the case of prisons, instituting systems of total confinement – in the case of the criminal courts, emergency measures arguably prompted a move *away* from their core function of delivering open justice.

None of this is to naturalize official responses to the COVID-19 pandemic and suggest that it could only ever have resulted in particular forms of intervention – the opening observation about historical approaches to managing disease spread in criminal courts demonstrates otherwise. As a further preliminary observation, it is worth noting, as researchers of disaster management have long pointed out,[1] that emergency measures can serve a political function. Such measures are frequently an extension of prior official thinking or in keeping with an existing direction of travel. As such, this chapter argues that when it comes to the work of the criminal court, the COVID-19 pandemic has hastened and legitimated a shift that was already underway in the preceding decades. It is a shift, to develop the earlier observation, that is likely to radically alter the function of the criminal court away from its historical role as a public space to 'see justice being done', as the famous legal aphorism has it.

The penultimate section of this chapter returns to this idea and considers what we might expect from post-pandemic justice in the criminal courts, in a context where the idea of openness is undergoing a radical revision. Here, the chapter suggests that we see the COVID-19 pandemic as participating in two key sets of trends, which we might see as giving rise to two distinct emerging models of adjudicatory justice: 'portal justice', where court processes and decisions become largely an administrative matter, and 'broadcast justice', where participation in court processes is mediated and often asynchronous. Before that, the chapter outlines the short- and mid-term impact of the COVID-19 pandemic on the work of criminal courts.

Assessing the short- and mid-term impact of the COVID-19 pandemic on criminal courts

In spring 2020, as Europe entered the first wave of the COVID-19 pandemic, the UK government introduced far-reaching emergency measures to deal with what was fast becoming a public health crisis. Just four years earlier, the country's preparedness for a serious outbreak of influenza had been tested in a cross-government simulation, Exercise Cygnus. While the Ministry of Justice had been part of that exercise, this was only to test responses in the area of offender management (House of Lords Select Committee on the Constitution, 2021: para 27).

The reorganization of court hearings during COVID-19 was, then, a development for which there had been little prior planning. What came to further impair the immediate response to the pandemic was the lack of digital infrastructure, in the lower criminal courts at least. A delayed and controversial court reform package, begun in 2016, had been directed towards modernizing court processes and buildings by, among other things, introducing a new digital case management system (the Common Platform), boosting information technology provision in court buildings and digitization of forms and processes (Acland-Hood, 2017). In 2018, the National Audit Office (NAO) undertook a review of the court reform programme in light of successive delays and was deeply critical of the management of the project, identifying a £61 million gap in funding (NAO, 2018: 4). At the point when the COVID-19 pandemic started, the court reform programme was still to deliver the wide-ranging technological change promised at its inception three years earlier.

This gives a sense of the broader context in which the government introduced emergency measures to manage criminal court casework during the COVID-19 pandemic. In the event, the decisions that halted and then reconfigured court hearings came quickly, over a ten-day period. On 17 March 2020, the Lord Chief Justice announced a temporary suspension of all new jury trials scheduled to run for more than three days (Courts and Tribunals Judiciary, 2020a). A week later, on 23 March, a further announcement strengthened these measures: new trials were suspended (with the exemption of priority cases) and no jury trials were to proceed unless adequate safety measures were in place (Courts and Tribunals Judiciary, 2020b). Two days later, on 25 March, the Coronavirus Act 2020 came into effect. This legal instrument, introduced to Parliament and passed by both Houses within six days, granted the government emergency powers to (among other things) restrict public gatherings, mandate mask wearing, detain people suspected of being infected with COVID-19 and prohibit certain public premises (such as shops) from opening to the public. Schedules 23–27 outlined specific measures for criminal courts, including the extended use of live video links for remote hearings and proceedings, and video transmission to enable public participation.

The immediate effect was a sharp and unprecedented increase in remote participation in court hearings. From 25 March to mid-June 2020 – the period of the first national lockdown – 80–90 per cent of all criminal hearings were carried out by audio or video link (House of Lords Select Committee on the Constitution, 2021: ch 2, fig 4). This was no doubt helped by the introduction in late April 2020 of a cloud-based video platform (CVP) to facilitate online hearings in both magistrates' courts and Crown Courts (House of Lords Select Committee on the Constitution, 2021: para 39). In England and Wales, most Crown Courts remained closed – with only urgent cases being heard in person – until June 2020, after which there was a gradual reopening (HM Crown Prosecution Service Inspectorate – HMCPSI, 2021: 10).

Looking beyond England and Wales, there are striking similarities in countries' reorganization of the work of lower criminal courts during the COVID-19 pandemic. With great consistency, most jury trials were adjourned, criminal courts were closed and hearings were moved (where possible) online, with only exceptional, high-priority cases taking place face to face (but with restrictions on in-person attendance, most notably for the public). Some jurisdictions were more ready for this shift than others. Puddister and Small (2020) provide an insight into how Canadian courts managed the COVID-19 pandemic. As a country where provinces have jurisdiction over lower courts, there were identifiable regional differences reflecting provinces' willingness to adopt technology and move away from in-person hearings. Kettiger and Lienhard (2021) outline the Swiss response and suggest that this jurisdiction was relatively underprepared for managing the impact of the pandemic on court processes, particularly in terms of courts' limited prior adoption of audiovisual technology. By contrast, for the Court of Justice of the European Union, the shift to new ways of working was helped significantly by the existence of a long-standing crisis plan for pandemics (Popotas, 2021).

The focus here is on the immediate impact of COVID-19 on court operations and the factors – specifically, prior adoption of live video link technology – that may have shaped this experience. As the first period of lockdown in the UK extended from one to two and then three months, it became evident that the medium-term impact would be a huge increase in case backlogs. In taking stock of this challenge, the HMCPSI noted that '[w]ithout some innovative thinking and solutions, the challenge of addressing the backlog is likely to be much more complex than dealing with the immediate crisis' (2020: 43). Magistrates' courts were less badly affected. The HMCPSI (2021: 11) reported that by August 2020, magistrates' courts were starting to finalize cases at a faster rate than they were receiving new ones. In Crown Courts, despite the introduction of various measures as part of a recovery package – extended opening hours and the creation of makeshift courts (so-called 'Nightingale courts') – by December 2020, the backlogs had increased to more than 53,000 cases (HMCPSI, 2021). The backlogs in these courts would continue to grow throughout much of 2021, reaching, at the end of June, an increase of 48 per cent since the start of the pandemic (NAO, 2021: 6).

In seeking to explain the persistence – indeed, continued growth – of the backlogs in court cases, the HMCPSI (2021) point to the complex set of resources needed to manage the situation (in particular, judges), an increase in case receipts (as a drop in crime during the pandemic gave police forces the opportunity to tackle their own backlogs) and historic underinvestment in courts and court services. 'It was not going to take much for the system to falter', noted the Crown Prosecution Service's chief inspector, adding that COVID-19 'was likely to be the event that finally broke the system' (HMCPSI, 2021: 6).

This was a view that was echoed by legal commentators – most notably The Secret Barrister in their lacerating Twitter updates – who were quick to point out that the backlogs of criminal cases that emerged during and after the COVID-19 pandemic were a product of existing, more long-term problems. Certainly, it is important to recognize that England and Wales entered the pandemic with significant court backlogs. The NAO points out that in the year *preceding* the pandemic, there was a 23 per cent increase in Crown Court backlogs (2021: 8). The factors mentioned previously that created these backlogs – lack of investment and staffing constraints – then deepened the impact of the pandemic on criminal courts.

The new ways of working that have been hastened by the pandemic – specifically, the move towards online processes and hearings – are seen by HM Courts & Tribunals Service (HMCTS) as key to long-term recovery of the court service, not least because they seem to answer to the pressing need for greater efficiency (HMCTS, 2019). The next section interrogates this proposition by considering the opportunities and challenges thrown up by these new ways of working in criminal courts. Before that, a caveat: a more granular look at the impact of COVID-19 on criminal courts reveals that the consequences have been uneven. There is, for example, significant regional variation – always part of the broader context for a discussion of criminal justice in England and Wales, and no less so when it comes to the impact of COVID-19. The overall 48 per cent increase in Crown Court backlogs across England and Wales from March 2020 to June 2021 (NAO, 2021: 6) hid considerable differences at a more local level. The NAO (2021: 9) note that while London saw a 72 per cent increase, the South West saw a far more modest 18 per cent increase in its backlog.

The NAO note too an unevenness in terms of case type, with serious sexual offence cases especially affected by the COVID-19 pandemic:

> Defendants accused of rape or serious sexual offences are typically more likely to plead not guilty compared with other offences. Cases with not guilty pleas typically take much longer to complete in the courts than cases where a defendant has pleaded guilty. Delays to jury trials have therefore disproportionately affected victims of these crimes: between 31 March 2020 and 30 June 2021, the number of sexual offence trial cases in the Crown Court backlog rose by 71%. (2021: 9)

Early in the pandemic, campaigners and activist-academics were warning of precisely this set of effects – that is, sexual violence cases would be disproportionately affected. This is due not just to the particular characteristics of these trials, as detailed earlier, but also, as outlined by Bradbury-Jones and Isham (2020), to the additional pressure put on intimate relations and victim-survivors' reduced access to support and services as a result of the stay at home order that was intermittently in place from spring 2020 to spring 2021. If we have seen the 'de-criminalisation of rape' over the last decade, as Dame Vera Baird (2020: 16) pointedly put it in the 2019/20 annual report of the Victims' Commissioner, the effects of the COVID-19 pandemic have surely accelerated this trend. This should give us pause to recognize that while in some areas the impact of the pandemic on the work of criminal courts is likely to be an operational matter, in others it may have more lasting effects on public confidence and victims' experiences of justice.

The long-term impact of COVID-19 on criminal courts: opportunities and challenges

Attending to the uneven impact of COVID-19-related measures on criminal courts should be a key point of focus for future research. So too should the question of whether the short-term emergency measures introduced during the pandemic can lead to more lasting innovation and, if so, to what effect. This is Wallace and Laster's (2021) chief concern. 'Will digital innovation stick?' they ask in an article outlining the opportunities afforded by the COVID-19 pandemic for instituting technological change in criminal court practice and process. Their focus is the Australian state of Victoria, a world-leading jurisdiction in terms of its embrace of live video links to allow witnesses to deliver testimony remotely and, in some instances, entire court hearings to be carried out online (so-called 'distributed hearings'). Victoria, as Wallace and Laster (2021) point out, might have been an 'early adopter' of court-based technology, but it has not seen 'sustained innovation' in this area. They usefully note the distinction between piecemeal practical solutions – in the Australian context, remote hearings as a way of managing geographical distance between court participants – and change of a more institutional and systematic nature.

In raising the prospect that meaningful change might require more than the sheer availability or repeat use of technology, Wallace and Laster (2021) make an observation that has long been a bedrock idea in science and technology studies: innovation is the product of interaction between people, institutions and technology. Walklate et al (2022) note something similar in a study exploring the effect of the COVID-19 pandemic on policing in England and Wales: modernization of process, they point out, contends with the parochialism of organizational practice, and in such a way that the latter can come to limit the former.

Wallace and Laster (2021) are broadly optimistic that the COVID-19 pandemic has sparked a set of changes that go beyond base-level adaptation. For this to happen, as they make clear, more is needed than an approach of add technology and mix. They draw attention to the role of leadership – the upper-level promotion of a vision – as well as changes to working practices that in turn shape organizational structures. We might add to this a clear sense of the accompanying system-level changes that are required – and their impact on users, processes and outcomes – as well as a sense of what is to be gained beyond mere efficiency and ease of access.

As Wallace and Laster (2021) note, one such gain is standardization of process and practice. There are no doubt other potential benefits coming from the digital transformation of criminal justice process and practice, such as the possibility that joined-up online systems lead to the integration of different parts of what is a multifaceted and often mal-coordinated criminal justice system. Implemented correctly, this is what an end-to-end case management system might allow for: smoother transitions and information-sharing across these different elements of the criminal justice system. Improved access – both in terms of access to justice for defendants and public access – is another potential gain, considering the possibility to signpost information online, funnel people through online processes and provide open access to data. So too is the possibility for decisions to be arrived at more quickly and outcomes circulated near instantaneously. This is the vision set out by the HMCTS (2019) when explaining the benefits of court reform – the perceived gains lie in greater consistency, speedier and more streamlined processes and better integration.

These are the perceived opportunities of digital reform in the criminal courts. In hastening a shift to online working, the COVID-19 pandemic has laid bare some of the barriers to achieving the official vision of digital transformation. It has, for example, revealed a set of practical constraints coming from insufficient resourcing. In an evaluation carried out by the HMCTS into the efficacy of remote hearings during the COVID-19 pandemic, one in five lay court users reported experiencing technological difficulties (and this rose to 30 per cent when the court user had accessed a hearing via video link; HMCTS, 2021a: 48).

As the House of Lords Select Committee on the Constitution (2021) notes, a lack of digital infrastructure to support remote hearings is a key barrier to long-term change. Their review emphasizes the lack of preparedness on the part of the HMCTS, highlighting, as this chapter has also done, the failure, prior to the pandemic, to bring about much-needed, long-anticipated modernization of court processes and practices. The committee also notes that the use of remote hearings declined sharply as the first period of national lockdown came to an end, such that '[b]y September 2020, the Crown Prosecution Service was making CVP applications in only approximately 15% of cases' (House of Lords Select Committee on the Constitution, 2021: para 66). The committee note a similar pattern in the use of remote remand hearings and, in doing so, cite the findings of a Criminal Justice Joint Inspection report which observed 'a clear judicial preference for in-person court attendance' (in House of Lords Select Committee on the Constitution, 2021: para 72).

For the Criminal Justice Joint Inspection (2021), as well as the House of Lords Select Committee on the Constitution (2021), this constitutes a lost opportunity. It is worth pausing, though, to reflect on why judges might prefer in-person court hearings. Some clues are provided by an anonymous blog post written by a district judge for a civil court, whose experiences might be usefully transposed to criminal courts (Anon, 2020). They note that when the technology to support remote hearings does not work – and, in line with the findings of the HMCTS (2021a) evaluation, they report that this was frequently their experience during the pandemic – it is obtrusive, potentially in such a way as to preclude court users from understanding processes and outcomes. They note too that remote proceedings necessarily reduce interaction between court participants. As they put it:

> The camera goes on, the phone is answered and we have no idea what we are likely to see or hear from those with pent up anger, or deep-rooted fear until that very moment.
>
> As the professionals in the equation, judges or advocates, we can become used to a new way of working and we may become more resilient, but for the parties this may be their one and only court

hearing. This is their one and only chance to participate, to engage, to understand. (Anon, 2020)

In other words, *even when the technology works seamlessly*, there are potential problems – here, notably, a lack of contextualizing detail to form a sufficient understanding of a party's intentions and state of mind – and the overall consequence of this is lay court participants not being able to participate fully.

There is a growing body of evidence within criminology to support this perspective. McKay (2018, 2020, 2022) sheds light on the impact of remote criminal hearings on defendants, a group that, it is worth reminding ourselves, is subject to special legal protections in court hearings (and, of course, at other stages of the criminal justice process). McKay (2022) argues that the use of live video links to connect an incarcerated defendant to a court hearing dissolves the boundary between prison and court, the effect being that the work of the latter (neutral arbitration and adjudication) is shaped by the meaning of the former (to detain and punish). Her 2018 book focuses on the prisoner experience of live video link appearances in court hearings as well as their use of this same technology to access legal advice and advocacy. Based on interviews with incarcerated defendants in New South Wales, Australia – but still relevant to understanding the impact of remote hearings in England and Wales – McKay (2018) carefully unpacks a range of problems, some related to technological failure and others to the changed (that is, reduced, less open) interpersonal communication between a defendant and their legal advocate. As a recent study by the Equality and Human Rights Commission (2020) observes, these factors are likely to be more grievous in their impact on defendants who have a 'cognitive impairment, mental health condition and/or neuro-diverse condition'.

McKay (2018) also raises a more general concern about the ways in which remote participation changes incarcerated defendants' relationship with justice. It is a concern raised too by Mulcahy (2008) in an early article about the shift towards online hearings: the move to remote participation necessarily 'dematerializes' a court hearing and reduces the symbolic features of justice. The risk is that a court hearing comes to seem more like a bureaucratic process than a meaningful public ritual concerned with fairness and justice.

As McKay (2018: 5) puts it: 'Technologies do not simply *replace* the old system, their intervention *transforms*.' Such an observation requires that we see criminal justice as a system in the first place, with elements and processes that contribute to (or hinder) higher-level goals and principles. To *not* see criminal justice in this way – to fail to recognize that technology transforms the operation of justice overall rather than simply transposing discrete processes – is to increase the risk of unintended consequences and perverse outcomes. The recent history of justice reform suggests an ongoing problem in this respect. A lack of systems thinking is evident, for example, in the recent cuts to legal aid, which sought to reduce government spending but in doing so increased costs in other parts of the social welfare system and increased pressure on already overstretched courts (for more on this, see Moore and Newbury, 2017).

The reorganization of criminal courts in response to the COVID-19 pandemic betrays, too, a fundamental lack of systems-level thinking, and this constitutes a further challenge in instituting effective long-term change to capitalize on the benefits of online working. The introduction of Nightingale courts is a striking example. Although a subsidiary part of the official response to COVID-19 (which, as discussed previously, in the main involved moving proceedings online), Nightingale courts tell us something about the government approach to the problem of court capacity.

Introduced in August 2020 as part of the HMCTS's recovery package, these makeshift courts provided additional estate resource and were part of an effort to reduce the huge increase in court backlogs across both the civil and criminal justice systems (HMCTS, 2020). They quickly proved insufficient. Anecdotal reports[2] from barristers suggested that the new court spaces were underused due to a lack of personnel, and due to restrictions on use, they heard mainly non-custodial crime and were unable to accommodate multi-hander trials[3] (Courtney-Guy, 2020). In spring 2021, the government responded by announcing the launch of so-called 'super courts' to provide additional temporary capacity for multi-hander trials, and at the same time, there was a move to allow more serious criminal cases to be heard in Nightingale courts (HMCTS, 2021b).

This development was a response to the problem of capacity during the pandemic, but it created new problems. In evidence to the House of Commons Committee of Public Accounts report on the backlog in criminal courts, the Deputy Mayor for Policing and Crime in London raised concerns about the lack of thoroughgoing, appropriate support in the new makeshift courtrooms for vulnerable victim-survivors (2022: RBC0005). The same month the report was published, news outlets ran a story about a rape trial involving a teenage victim whose parents were told that there would not be enough space for them to attend the hearing in the allocated Nightingale court (Syal, 2022).

The introduction of Nightingale courts was, as *The Law Society Gazette* succinctly put it, 'like taking a bucket to a house fire' (Hyde, 2020). It revealed not just a serious underestimation of the scale of the problem, but also a lack of thinking about the complexities of the backlogs, the nature of criminal hearings (crucially, from a court user perspective) and the knock-on effects of decisions that answer singularly to efficiency, without regard for other important measures of justice.

One especially neglected measure of justice – not just during the COVID-19 pandemic, but in broader government discussions about court reform and a move to online hearings – is the degree to which court processes and outcomes are accessible to the public. This is an especially pressing challenge in negotiating a more long-term, scaled-up move towards online hearings. As a distinctively public-facing part of the criminal justice system, in common law jurisdictions at least, criminal courts must make their processes and decisions available for public scrutiny. The 18th-century jurist and philosopher Jeremy Bentham famously saw this as a matter of democratic principle. The physical co-presence afforded by open courts, he argued, meant that they could serve as both schools and theatres of justice, and – a more immediately obvious function of the open court – the public's presence would serve as a check on judges' authority and witnesses' testimony (Bentham, 1843).

The move to online hearings during the COVID-19 pandemic – and the restricted access to the limited hearings that did take place in person – very significantly reduced public and media access to criminal courts. This came at precisely the point when a new and controversial legal instrument, the Coronavirus Act 2020, was introduced. Transform Justice sought to observe court hearings throughout the first period of national lockdown and recorded a grievous lack of organization and access. In a blog post outlining the consequences of this new, and temporary, form of 'closed justice', the organization note a before-pandemic situation where 'you could wander into any criminal court, have a look at the court lists and sit in the public gallery to observe'. The government's stay at home order meant that

> for the first time in hundreds of years there are in effect no open criminal courts. Journalists have been invited to 'digitally observe' some hearings but there are few enough court reporters at the best of times, and they (understandably) usually focus on the Crown Court. So that means magistrates' courts are closed – journalists are not covering hearings and the public can't access them. (Transform Justice, 2020)

They go on to detail the implications of this, both in terms of a likely increase in miscarriages of justice, as a result of the lack of outside scrutiny, and the problems arising from defendants' and witness' mediated, and so more partial, participation in the justice process.

It is tempting here to think of this challenge as easily surmountable with better technology and planning. Pre pandemic, there was a move towards as-live streaming of court proceedings – most notably and successfully in The Supreme Court – and so it is possible to imagine a likely transition to streaming full online hearings in such a way that emulates the conditions of the open court. To borrow from McKay (2018), it is important to recognize that such a transition would transform, rather than simply replace, public access to the courtroom and, in turn, the meaning of the open court. There is limited research in this area, but what does exist suggests that production choices in the creation of as-live courtroom footage shape public reception (Moore et al, 2021), that the lack of a physical connection between court personnel and lay viewers changes the performances of lawyers (Flower and Ahlefeldt, 2021) and that in circulating courtroom footage, media platforms such as YouTube tend to decontextualize adjudicatory outcomes (Revier, 2021). In other words, the mediated court is different in kind to Bentham's open court. In other ways besides, we are moving away from the open court of yesteryear. The next section considers more fully what might be emerging in its place.

Imagining post-pandemic justice: the emergence of portal justice and broadcast justice

This chapter started with an observation about historical responses to the threat of disease spread in the courtroom, and it did so in order to suggest that the management of criminal courts during the COVID-19 pandemic was not an inevitable response. Instead, we should see the response as a course of action that answers to, and tells us important things about, the perceived role and function of criminal courts. The official response tells us, for example, which court processes, or elements thereof, are seen as fundamental to the operation of justice and which are seen as superfluous to the main task at hand. Those ideas – about what the criminal court is, in essence – stick, even as certain adaptations and uses of technology might be short-lived. One such sticky idea is that of the virtual court. As previously discussed, the move towards online hearings – much vaunted pre pandemic, and also much delayed – has in practice been mired with problems related to poor technology, lack of system-level thinking and lack of consideration about how to make courts accessible to the media and public. Nonetheless, this remains the direction in which we are headed in England and Wales – after all, the Ministry of Justice has pre-empted the shift, by closing 51 per cent of its physical court estate over the last decade (House of Commons Library, 2020). This penultimate section shifts focus away from the COVID-19 pandemic to consider the overall direction of court and criminal justice reform. It places the move to online hearings alongside other key trends and developments to consider the terrain of post-pandemic justice in the criminal court. From here, the chapter points to the emergence in England and Wales of two distinct models of criminal justice that are set to take the place of the open court: portal justice and broadcast justice. This section proceeds by setting out the key features of each of these emerging models.

Let's start with portal justice. The main impetus here is the desire for greater efficiency. This is the end goal of the current court reform programme in

England and Wales — fewer staff, fewer court buildings and a leaner, less expensive court system (NAO, 2018). Digitization of forms and processes as well as a move to online hearings are seen as key to this, and the expectation is that they will also make things easier, cheaper and more streamlined for court users. This vision of the future is one in which the everyday court user will, in the comfort of their own home, be able to complete processes that would have previously involved arduous trips to court, thus 'enabling justice unrestricted by physical location' (HMCTS, 2021a: 19). Take, by way of example, the Ministry of Justice and HMCTS's response to the 2016 consultation on court reform:

> In a society where people transact digitally in so many aspects of life, they expect a service to be available when they need it. Access to justice cannot, therefore, be defined solely by proximity to a court or tribunal building. It must be defined by how easy it is for people — witnesses, victims, claimants, police and lawyers — to access the service they need, however they choose to do so. (2016: 4)

Here, we see a new understanding of access to justice, where processes should be as friction-free as possible, available 24/7 and a simple matter of logging in to an online portal to complete a form or pay a fee.

This new form of portal justice is becoming increasingly dominant, facilitated not just by the court reforms outlined in this chapter, but also by other, parallel developments. These include the introduction in 2015 of the single justice procedure (SJP) to deal with minor criminal offences, such as fare evasion, speeding offences and non-payment of television licence fees. SJP notices can be issued by a range of bodies — most usually the police, but also Transport for London and rail companies — and if a defendant enters a guilty plea via the dedicated online portal, the case will be decided by a magistrate without a court hearing (Jones, 2021). The SJP has been the subject of considerable criticism by legal campaigners and magistrates. The Magistrates Association, for example, has raised concerns about the lack of transparency concerning processes and outcomes, the lack of legal advice for defendants and the possibility that in moving this part of criminal court process behind closed doors, 'the system may appear to be administrative rather than judicial' (Magistrates Association, 2021). These problems came into stark focus during the COVID-19 pandemic. The SJP was used to charge a large number of people for disobeying the COVID-19-related emergency measures, and as a group of legal campaigners noted at the time, this meant that these cases were subject to less scrutiny than those processed in open court (Fair Trials et al, 2021). While the CPS reviewed charges brought under the new coronavirus-related legislation — and discovered a staggering rate of misapplication of the new regulations, leading to a third of the charges they reviewed being overturned – SJP cases were omitted from this review (Fair Trials et al, 2021).

A key problem with portal justice, then, is that it lacks the more traditional features of openness which allow for public scrutiny of decisions and process. The increased reliance on algorithms to decide criminal justice penalties is likely to exacerbate this problem – and it is worth noting here that a key feature of the Judicial Review and Courts Bill 2021, under review in the House of Lords at the time of writing, is the introduction of automated online conviction and penalty for those who plead guilty to minor criminal offences.

Given that most cases processed by our criminal justice system are minor offences, it might reasonably be suggested that portal justice is set to become the dominant, everyday model. For serious offences, another model of justice is likely to become dominant, one that at the same time as being reserved for a minority of cases will also be far more visible to the public. These cases will proceed to trial and will involve defendants in docks and the recognizable accoutrements of the criminal court. They will also – in a departure from the open court as was – depend to an ever-increasing degree on pre-recorded testimony, live video link participation from some court participants and the creation of video streams for public consumption. We might think of this emerging model as broadcast justice.

Again, the impact of the COVID-19 pandemic on practices in criminal courts sits alongside parallel developments in ushering in this second core model of justice. The COVID-19 pandemic catapulted criminal courts into a situation where most hearings required the online participation of defendants, witnesses and court personnel. Pre pandemic, we saw a slow reconfiguration of public access to court hearings, commensurate with an overall move towards online hearings and hybrid hearings. There has been a global shift over the past 20 years towards the introduction – in some cases, reintroduction – of cameras to courtrooms so that barristers' summing-up speeches, judges' sentencing remarks and, in some jurisdictions, whole trials are filmed and circulated via online platforms (Moore et al, 2021). Pressure from media companies is a key factor here. Just as these organizations have de-invested in court journalists over the last decade, they have become more dependent on audiovisual content as their operations have (also) moved online, and the mega-trials of the 1990s in the United States – the much-publicized court cases involving O.J. Simpson and Michael Jackson – have in turn demonstrated that big criminal court cases make for easy copy (Moore et al, 2021).

It is tempting to see broadcast justice as the obverse of portal justice – that is, as pushing court processes into the spotlight of public scrutiny as opposed to moving them behind closed doors. This, though, is to ignore the very distinctive form of publicity brought by the emerging model of broadcast justice – one that, again, marks it out as different from the open court as was. For one thing, as McKay's (2018) research indicates, the increased reliance on remote connections to a hearing reshapes participation in such a way that the possibility for interaction is limited and, with this, the felt presence of others. As with broadcast media more generally, the relationship between actors and audience is such that the former make appearances and the latter remain at a distance, able to select which bits of proceedings they want to watch. Liveness, long a core feature of the open court, becomes less important when the roles of court participants are reconfigured in this way, and so one of its likely consequences is that different forms of participation – by defendants, witnesses, the public – become asynchronous.

Conclusion

This chapter sought to outline the immediate impact of COVID-19 on criminal courts and explore the opportunities afforded by the new ways of working that emerged during the pandemic, as well as the challenges to more wholesale change. The chapter noted that – in common with other jurisdictions – the reorganization of work in the criminal courts during the COVID-19 pandemic largely involved a move to online hearings. This has long been part of the government's aspirations for court reform. England and Wales is currently in the midst of a £1 billion reform programme that seeks to introduce a new end-to-end case management system, digitize forms and processes, and (where possible) boost remote participation in hearings.

This chapter outlined some of the problems encountered during the COVID-19 pandemic in moving the work of the criminal court online, and in doing so it identified a set of barriers to longer-term plans for court reform. The discussion focused on three key challenges. The first is a lack of suitable digital infrastructure. The second is a lack of systems-level thinking and, as part of this, concern for how one set of changes (such as a move to online practice) might impact on other parts of the justice system. The third is a lack of consideration for media and public access to the criminal court. Although it is tempting to think better technology is the solution to each of these problems, this chapter has urged caution in this respect. More research is needed to understand the ways in which technology might come to transform – rather than simply transpose – existing processes and forms of participation and how, in turn, this might change the meaning and operation of justice.

The chapter's penultimate section moved on to discuss the impact of COVID-19 on the criminal court in broader context and consider what we might expect from the post-pandemic criminal court. I argued that we are seeing the emergence of two distinctive models of adjudicatory justice. One relies on the courtroom as a space of ritual and hierarchy and, to this degree, retains features of the open court as was. Its reliance, too, on audiovisual technology – from witnesses' pre-recorded testimonies to defendants' appearances via video link for remand hearings and the public's consumption of broadcast streams of judges' summing-up remarks – means that it is reconfiguring participation in court hearings. The other emerging form of justice is more administrative in nature, more private and perfunctory. It too moves part of the work online, this time to portals for filling out and submitting forms and completing processes. Earlier, I suggested that we might usefully think of these two models of justice as broadcast justice and portal justice, respectively. The official response to the COVID-19 pandemic might have hastened the shift towards these new approaches to justice, but the ideas that underpin these developments – most important, perhaps, the prizing of online access over the more traditional features of the open court – have been with us for longer and will no doubt play a key role in shaping policy in the post-pandemic world.

Notes

[1] See, for example, Fassin and Pandolfi (2013) or Agamben (2004).
[2] As an aside here, there is a lack of data that tracks the use and outcomes of Nightingale courts and the effectiveness COVID-19-related measures in criminal courts more generally. This has seriously limited the possibility for evaluation of 'what works' (and does not) and, in itself, constitutes a challenge moving forward.
[3] Multi-hander trials involve a large number of defendants (typically, they are cases of gang-related crime, drug trafficking and money laundering).

References

Acland-Hood, S. (2017) 'We're delivering reform – and starting to make a difference', *Inside HMCTS*, [online] 28 September, Available from: https://insidehmcts.blog.gov.uk/2017/09/28/were-delivering-reform-and-starting-to-make-a-difference/

Agamben, G. (2004) *State of Exception*, Chicago: University of Chicago Press.

Anon (2020) 'Remote justice – a view of the pros and cons from an anonymous judge', *Transform Justice*, [online] 6 November, Available from: www.transformjustice.org.uk/remote-justice-a-view-of-the-pros-and-cons-from-an-anonymous-judge/

Baird, V. (2020) *2019/20 Annual Report*, HC 625, London: Victims Commissioner.

Bentham, J. (1843) 'Publicity in courts of justice', in J.H. Burton (ed) *Benthamiana: Or, Select Extracts from the Works of Jeremy Bentham*, Edinburgh: William Tait, pp 115–16.

Bradbury-Jones, C. and Isham, L. (2020) 'The pandemic paradox: the consequences of COVID-19 on domestic violence', *Journal of Clinical Nursing*, 29(13): 2047–9.

Courtney-Guy, S. (2020) 'Nightingale court set up to deal with huge backlog is still being underused', *Metro*, [online] 23 August, Available from: https://metro.co.uk/2020/08/23/nightingale-court-not-used-enough-despite-huge-criminal-case-backlog-13163357/

Courts and Tribunals Judiciary (2020a) *Coronavirus (COVID-19): Jury Trials, Message from the Lord Chief Justice*, [press release] 17 March.

Courts and Tribunals Judiciary (2020b) *Review of Court Arrangements due to COVID-19, Message from the Lord Chief Justice*, [press release] 23 March.

Criminal Justice Joint Inspection (2021) *Impact of the Pandemic on the Criminal Justice System: A Joint View of the Criminal Justice Chief Inspectors on the Criminal Justice System's Response to Covid-19*, [online] Available from: www.justiceinspectorates.gov.uk/hmicfrs/wp-content/uploads/2021-01-13-State-of-nation.pdf

Equality and Human Rights Commission (2020) 'Inclusive justice: a system designed for all', [online] Available from: www.equalityhumanrights.com/en/publication-download/inclusive-justice-system-designed-all

Fair Trials, Big Brother Watch, Transform Justice, Howard League for Penal Reform, APPEAL and Commons Law CIC (2021) *Single Justice Procedure: Unlawful Coronavirus Prosecutions and Convictions Behind Closed Doors*, Letter to Secretary of State for Justice, [online] 1 June, Available from: www.fairtrials.org/app/uploads/2022/01/Single-Justice-Procedure-Joint-letter-June-2021.pdf

Fassin, D. and Pandolfi, M. (2013) *Contemporary States of Emergency: The Politics of Military and Humanitarian Interventions*, New York: Zone Books.

Flower, L. and Ahlefeldt, M. (2021) 'The criminal trial as a live event: exploring how and why live blogs change the professional practices of judges, defence lawyers and prosecutors', *Media, Culture and Society*, 43(8): 1480–96.

Godfrey, B., Richardson, J.C. and Walklate, S. (2021) 'The crisis in the courts: before and beyond Covid', *The British Journal of Criminology*, 62(4): 1036–53.

HMCPSI (HM Crown Prosecution Service Inspectorate) (2020) *CPS Response to COVID-19: 16 March to 8 May 2020*, Publication No CP001: 1272, London: HMCPSI.

HMCPSI (2021) *CPS Response to COVID-19: Dealing with Backlogs*, Publication No CP001: 1281, London: HMCPSI.

HMCTS (HM Courts & Tribunals Service) (2019) 'Guidance: HMCTS reform programme projects explained', [online] Available from: www.gov.uk/guidance/hmcts-reform-programme-projects-explained

HMCTS (2020) *COVID-19: Update on the HMCTS Response for Criminal Courts in England & Wales*, London: HMCTS.

HMCTS (2021a) *Evaluation of Remote Hearings during the COVID-19 Pandemic: Research Report*, London: HMSCTS.

HMCTS (2021b) *More Courts to Speed Up Justice*, [press release] 17 February.

House of Commons Committee of Public Accounts (2022) *Reducing the Backlog in Criminal Courts*, Forty-third Report of Session 2021–22, HC 643, London: House of Commons.

House of Commons Library (2020) 'Data dashboard. Constituency data: magistrates' court closures', [online] 13 May, Available from: https://commonslibrary.parliament.uk/constituency-data-magistrates-court-closures/

House of Lords Select Committee on the Constitution (2021) *COVID-19 and the Courts*, 22nd Report of Session 2019–21, HL 257, London: House of Lords.

Hyde, J. (2020) 'Nightingale courts are like taking a bucket to a house fire', *The Law Society Gazette*, [online] 20 July, Available from: www.lawgazette.co.uk/commentary-and-opinion/nightingale-courts-are-like-taking-a-bucket-to-a-house-fire/5105073.article

Jackson, S. (1978) *The Old Bailey*, London: W.H. Allen.

Jones, S. (2021) 'Explaining the Single Justice Procedure in the magistrates' court', *Inside HMCTS*, [online] 26 October, Available from: https://insidehmcts.blog.gov.uk/2021/10/26/explaining-the-single-justice-procedure-in-the-magistrates-court/

Kettiger, D. and Lienhard, A. (2021) 'Swiss courts facing the challenges of COVID-19', *International Journal of Court Administration*, 12(2): 5. doi: 10.36745/ijca.380.

Magistrates Association (2021) *Position Statement: Single Justice Procedure*, Document number 21/19, [online] 30 March, Available from: www.magistrates-association.org.uk/Portals/0/19%20Single%20Justice%20Procedure_1.pdf

McKay, C. (2018) *The Pixelated Prisoner: Prison Video Links, Court 'Appearance', and the Justice Matrix*, Abingdon: Routledge.

McKay, C. (2020) 'Glitching justice: audio visual links and the sonic world of technologised courts', *Law Text Culture*, 24: 364–404.

McKay, C. (2022) 'Digital justice and video links: connecting and conflating courtroom and carceral space', in K. Duncanson and E. Henderson (eds) *Courthouse Architecture, Design and Social Justice*, Abingdon: Routledge, pp 191–221.

Ministry of Justice and HMCTS (2016) *Response to the Proposal on the Provision of Court and Tribunal Estate in England and Wales*, London: Ministry of Justice.

Moore, S. and Newbury, A. (2017) *Legal Aid in Crisis: Assessing the Impact of Reform*, Bristol: Policy Press.

Moore, S., Clayton, A. and Murphy, H. (2021) 'Seeing justice being done: courtroom filming and the deceptions of transparency', *Crime, Media, Culture*, 17(1): 127–44.

Mulcahy, L. (2008) 'The unbearable lightness of being? Shifts towards the virtual trial', *Journal of Law and Society*, 35(4): 464–89.

NAO (National Audit Office) (2018) *Early Progress in Transforming Courts and Tribunals*, Session 2017–19, HC 1001, London: National Audit Office.

NAO (2021) *Reducing the Backlog in Criminal Courts*, Session 2021–22, HC 732, London: National Audit Office.

Popotas, C. (2021) 'COVID-19 and the courts: the case of the Court of Justice of the European Union (CJEU)', *International Journal of Court Administration*, 12(2): 4. doi: 10.36745/ijca.381.

Puddister, K. and Small, T.A. (2020) 'Trial by Zoom? The response to COVID-19 by Canada's courts', *Canadian Journal of Political Science*, 53(2): 373–7.

Revier, K. (2021) 'The "worst of the worst": punitive justice frames in criminal sentencing clips on YouTube', *Contemporary Justice Review*, 24(4): 436–56.

Syal, R. (2022) 'Nightingale court tells parents of victim of alleged rape there is no room for them at trial', *The Guardian*, [online] 13 February, Available from: www.theguardian.com/uk-news/2022/feb/13/nightingale-court-tells-parents-of-victim-of-alleged-there-is-no-room-for-them-at-trial

Transform Justice (2020) 'Is closed justice a price worth paying to keep courts running?', *Transform Justice*, [online] 3 April, Available from: www.transformjustice.org.uk/is-closed-justice-a-price-worth-paying-to-keep-courts-running/

Walklate, S., Godfrey, B. and Richardson, J. (2022) 'Changes and continuities in police responses to domestic abuse in England and Wales during the Covid-19 "lockdown"', *Policing and Society*, 2(2): 221–33.

Wallace, A. and Laster, K. (2021) 'Courts in Victoria, Australia, during COVID: will digital innovation stick?', *International Journal of Court Administration*, 12(2): 9. doi: 10.36745/ijca.389.

4

COVID-19 and Community Sanctions

Sam Ainslie, Andrew Fowler, Jake Phillips and Chalen Westaby

Introduction

The coronavirus pandemic sent shockwaves around the world, resulting in radical changes to how people in all sectors were expected to do their jobs. The probation service was no exception, with the National Probation Service (NPS) in England and Wales introducing the exceptional delivery model (EDM) following the announcement of the first lockdown on 23 March 2020. This chapter focuses on the impact these changes had on the service, staff and people under supervision. The EDM led to unpaid work (UPW) ceasing (temporarily at least), a pause to the delivery of accredited programmes for all but the highest-risk individuals (which were delivered on a one-to-one basis) and most court-related activities being suspended (Phillips, 2020). The EDM mandated the completion of assessments to review risk management actions and sentence plan objectives for all individuals subject to community supervision (House of Commons Justice Committee, 2020a; Napo, 2020) and determine the method and frequency of supervisory meetings under the new model of delivery (Napo, 2020). Face-to-face meetings with people on probation were reduced in frequency to enable people to adhere to the 'stay at home' message, and most probation practitioners quickly transitioned to working from home. Face-to-face meetings were limited to people assessed as posing a very high risk of harm, prison leavers reporting for their initial appointment, people managed in accordance with counterterrorism legislation and, finally, those without access to remote communication. Where face-to-face meetings were deemed necessary, these were conducted at a probation office and/or via doorstep visits at the client's home.

Remote communication thus became the primary method for delivering community supervision. Clients were contacted by telephone, WhatsApp and Skype, with video messaging to be used wherever possible (Napo, 2020). Remote supervision was considered inferior when compared to traditional face-to-face contact, so contact requirements were increased to twice the frequency (Napo, 2020). As the pandemic progressed, this requirement was relaxed to allow greater professional judgement, ameliorate logistical difficulties and respond to a perception that these additional reporting requirements were too onerous for people under supervision.

Step Two of the *Probation Roadmap to Recovery* (HM Prison and Probation Service – HMPPS, nd) started on 6 July 2021 with reductions in doorstep visits and increased face-to-face contact. This was achieved by reopening some offices and extending the opening hours of others (Ministry of Justice, 2021b). In June 2021 – when the privatized community rehabilitation companies and public sector NPS merged to create the Probation Service – new national standards were introduced (HMPPS, 2021a). These state that contact can be blended in nature (depending on the nature and level of risk posed by the person under supervision) but that 'direct face to face contact ... remains central to the supervision process' (HMPPS, 2021a: 15). That said, the new Target Operating Model (HMPPS, 2021b: 52) states the Probation Service will adopt a 'blended approach to contact (applying learning from COVID-19 delivery arrangements)', so we can assume that some of these developments introduced as a direct response to the pandemic are here to stay for the long term.

In this chapter, we draw on a range of research studies and policy developments to consider how these changes impacted on the capacity for probation to achieve its main objectives (delivering and enforcing court sentences, facilitating rehabilitation, reintegration and reducing reoffending, and public protection). We also consider the impact these changes had on the experiences of those people involved in probation services, including staff and clients, and we conclude with some discussion of the implications of the pandemic on the future of probation practice. Throughout the chapter we draw on data from research we conducted during the pandemic, which took place as part of a larger study that had been designed to evaluate the revised staff supervision framework (the Reflective Practice Supervision Standards, formerly known as the Supervisory Line Management and Meetings Framework). As part of this, we conducted a survey of all staff in the NPS just prior to the pandemic and then interviewed practitioners and managers between January and March 2021 about their experiences of staff supervision, well-being and, more broadly, the emotional labour of probation practice. We have published the findings from this study elsewhere (Phillips et al, 2021; Westaby et al, 2021; Phillips et al, 2022).

Due to the timing of the interviews, participants often talked about what practice had been like during the pandemic. The primary focus of the study will have shaped our data, but the data also reflect the feelings and priorities of our participants, who were given freedom to steer the content of interviews. In total, we interviewed 61 people: 28 senior managers or senior probation officers (SPOs); 30 frontline practitioners – probation officers (POs) and probation service officers (PSOs), and Residential Workers – as well as 3 learning and development POs who had been involved in delivering the supervision framework training the broader study was evaluating. Participants were from a wide range of operations, such as case management, courts, prisons, approved premises and victim liaison units. The sample generally reflected the gender make-up of the NPS, with 43 women and 18 men taking part. The research was approved by Sheffield Hallam University's Research Ethics Committee and agreed by the HMPPS National Research Committee. Additionally, the NPS senior leadership team approved the research, providing us with access to all divisions in England and Wales. Interviews were 45–90 minutes long, and these were transcribed and analyzed to identify key themes that emerged in interviews. One team member collated and coded all instances where the pandemic was referenced, and this was then recoded by other team members to ensure accuracy of interpretation through reflexive thematic analysis (Braun and Clarke, 2006).

Achieving the aims of probation practice during the pandemic

We start our analysis by considering the impact of the EDM on the ability of the NPS to meet its statutory obligations and be 'effective'. We then ask how the pandemic affected its ability to undertake its core functions of delivering and enforcing court orders, managing risk and protecting the public, and delivering rehabilitation and supporting desistance. These different objectives align with the overarching mission of the Probation Service (which has the strapline 'assess, protect, change'), the purposes of sentencing as laid out in the Criminal Justice Act 2003, and what we know about why POs themselves do the job and how they define quality practice (Shapland et al, 2012). Although not mutually exclusive, the objectives are sufficiently different to have different outcomes or measures of 'success', and we draw on these as we progress through our discussion.

Punishment, enforcement and compliance

The pandemic had a profound effect on the way sentences were imposed by the court and subsequently delivered. Here, we consider the delivery of these sentences, focusing on the implications for 'punishment' and how probation staff enforced orders and maximized compliance. Since the Legal Aid, Sentencing and Punishment of Offenders Act 2012, all community sentences must contain a 'punitive element'. The Act defines punitive elements as curfews, exclusion zones and prohibited activities, but it is most often implemented through the imposition of UPW requirements. Undertaking a set number of hours of UPW within the community is a significant restriction on liberty as well as an opportunity to make reparation and build skills that can support rehabilitation. The suspension of UPW, then, severely impacted the ability of probation services to deliver 'punishment' on behalf of the court and restricted the ability of people on UPW to give back to the community as a form of reparation. This quickly led to a backlog in the number of hours of UPW that were to be completed, resulting in several important implications for the delivery of punishment. First, it raised the risk of a perception that people were not being appropriately punished. Second, the backlog risked leading to potential capacity issues once UPW was restarted during the recovery period. One solution to this – implemented by the Scottish Government – was to reduce the number of hours by 35 per cent across all cases, except for those sentenced for domestic abuse, sexual offences and stalking (Casey et al, 2021). Such a move raises questions about the state of community sentences during the pandemic and the extent to which they are parsimonious, productive or proportionate (McNeill, 2018). For example, we might ask whether these newly reduced sentences result in proportionate punishments for people sentenced before the pandemic, and during and after the pandemic lockdowns. Similarly, we could also ask whether the original sentence was actually parsimonious if, later on, a reduced sentence is seen to deliver an acceptable 'amount' of punishment.

Curfews (with or without electronic monitoring) are another method of punishment available to sentencers as part of community sanctions. While, in the period from January to March 2021 compared to the same period in 2020, there was a noticeable reduction (of 21 per cent) in the number of UPW commencements, there was an increase (of 17 per cent) in curfew requirement commencements, suggesting that UPW was replaced – temporarily at least – as the main method for delivering punishment in the community in this period (Ministry of Justice, 2021a). Lockdown legislation introduced a form of curfew or home detention for all but those deemed to be 'essential' workers, and although this fails to account for differences in levels of poverty and quality of housing between the 'offending' population and the 'general' population, it does raise questions about whether the wide-reaching restrictions on everyday life reduced the marginal effect of imposing a curfew requirement. The punitive pains associated with the visible stigma of an electronic tag and lack of autonomy (Payne and Gainey, 1998) would have been reduced given the lack of freedom to interact with others in community settings. By contrast, the recognized pain of family dysfunction (Payne et al, 2014) could have been exacerbated for many by virtue of longer periods spent at home, and this is particularly concerning given the documented increase in reporting of domestic abuse during the pandemic (Office for National Statistics, 2020). Ultimately the 'pain' of a sanction is subjective and best articulated by those who have lived experience, so to truly understand the impact of serving a curfew during the pandemic, further research is required. Given the stated intention to further increase the use of curfews and electronic monitoring (as set out in the *Smarter Approach to Sentencing* White Paper; Ministry of Justice, 2020), such research would be vital for shaping understanding of the 'calculus of compliance' (Nellis, 2020: 1) and the burden that such modes of punishment place on service users and their families.

In addition to inhibiting the ability of probation services to deliver punishment, the EDM curtailed probation practitioners' capacity to enforce sentences. For example, if a client was deemed to be in breach of their order, cases could not be returned to court for breach during the original lockdown. On a theoretical level, this could impact on perceptions of legitimacy of the service should practitioners be unable to enforce sentences, and this suggests an area for future research. Other types of enforcement activity – such as recall for those on licence after release from prison – remained available. However, here we see accentuated ethical and human rights tensions given COVID-19 infection rates in prisons, the lack of opportunity for prisoners to have family and legal visits, and the response by the prison service, which involved locking people in their cells for almost 24 hours per day to prevent infection (see Chapter 5, this volume). Although the context for complying with human rights obligations is not quite the same for probation as it is for prisons (which are part of covered by the National Preventive Mechanism and must comply with the Optional Protocol to the Convention against Torture and Other Cruel, Inhuman or Degrading Treatment or Punishment and), such considerations may have shaped practitioner decisions around recall and enforcement in ways that are not observable in compliance and enforcement statistics.

'Effectiveness and compliance are, in the field of community penalties, topics that are inextricably linked' (Bottoms, 2013: 89). Compliance can be measured through either tangible (and often binary) measures – such as attending appointments, providing clean drug tests, absence of reconviction and successful completion of requirements – or less tangible behaviours – such as the engagement and cooperation of the person on probation. 'Formal compliance' – that is, 'behaviour which technically meets the minimum specified requirements of the order' – was both facilitated and hindered by the pandemic (Robinson and McNeill, 2008: 434). As mentioned earlier, the EDM largely removed the requirement for face-to-face contact in favour of remote communication, particularly telephone calls. This meant that for most, answering the phone was all that was required to ensure they were formally complying with their order, and for some of these individuals, this was considered easier than the requirement to attend an office. As one practitioner in a study by Dominey et al said: '*they just pick up their phone … At the end of the day, they've answered you and you've contacted them*' (2021: 403).

Getting people 'through their orders' has long been a strategy of practitioners who work in a system which has become managerial in its approach to measuring 'good' practice, with many practitioners in Phillips's (2016) study relying on making contact remotely or changing the conditions of an order to make it easier for people to formally comply. Many of the changes to practice that were introduced as part of the EDM would have made 'technical compliance' (Robinson and McNeill, 2008) easier to facilitate. While a lack of face-to-face contact and probation offices being closed meant activities such as drug tests were more difficult to administer, they also became unnecessary as the service sought to reduce the amount of face-to-face contact.

Distinct from 'formal compliance', Robinson and McNeill argue that '[s]ubstantive compliance … implies the active engagement and co-operation of the offender with the requirements of his or her order' (2008: 434). We would suggest this was made more difficult by the pandemic. The EDM changed the priorities of supervision – rather than engagement, practitioners were asked to manage risk through doorstep visits and regular check-ins. Practitioners found this way of operating challenging for risk assessment and antithetical to engagement (Phillips et al, 2021). Moreover, remote communication made it more difficult to achieve the engagement required to achieve substantive compliance. It is not difficult to imagine the challenges faced by staff when trying to actively engage individuals in their sentence planning, take individualized approaches and develop productive relationships with people they have never met and only communicate with by phone. Indeed, practitioners in both our study and Dominey et al's (2021) suggested that remote communication was particularly difficult when it came to people they had not met prior to the pandemic and that this hindered their ability to develop constructive working relationships.

In Weaver et al's (2021) research on compliance with criminal justice interventions in Scotland, three key elements that shape noncompliance were identified: motivational postures and attitudinal stances; systemic structural and social influences; and impacts and effects of interactions with authorities. Passive disengagement (as opposed to overt hostility towards supervision) was seen to result from the pull of other concerns that undermine the salience of community sanctions and override concerns about the consequences of noncompliance. In 'normal' times, these concerns are likely to include a myriad of social and structural issues that impact on willingness to comply. It is reasonable to argue that the pandemic and resulting restrictions were a significant concern with the potential to impact on motivation to fully engage with community sanctions and, thereby, increase the potential for passive disengagement. Furthermore, supervision delivered in line with the EDM has the potential to result in perceptions of procedural injustice given Weaver et al's (2021) findings that this is most linked to the brief nature of most interactions, inadequate support and the outcome of risk-centric decision making. Put simply, remote communication methods could be perceived by some people on probation as superficial, lacking in substantive help or devoid of care and concern. Similarly, doorstep visits risk contributing to a sense of surveillance and monitoring but without the concomitant commitment to support and assistance that is expected by the individuals under probation supervision.

Finally, we would suggest that the pandemic changed the nature of structural barriers to compliance. Barriers to compliance include unstable accommodation, financial problems, lack of community ties, unemployment and literacy issues. Staff have been found to work to overcome such structural barriers to make compliance easier (Phillips, 2016; Ugwudike and Phillips, 2019). The pandemic will have made some of these barriers more acute, and remote supervision will have limited the ability of staff to deal with them. Indeed, participants in our research highlighted how remote communication made it easier for service users to comply formally (because of the removed structural barrier of having to travel) but more difficult to know exactly how the service users were getting on:

'Obviously it's the ones on the telephone that you can't get a sense of how they're looking or whatever, but I feel that most of them have been quite open and so actually sometimes there is a bit of a relief, I think, that they're not having to perhaps trapse in for another appointment or come in to an office or whatever.' (Ava PSO Courts)

'Mine are loving it, if I'm being honest. It's so much easier for them. They've got to pick up the phone once a week and have a 20-minute phone conversation, but I don't think you get the same engagement out of them. You don't get the same information. You can't have the same conversations, because they're sat at home in their living room with their partner and kids in the same room and you've got to talk about offence-related things, and they don't want to have those conversations in front of their family. So, engagement's just not there.' (Esther Professional Qualification in Probation [PQiP])

When it comes to punishing people on behalf of the court, enforcing orders and maximizing compliance, we can identify countervailing effects of the pandemic and the EDM. On the one hand, the delivery of sentences was more difficult because the service's ability to deliver punitive elements of the sentencing framework was affected; substantive compliance was also more difficult to achieve and enforcement more challenging. On the other hand, formal compliance became more feasible and some orders were more parsimonious, because people on probation had to adhere to fewer requirements as UPW and other programmes were paused.

Managing risk and public protection

The focus of probation practice during the pandemic was 'offender management and risk supervision' (Buckland, in House of Commons Justice Committee, 2020b: Q58), highlighting the enduring importance of this aspect of probation practice. To this end, policy makers focused on how to supervise clients by managing risk effectively and prioritizing individuals assessed as posing a high or very high risk of harm. In England and Wales, practitioners could see low- or medium-risk clients face to face, but only where there was a perceived increase in risk. Risk management has long been a key objective of probation, and it is interesting that during the pandemic it resurfaced as the main method of allocating resources. As such, doorstep visits were introduced for high- and very high-risk clients to allow 'staff to have sight of the offender at the address whilst also facilitating a discussion' (Napo, 2020: 1). Despite this, doorstep visits were considered 'a poor substitute for proper face-to-face supervision and proper home visits' (Russell, in House of Commons Justice Committee, 2020a: Q15), yet they continued to be used as a legitimate way of assessing risk. Probation staff in our study complained that using doorstep checks as a risk management tool was time-consuming (partly because of the need for two practitioners to go on each visit) and mostly ineffective:

> 'We still have to see people at home, but we do these doorstep checks. You go and knock on the door, stand two meters back and say hello and how are you doing and, sorry, we can't talk about that on the street, and that's it really. That's a doorstep check. Apparently that's meant to be a risk management tool.' (Paul PO Generic)

Despite having ineffective tools to assess clients, probation staff remained conscious of being held to account with respect to potential serious further offences and felt that they would be held responsible for failing to gather enough information to assess risk or meaningfully engage with their clients:

> 'Basically all they were doing was checking that the person was at the house at that point, but people have felt ... it has been really difficult to get information to do formulations with, so they've kind of shied away a bit from having those conversations about some of the childhood trauma experiences, and rightly so ... So all of that, and people have

said it hasn't felt like doing what I should do, which has been very difficult for officers ... then there was worries around will I be hauled up for this?' (Dionne PO Offender Personality Disorder pathway)

We have argued elsewhere (Phillips et al, 2021b) that the restrictions on face-to-face contact led to practitioners, in McNeill's (2020) words, 'defaulting to welfare checks and/or a basic form of surveillance', reinforcing the idea that substantive compliance was difficult to achieve. Moreover, we identified an overarching perception among practitioners that the organization was seeking to cover its back at all costs:

> There was a lot of pressure to carry on regardless, but carry on doing more regardless as well. So that's taken its toll on everyone. (Zachary PO Generic)

> So that makes me really cross because to me that's not about actually managing risk, that's a back covering exercise in case something goes wrong. Somebody kills somebody, god forbid, during lockdown and they want to cover themselves. (Charmaine PO Generic) (Quoted in Phillips et al, 2021: 435)

Dominey et al also discovered that staff found risk assessment in the pandemic difficult, partly because of the need to communicate remotely: 'Practitioners were particularly concerned that the loss of sensory feedback reduced their ability to make accurate judgments about risk' (2021: 400). In relation to risk management we can observe, then, a real tension between preventing the spread of COVID-19 and doing effective or quality work. At times, people struggled because they had to remain physically distanced, while at other times, they wanted to remain physically distant because the only alternatives were ineffective and served to put people at risk of either spreading the virus or doing work which was perceived to be solely about covering their back. A further consideration here is the way in which COVID-19 shaped the risk that people posed in the first place:

> 'Sometimes you've just felt that there have been more people that are being ... there are people out there that haven't been given credit for the fact that they've actually reduced their own risks by actually adhering to COVID restrictions, and not all of those have led to an increase in DV [domestic violence] or sexual crimes being committed.' (Zachary PO Generic)

Zachary's comment suggests that solely focusing on managing risk and public protection fails to take into consideration the fact that, on the whole, by complying with COVID-19 restrictions, people on probation were also reducing the risk they posed. Managing risk has long been the 'raison d'etre' Kemshall (1998) of the probation services, yet remote communication and the need for social distancing made risk assessment, risk management and, by implication, public protection more difficult.

Rehabilitation, supporting desistance and working relationally

It is a long-standing belief among probation staff that relational engagement with individuals is 'at the heart of the probation enterprise' and that rehabilitation is a core endeavour of this relational work (Senior et al, 2016; see also Burnett and McNeill, 2005; Phillips, 2013). The development of effective working relationships between probation practitioners and service users enables probation workers to manage risk, protect the public and induce compliance, but this also contributes towards an equally important value to which probation practitioners are committed: belief in the service user and their capacity to change (Lewis, 2014).

Despite challenges around 'using' criminal justice to rehabilitate people, rehabilitation has survived as a legitimate correctional penal policy by adapting to three dominant discourses. According to Robinson (2008), rehabilitation is now: utilitarian by becoming justified on the grounds of protecting the public from harm; managerialist by making use of prescribed processes and interventions determined by risk and measured via quantitative outcomes; and expressive in that it is a punishment in its own right rather than an alternative to punishment. We would suggest that rehabilitative work during the EDM suffered along each of these lines. McNeill (2012) identifies four forms of rehabilitation: personal, social, moral and legal. Personal rehabilitation relates to promoting positive individual-level change, and as already mentioned, this was incredibly difficult to achieve through remote communication and doorstep visits. As one participant said:

> 'I'm struggling to work out how to do workbooks. I know it's a mental block that I haven't delivered a workbook over the phone – I'm used to having a bit of paper there between us and going through it, and they've got a bit of paper ... so, yeah, I've kind of put it off.' (Isabela PO Generic)

Moral rehabilitation relates to offenders making reparation as a means of restoring their social position, and social rehabilitation relates to recognition and acceptance of the ex-offender within the community. This occurs via interventions such as UPW or restorative justice, which were prevented from taking place by the EDM. Rehabilitation can also be '*social* in the sense that rehabilitation seeks to promote the restoration or establishment of social bonds that will support the (re)integration of the individual into the community and in doing so, strengthen collective efficacy of society itself' (Burke et al, 2023: 19). The pandemic posed serious challenges to this way of working with people on probation:

> 'It's been much more difficult because there's less resources there to help them. Less activities, more restrictions, so it's been much more difficult.' (Abby PO Generic)

Rather than probation rehabilitating people, the 'desistance paradigm' (McNeill, 2006) asks us to think about doing probation *with* people rather than *to* them. Thus, desistance-focused probation practice empowers people to make their own decisions about where they want to be in their lives and supports them to get there. We can, thus, consider 'effectiveness' by thinking about how practitioners were (un)able to perform their role in a way which supported the preconditions for desistance. Being a 'counsellor' who develops motivation and 'holds hope' was difficult during the pandemic, particularly given the impact of lockdown on our participants' own emotional wellbeing (see the next section).

Empowering clients and promoting a sense of agency in the context of widespread restrictions on 'normal life' and building trusting working relationships will have been constrained by the pandemic. Additionally, the difficulties in delivering programmes and one-to-one supervision made it difficult for practitioners to perform the role of 'educator', where they seek to develop human capital, normally through programmes, rehabilitation activity requirement interventions and structured work to improve cognitive skills. Finally, working remotely made it difficult to advocate on behalf of clients; accessing services to support social capital growth was severely restricted given the lack of community services which normally work with and alongside probation interventions. In short, the pandemic and the EDM had serious implications for both the social-relational and structural dimensions of the desistance process which practitioners are expected to assist (McNeill, 2006).

Ultimately, to be effective in assisting desistance, practitioners need to provide practical help and resources alongside 'sustained positive feedback and encouragement' (Villeneuve et al, 2021: 75). This was especially difficult for practitioners when examined through the lenses of emotional literacy (Knight, 2014) and emotional labour (Fowler et al, 2018). Emotional labour requires the worker's emotional displays to conform to feeling rules or display rules established by the organization (through, for example, induction, recruitment, policy and staff supervision) and as a result of becoming occupationally acculturated within their chosen profession (Hochschild, 1983; Rafaeli and Sutton, 1989; Ashforth and Humphrey, 1993; Adams and Mastracci, 2019). Display rules can also be societal, and these more general norms often influence organizational and occupational display rules (Ekman and Friesen, 1975; Ashforth and Humphrey, 1993). Probation staff are expected to perform emotional labour because of such display rules (Fowler et al, 2018; Westaby et al, 2019), which can be achieved through surface or deep acting. Surface acting is the feigning of outward emotional displays, which disguises incongruous inner feelings; deep acting is where a worker attempts to align their feelings with outward emotional displays, either through experience or by training their imagination (Hochschild, 1983). Emotional labour is one way in which practitioners contribute to the overarching goals of an organization, and so any changes to emotional labour expectations are likely to impact on how 'effective' practitioners are.

Emotional labour performed by probation staff prior to the pandemic was primarily face to face, but the EDM prioritized remote communication. As McNeill (2020: 1) points out, '[p]ractitioners are used to reading and relying on non-verbal cues to guide their interventions', so for some of the participants in our study, the lack of face-to-face contact made it difficult to determine the emotional labour they needed to perform:

'I found it very difficult trying to manage from afar with just telephone calls, and I think nothing can replace that face-to-face structure that you have with your service user, because you can read their body language, you can see if their eyes are dark, you know, you're picking up on all these things that are going on, if there's a change in their appearance. All that was missing, because also I couldn't do a home visit either because I was shielding completely. I've got to be honest, I was worried constantly that I wasn't picking up on important issues or that the phone calls were becoming quite static, because on the whole people were doing what they needed to do and were staying in, so there wasn't really anything to discuss.' (Nettie PSO Generic)

This reflects findings from other studies, with Dominey et al (2021), for example, noting that staff found it difficult to establish satisfactory supervisory relationships over the telephone. Even so, our participants reported that where there was an established working relationship, the adjustment to voice-to-voice contact was easier:

'the only ones that I've really had that I've allowed telephone contact with is the ones that I've got a really good established relationship with, so on the phone I can ... I know their confident enough to tell me when they're not coping, they're confident enough to say "I need to see you", and then I do then see them in the office, regardless.' (Abby PO Generic)

Sturm et al (2021) found that telephone calls were difficult where there was no working alliance between the probation practitioner and the client or where English was not the service user's first language (Dominey et al, 2021). Where a probation staff member had no prior relationship with an individual on probation, this proved to be a barrier to developing a working relationship and inevitably affected their ability to work with the client towards rehabilitation:

> 'I hate it with a passion. I've got a few offenders who have come out and it's been during lockdown, and you just feel as though you just don't know them. I really feel as though I struggle to get to grips with people more recently. I much prefer the relationships that I've developed prior to lockdown, because I feel as though they are more trusting as well, so they will talk a bit more freely ... it tends to be phone calls, and again, for the phone call, you just don't feel as though you've got that level of the relationship.' (Violet PSO Generic)

Trying to rehabilitate people on probation in 'normal' times is challenging, and rehabilitation as a penal strategy is a difficult one to justify. To do so during a pandemic appears to be even more difficult. Indeed, regardless of the lens we have used to examine rehabilitation in the pandemic, this element of probation practice has been severely affected. That said, the flexibility that remote communication provides may prove useful in the longer term (Sturm et al, 2021), and the lack of data on the impact of this on longer-term compliance, reoffending rates and desistance (as difficult as that is to measure) means it is difficult to fully assess the impact of the pandemic in this area.

Impact on staff of working in probation in the pandemic

The boundary between work and family life and how this can be managed effectively is an important consideration in the well-being of probation staff. There is no single correct way to manage the boundary between work and family life. While one person may carefully divide the two, another may allow their work life to overlap with their personal life (Kossek, 2016). Where work spills over into family lives, work–family conflict can arise and impact on well-being (Westaby et al, 2016), and our data suggests this was exacerbated by the pandemic:

> 'It's the appropriateness of it, isn't it? And I think that is one of the things that was missed at the beginning of this pandemic. If you can work from home, then work from home. So we physically can work from home – but having a detailed MAPPA [multiagency public protection

arrangement] meeting when you're talking about somebody's sexual offending isn't appropriate when you've got children around. I think that is something that the service failed to acknowledge, that actually the nature of our work is not child-friendly, is it? We don't have children coming to the office, for a very good reason. And my kitchen is now my office, and on top of that my husband also works for the service, he works with offenders, so we are both working in the kitchen, and we have all that juggle going on as well.' (Vicki PSO Victim liaison officer)

Our participants reported that having to do their work at home meant they could not easily detach from the 'emotional dirty work' (Ward and McMurray, 2020) expected of them. As Ursula (SPO Generic) states, there was no "safe space to switch off". The pandemic also resulted in staff working longer hours and needing more flexible work patterns because of caring for children and/or vulnerable family members (HM Inspectorate of Probation, 2020; Norton, 2020), resulting in even more acute work–family conflict.

Given the emotionally demanding work required of probation practitioners, it is important to consider the amount of work expected from staff. Probation staff in the NPS find their work to be 'relentless' (Phillips et al, 2016), and increasing workloads and complexity of cases only serves to decrease their well-being. In a study of POs in the United States, it was also found that probation staff who supervise more service users with mental health concerns are affected more negatively in terms of their own mental and emotional well-being (Gayman et al, 2018). Prior to the pandemic, staffing issues were already present within the NPS: the NPS reported over 600 vacancies in England and Wales in June 2019 (HM Inspectorate of Probation, 2019: 4), and the pandemic exacerbated already high workloads. With no workload compensation granted to practitioners, this created additional pressures for probation staff:

'In fact, what they did … was double the number of times we have to have contact with people. They increased the level of contact we had to have … if you try and do everything that you're supposed to in the job, and we have seen it time and time again, those people burn out and they go off, or they become managers because they don't want to do it any more. It's just impossible to do that … So, yeah. COVID made that much more difficult, because they were really on top of the tracking systems, as in the monitoring systems, to make sure that you're having the contacts that you had to have, and you'd literally double.' (Zachary PO Generic)

'So I am now working longer. Whereas when I was in the office, I wouldn't mind staying longer, because there at least I know when it's done, it's done, and I'm not taking it back home with me.' (Charmaine PO Generic)

To ensure the continued well-being of staff, it is important to have access to both organizational and peer support (Lee, 2017), and a number of practitioners in our study felt unsupported by their line manager at crucial points during the pandemic:

'It was the start of COVID, working a lot from home, nearly all the time from home really ... I had this man I'd been working with for about six months became really, really aggressive and threatening. It was all over WhatsApp. It was on the phone. I don't think it was because I was in my own home or what, but it felt really, really threatening ... I asked for quite a lot of support with that, but I didn't feel I got it. It felt very much like, well, you know, we have difficult people all the time and we deal with them. And it was like, well, actually this felt really different, it felt really targeted, it felt very personal. But I didn't get anything back really. So it's stuff like that really that I feel is missing, feeling that sometimes that's the support I need sometimes that we just don't get.' (Gabrielle PO Generic)

That said, SPOs in our study were mindful of the additional emotional toll working in accordance with the EDM had taken on their staff. And it is clear from discussions with some frontline practitioners that they were gaining support from the NPS through SPOs:

'You build up a resistance and an ability to be able to cope with separating the work from home, and [my SPO has] gone through the process of talking about that, so how can you do that, what's going to be useful for you, what do we not need to do, what do we need to do, you know, going through that kind of process ... We talked about, okay, so what can you do in terms of having space? What about having somewhere different to work, all those kinds of things, and this is something we just kind of talked about. Yeah. It's been a process of us having a conversation, which I imagine she's had with lots of other people as well.' (Kian PO Trainer)

Moreover, providing emotional support to frontline practitioners has in turn placed additional emotional strain on SPOs, who were also trying their best in a difficult situation:

'There is always time when a staff member will be struggling or will be completely emotional about something or has a really bad week, but it's just been more frequent. And that has meant a lot more energy has had to go into that, and when you're having those conversations with staff, you yourself as an SPO are absorbing that as well, so you are then carrying it around and that has been really tough. I've had periods where I've been quite upset off the back of having conversations with individuals and the team as a whole, because you just want to be doing your best for people. It's really hard to support everyone and make things good for people. You just can't do it, so you end up feeling "Oh have I done enough? Is there something more? I wish I could take that off you." But you are just doing your best really.' (Ursula SPO Generic)

The most significant impact on staff well-being came from the lack of opportunity to engage in collective emotional labour and offload with other colleagues as a coping mechanism (Fowler et al, 2018). 'Communities of coping' (Korczynski, 2003) enable service workers to turn to each other for emotional support. While some participants described being able to gain support from peers in alternative ways during the pandemic, working from home has generally been detrimental in terms of staff peer support:

'The thing that I missed the most was the unquantifiable exchanges that you have with your colleagues all the time, who've just heard you have a difficult phone call or a difficult exchange, and you can release the pressure of that … it took me a long while to realize how important that was and how hard it was to work without it. That sort of glue or whatever it was that was helping us manage that has gone, and it's made it much more important for us to acknowledge the emotional impact of the work.' (Brianna SPO Generic)

'Yeah. It's more difficult really, I think. I've got a couple of people I'm quite close to that I would ring up just for a chat about things, but I think most people you only contact them if there's a work-related issue. Certainly, in the office, you could be making a cup of coffee and someone will walk in and say are you all right? You go, no! You barge into it, sort of thing!' (Gabrielle PO Generic)

Remote supervision appears to have taken its toll on people working in the service. The sensorial nature of penal supervision – using senses to assess and understand where someone is and where they are going – and communicating by phone made this difficult and, in the words of one participant in Dominey et al's (2021: 399) study, 'demanding and tiring'. We already know that probation work is hard because of the nature of the work – the pressures of talking about sensitive issues, dealing with high workloads and managing so-called high-risk people can take its toll. Working from home combined with remote supervision methods and increased frequency of contact with people made doing probation work even more difficult in the pandemic. Our own research and that of others in the field of probation suggest that the pandemic has exacerbated many of the pre-existing issues.

Probationers' experience of being under supervision during the pandemic

There is a small body of literature exploring the lived experience of people on probation. Our own participants noted that it became more difficult to provide the services their clients would normally rely on:

> 'Up to recently as well in the last three, four years, I ran a mental health group at [location] and at [location] as well, which was very much service user led really, looking at people's emotional well-being, sort of coping with being on probation, coping with release from prison and stuff like that. Well, that's stopped with COVID at the moment.' (Gabrielle PO Generic)

Gabrielle's take here is that people's experiences will have been negative, but staff are poor proxies for understanding service users' experiences. In their study of justice-affected people in Scotland, Casey et al (2021) found that people reported reduced access to support services because of difficulties in accessing online services. Casey et al (2021) highlight that some people under supervision reported restricted access to technology and others were prohibited from using the internet as part of the sentence conditions. At a time when all aspects of life pivoted to online, the experiences of people under probation supervision during the pandemic are likely to have been particularly acute.

Despite this, participants in Casey et al's study suggested that their supervision had become looser, because they 'could just "go through the motions" by phone' (2021: 484). On the other hand, Dominey et al (2021) found that remote communication afforded both parties greater accessibility and this could enable more proactive and reciprocal forms of communication which had not been available before the pandemic. For some service users, this meant supervision became easier and less disruptive to their lives:

> 'I'm actually much happier. It always seemed a chore to go to the office. Sometimes it would take an hour to get there just for a 10-minute meeting.' (Service user quoted in HM Inspectorate of Probation, 2021: 4)

However, the NPS's move to remote supervision impacted negatively on some clients. User Voice (2021) reports that while remote supervision suited some people under probation, certain vulnerable clients struggled due to a lack of support systems (see also Dominey et al, 2021). Remote communication increases the chances for miscommunication or lack of communication between probation staff and clients, and this risks creating further anxiety:

> 'Got a text message telling me that I have an appointment in the office, but I've already sorted that with my case manager and it's a phone call, not me going into the office. It's confusing when the case manager tells me one thing and a text message is telling something different. Causes me stress and anxiety.' (Service user quoted in User Voice, 2021: 9)

> 'I have not heard anything since before Christmas. I have had 2 calls scheduled but nobody has rang. I have tried to get hold of my PO but was told that she was on sick and someone else would ring but nobody ever has. I don't have long to go so don't want anything to go wrong.' (Service user quoted in User Voice, 2021: 8)

Like probation practitioners, clients noted the difficulty in developing a rapport and good working relationship with the probation staff:

> 'I didn't meet my officer while in prison and I thought it wasn't OK for someone I had never even met to be making such massive decisions about me and my life.' (Service user quoted in HM Inspectorate of Probation, 2021: 4–5)

The pandemic extended periods of supervision because final review meetings were delayed (Casey et al, 2021) and, as discussed earlier, people undertaking UPW were not able to complete this within the planned time frame. This has impacted negatively on clients, not only in terms of potentially extending their order, but also with respect to the uncertainty it brings in terms of when their order will end and whether they might be recalled for not completing work:

> 'I need help with my CP [Community Payback] – I don't know anything – not knowing what I'm doing or if I'm going to be recalled for not attending CP- no one has told us anything about what is going on – until now- thank you for keeping me up to date jason – why can't they just do the same as what you are doing.' (Service user quoted in User Voice, 2021: 10)

> 'I have not heard a thing about when I can complete my hours. I only have 6 hours left and feel as though I am in limbo until I can finish

them. Not sure how long this is going to go on for, surely I could do them with some social distancing or whatever, shops and pubs are open so why can't unpaid work be done?' (Service user quoted in User Voice, 2021: 10)

'Lockdown affected me mostly because I wanted to get going but everything was, and still is, at a standstill.' (Service user quoted in HM Inspectorate of Probation, 2021: 5)

People on probation also raised concerns about where they would access support when their order finished. They had come to rely solely on their PO due to a lack of support elsewhere, and they felt unprepared for life after their order:

'I'm off my order soon, so the phone calls will drop off a cliff. I do worry as there is nowhere else to get support at the moment and probation have been helping with more than just reoffending. They've been there the whole time, and filled the gaps of other services.' (Service user quoted in HM Inspectorate of Probation, 2021: 6)

There were, then, countervailing themes in that 'while less may have been demanded of some of those subject to unpaid work requirements, the social marginalisation associated with supervision has been exacerbated, and the pains of being suspended in punitive limbo have also been sharpened' (Casey et al, 2021: 489). That said, more research clearly needs to be done to understand how people under probation supervision experienced the pandemic. Such research will have potentially important findings about what went well in probation during the pandemic and what lessons should be learned from this unplanned transition to remote working.

Conclusion

The challenges for probation services and those on probation during the pandemic are clear to see. We have shown that meeting the statutory aims of probation has been challenging, and now we consider what this means for the future of probation. Our analysis suggests it was difficult to deliver the key objectives of probation in the context of paused UPW, closed courts and restricted access to support services and traditional ways of developing relationships with people on probation. The understanding of 'compliance' shifted to surface-level assessments as the sensorial qualities of informed risk assessment were inhibited due to remote communication. Similarly, we have heard that while people on probation did not have access to the same support services, they successfully managed their own risk and adhered to the government's message to 'stay at home'. This reveals important questions, opportunities and observations about the future direction and nature of the Probation Service.

The pandemic brings to the fore key questions about the aims of probation work and how these should be achieved. The experiences of staff and supervised individuals were, in many ways, intensified and became less satisfactory. Moreover, the pandemic raises questions about how equity and proportionality are implemented in sentencing; how the burden of punishment is experienced by people on probation; how compliance should be measured; and what the role of co-production should be in compliance. Finally, some broader questions become more pronounced in this context: What is the role of the senses in risk assessment? How can remote communication be used in the context of rehabilitative work? What is an appropriate caseload in terms of risk, complexity of need and volume? And, finally, what support do probation workers require to deal with the toll that their practice can take?

There is currently no data on the impact of the EDM on compliance, reoffending and desistance, and it might be wise to see what transpires before making recommendations. However, we can confidently say probation staff continued to support people on probation, their colleagues and the community during, and in spite of, the pandemic. While coping with their own pressures of lockdown, social distancing and COVID-19, the desire for a welfare-orientated approach in probation became prominent rather than being hidden, apologetic and behind the scenes. Looking ahead to the newly unified Probation Service in England and Wales, there is an opportunity to create a service which prioritizes certain aims and objectives (Ainslie, 2021), building on learning from Transforming Rehabilitation and the pandemic:

> Therefore, in probation, our aim is to use recovery work not simply to return to business as usual as quickly as possible, but to transition to a reformed, unified model of probation. Our Recovery Programme will ensure that everything we do pulls together to deliver the probation system we want for the future and that we have a consistent approach to achieving this which maintains continuity of essential service delivery and minimises disruption to front line delivery. This presents opportunities of learning and innovation for potentially new ways of working, and to build a more resilient service which is better prepared for any future emergencies. (Ministry of Justice, 2021b: Q17)

If this new model is to succeed, we would suggest it is time to harness the experiences of people on probation in the vision of this new 'resilient' service. The support one participant experienced from clients during the pandemic revealed the humanity at the core of the probation endeavour:

'What COVID has done as well is every now and again I've had an offender turn round and I've asked them how they are, they've turned round and said how are you though? How are you coping through all of this? You don't always get that in this job. It means a lot sometimes. It's nice of them to say it and it's nice to hear it, but you don't hear it often enough in this job from people that you're working with or colleagues or partnerships.' (Zachary PO Generic)

These insights have a great deal to teach us about how probation might move forward. Rather than being focused almost exclusively on risk – as happened with the EDM and which many of our participants eschewed – probation might start to move towards a re-emergence of the 'radical socialist model' in which the commitment to social reform, community change and empowerment of service users comes to the fore (Ainslie, 2021: 44). The pandemic forced the state to intervene in society to protect the vulnerable (for example, through the furlough scheme and the all-out project to put homeless people into accommodation) in a way not seen since the Second World War. Perhaps this represents an opportunity for such an approach to be adopted and pursued by organizations and practitioners who are responsible for working with one of the most vulnerable groups of people in society, however tainted the former may be. Rather than referring to welfare-focused probation work as 'old school', we would argue that this form of practice should more visible and acceptable. If the pandemic allows for this, then at least one good thing could be rescued from the ashes of this otherwise devastating crisis.

To conclude, in this chapter we have presented analysis of previously published literature and new research data to argue that the pandemic made it difficult for probation services to achieve their official objectives. In response to the pandemic, probation services initially reverted to risk assessment as the main focus of practice, with staff working from home but finding it difficult to engage people substantively by phone and video call. This way of working took its toll on staff, who struggled with reduced access to communities of coping and increased demands around the performance of emotional labour. That said, the increased flexibility afforded by remote working appeared to work well for some people. One such group was the people under supervision who, despite losing access to systems of support, found the experience less "tight". The pandemic recovery period in conjunction with the ongoing move towards a unified service provides the opportunity to rethink the way probation defines its overarching aims and objectives. We would argue that this period should be used to find the balance between making probation more flexible and responsive to the needs of people on the caseload (through, for example, the potential benefits of remote communication) and, at the same time, protecting the well-being of staff and individuals on probation from the loneliness that characterized so many people's experiences of life in lockdown.

References

Adams, I.T. and Mastracci, S.H. (2019) 'Hidden in plain sight: contrasting emotional labour and burnout in civilian and sworn law enforcement employees', in J. Phillips, C. Westaby, A. Fowler and J. Waters (eds) *Emotional Labour in Criminal Justice and Criminology*, Abingdon: Routledge, pp 185–95.

Ainslie, S. (2021) 'Probation: what next and who decides?', *Probation Quarterly*, 21: 42–5.

Ashforth, B.E. and Humphrey, R.H. (1993) 'Emotional labor in service roles: the influence of identity', *The Academy of Management Review*, 18(1): 88–115.

Bottoms, A. (2013) 'Compliance and community penalties', in A. Bottoms, L. Gelsthorpe and S. Rex (eds) *Community Penalties: Change and Challenges*, Abingdon: Routledge, pp 87–116.

Braun, V. and Clarke, V. (2006) 'Using thematic analysis in psychology', *Qualitative Research in Psychology*, 3(2): 77–101.

Burke, L., Carr, N., Cluley, E., Collette, S. and McNeill, F. (2023) 'Introduction: reforming, reimagining and moving forward: for what purpose?', in L. Burke, N. Carr, E. Cluely, S. Collette and F. McNeill (eds) *Reimagining Probation Practice: Re-forming Rehabilitation in an Age of Excess*, Abingdon: Routledge, pp 1–28.

Burnett, R. and McNeill, F. (2005) 'The place of the officer-offender relationship in assisting offenders to desist from crime', *Probation Journal*, 52(3): 221–42.

Casey, R., McNeill, F., Barkas, B., Cornish, N., Gormley, C. and Schinkel, M. (2021) 'Pervasive punishment in a pandemic', *Probation Journal*, 68(4): 476–92.

Dominey, J., Coley, D., Ellis Devitt, K. and Lawrence, J. (2021) 'Putting a face to a name: telephone contact as part of a blended approach to probation supervision', *Probation Journal*, 68(4): 394–410.

Ekman, P. and Friesen, W.V. (1975) *Unmasking the Face: A Guide to Recognizing Emotions from Facial Clues*, Englewood Cliffs, NJ: Prentice-Hall.

Fowler, A., Phillips, J. and Westaby, C. (2018) 'Understanding emotions as effective practice: the performance of emotional labour in building relationships', in P. Ugwudike, P. Raynor and J. Annison (eds) *Evidence-based Skills in Community Justice: International Research on Supporting Rehabilitation and Desistance*, Bristol: Policy Press, pp 243–62.

Gayman, M.D., Powell, N.K. & Bradley, M.S. (2018) 'Probation/parole officer psychological well-being: the impact of supervising persons with mental health needs', *Am J Crim Just*, 43, 509–29.

HM Inspectorate of Probation (2019) *An Inspection of Central Functions Supporting the National Probation Service*, Manchester: HM Inspectorate of Probation.

HM Inspectorate of Probation (2020) *A Thematic Review of the Exceptional Delivery Model Arrangements in Probation Services in Response to the COVID-19 Pandemic: A Review by HM Inspectorate of Probation*, Manchester: HM Inspectorate of Probation.

HM Inspectorate of Probation (2021) *Service User Perspectives on How Probation Is 'Getting Back to Normal' after the COVID-19 Pandemic*, [online] Available from: www.justiceinspectorates.gov.uk/hmiprobation/wp-content/uploads/sites/5/2021/02/210210_Epic_Report_3-2.pdf

HMPPS (HM Prison and Probation Service) (nd) *Probation Roadmap to Recovery*, [online] Available from: www.gov.uk/government/publications/covid-19-probation-roadmap-to-recovery

HMPPS (2021a) *National Standards 2021: Supporting Transition to the Unified Model*, https://assets.publishing.service.gov.uk/government/uploads/system/uploads/attachment_data/file/998799/National_Standards_2021_-_Supporting_transition_to_the_Unified_Model_-_June_2021__in_English_.pdf

HMPPS (2021b) *The Target Operating Model for Probation Services in England and Wales*, [online] Available from: https://assets.publishing.service.gov.uk/government/uploads/system/uploads/attachment_data/file/1061047/MOJ7350_HMPPS_Probation_Reform_Programme_TOM_Accessible_English_LR.pdf

Hochschild, A.R. (1983) *The Managed Heart: Commercialization of Human Feeling*, Berkeley, CA: University of California Press.

House of Commons Justice Committee (2020a) *Oral Evidence: Coronavirus (covid-19) Impact on Prison, Probation, and Court System*, HC 299, [online] Available from: https://committees.parliament.uk/oralevidence/283/html/

House of Commons Justice Committee (2020b) *Oral Evidence: The Work of the Lord Chancellor*, HC 225, [online] Available from: https://committees.parliament.uk/oralevidence/248/pdf/

Kemshall, H. (1998) *Risk in Probation Practice*, Farnham: Ashgate.

Knight, C. (2014) *Emotional Literacy in Criminal Justice: Professional Practice with Offenders*, Houndmills: Palgrave Macmillan.

Korczynski, M. (2003) 'Communities of coping: collective emotional labour in service work', *Organization*, 10(1): 55–79.

Kossek, E.E. (2016) 'Managing work–life boundaries in the digital age', *Organizational Dynamics*, 45(3): 258–270.

Lee, R. (2017) 'The impact of engaging with clients' trauma stories: personal and organizational strategies to manage probation practitioners' risk of developing vicarious traumatization', *Probation Journal*, 61(4): 372–87.

Lewis, S. (2014) 'Exploring positive working relationships in light of the aims of probation, using a collaborative approach', *Probation Journal*, 61(4): 334–45.

McNeill, F. (2006) 'A desistance paradigm for offender management', *Criminology and Criminal Justice*, 6(1): 39–62.

McNeill, F. (2012) 'Four forms of "offender" rehabilitation: towards an interdisciplinary perspective', *Legal and Criminological Psychology*, 17(1): 18–36.

McNeill, F. (2018) *Pervasive Punishment: Making Sense of Mass Supervision*, Bingley: Emerald Publishing.

McNeill, F. (2020) 'Penal supervision in a pandemic', *The Scottish Centre for Crime & Justice Research*, [online] Available from: https://sccjrblog.wordpress.com/2020/05/04/penal-supervision-in-a-pandemic/

Ministry of Justice (2020) *A Smarter Approach to Sentencing*, CP 292, [online] Available from: www.gov.uk/government/publications/a-smarter-approach-to-sentencing

Ministry of Justice (2021a) 'Offender management statistics quarterly: January to March 2021', [online] 29 July, Available from: www.gov.uk/government/statistics/offender-management-statistics-quarterly-january-to-march-2021/offender-management-statistics-quarterly-january-to-march-2021

Ministry of Justice (2021b) *Written Evidence from Ministry of Justice*, [online] Available from: https://committees.parliament.uk/writtenevidence/12400/html/

Napo (2020) *Additional Guidance in Light of the Most Recent Government Covid 19 Guidance*, [online] 24 March, Available from: www.napo.org.uk/sites/default/files/COVID%2019%20Guidance.pdf

Nellis, M. (2020) 'Electronic monitoring curfews: back with a vengeance', *Centre for Crime and Justice Studies*, [online] 14 December, Available from: www.crimeandjustice.org.uk/resources/electronic-monitoring-curfews-back-vengeance

Norton, S. (2020) 'COVID-19 pandemic: practitioner reflections on probation practice', *Irish Probation Journal*, 17: 183–90.

Office for National Statistics (2020) 'Domestic abuse during the coronavirus (COVID-19) pandemic, England and Wales: November 2020' [online] Available from: www.ons.gov.uk/peoplepopulationandcommunity/crimeandjustice/articles/domesticabuseduringthecoronaviruscovid19pandemicenglandandwales/november2020

Payne, B.K. and Gainey, R.R. (1998) 'A qualitative assessment of the pains experienced on electronic monitoring', *International Journal of Offender Therapy and Comparative Criminology*, 42(2): 149–63.

Payne, B.K., May, D.C. and Wood, P.B. (2014) 'The "pains" of electronic monitoring: a slap on the wrist or just as bad as prison?', *Criminal Justice Studies*, 27(2): 133–48.

Phillips, J. (2013) 'Understanding "the relationship" in English probation practice', in I. Durnescu and F. McNeill (eds) *Understanding Penal Practice*, Abingdon: Routledge, pp 122–38.

Phillips, J. (2016) 'Myopia and misrecognition: the impact of managerialism on the management of compliance', *Criminology and Criminal Justice*, 16(1): 40–59.

Phillips, J. (2020) 'Delivering probation during the Covid-19 pandemic', *The Sheffield Institute for Policy Studies*, [online] 30 April, Available from: https://sheffieldinstituteforpolicystudies.com/2020/04/30/delivering-probation-during-the-covid-19-pandemic/

Phillips, J., Ainslie, S., Fowler, A. and Westaby, C. (2022) '"What does professional curiosity mean to you?" An exploration of professional curiosity in probation', *The British Journal of Social Work*, 52(1): 554–72.

Phillips, J., Westaby, C., Ainslie, S. and Fowler, A. (2021) '"I don't like this job in my front room": practising probation in the COVID-19 pandemic', *Probation Journal*, 68(4): 426–43.

Phillips, J., Westaby, C. and Fowler, A. (2016) '"It's relentless": the impact of working primarily with high-risk offenders', *Probation Journal*, 63(2): 182–92.

Rafaeli, R. and Sutton, R.I. (1989) 'The expression of emotion in organizational life', in L.L. Cumming and B.M. Staw (eds) *Research in Organizational Behavior* (Vol 11), Greenwich, CT: JAI Press, pp 1–42.

Robinson, G. (2008) 'Late-modern rehabilitation: the evolution of a penal strategy', *Punishment & Society*, 10(4): 429–45.

Robinson, G. and McNeill, F. (2008) 'Exploring the dynamics of compliance with community penalties', *Theoretical Criminology*, 12(4): 431–49.

Senior, P., Ward, D., Burke, L., Knight, C., Teague, M., and Chapman, T., et al (2016) 'The essence of probation', *British Journal of Community Justice*, [online] 15 March, Available from: https://mmuperu.co.uk/bjcj/articles/the-essence-of-probation/

Shapland, J., Bottoms, A., Farrall, S., McNeill, F., Priede, C. and Robinson, G. (2012) *The Quality of Probation: A Literature Review*, Sheffield: Centre for Criminological Research, University of Sheffield.

Sturm, A., Robbers, S., Henskens, R. and de Vogel, V. (2021) '"Yes, I can hear you now ..." Online working with probationers in the Netherlands: new opportunities for the Working Alliance', *Probation Journal*, 68(4): 411–25.

Ugwudike, P. and Phillips, J. (2019) 'Compliance during community-based penal supervision', in P. Ugwudike, H. Graham and F. McNeill (eds) *Routledge Companion to Rehabilitative Work in Criminal Justice*, Abingdon: Routledge, pp 870–80.

User Voice (2021) *Coming Out of COVID: Solutions from the User Voice*, London: User Voice.

Villeneuve, M.-P., Dufour, I.F. and Farrall, S. (2021) 'Assisted desistance in formal settings: a scoping review', *The Howard Journal of Criminal Justice*, 60(1): 75–100.

Ward, J. and McMurray, R. (2020) *The Dark Side of Emotional Labour*, Abingdon: Routledge.

Weaver, B., Piacentini, L., Moodie, K. and Barry, M. (2021) 'Exploring and explaining non-compliance with community supervision', *The British Journal of Criminology*, 61(2): 434–55.

Westaby, C., Fowler, A. and Phillips, J. (2019) 'Managing emotions in probation practice: display rules, values and the performance of emotional labour by probation practitioners in their interactions with clients', *International Journal of Law, Crime and Justice*, 61: 1–11.

Westaby, C., Phillips, J. and Fowler, A. (2016) 'Spillover and work–family conflict in probation practice: managing the boundary between work and home life', *European Journal of Probation*, 8(3): 113–27.

Westaby, C., Phillips, J., Fowler, A. and Ainslie, S. (2021) *An Evaluation of the Implementation of Reflective Practice Supervision Standards in the National Probation Service*, Sheffield: Sheffield Hallam University.

5

COVID-19 in Custody: Responding to Pandemics in Prisons in England and Wales

Christopher Kay

Introduction

The introduction of the first cases of COVID-19 in England and Wales saw a sudden and significant strain placed on a range of public services, with general practitioner surgeries, hospitals, schools, adult social care and others having to adapt quickly to life with the virus. While the impact of the pandemic on such services cannot be denied, the virus also posed a 'very real threat … to our other, often unfairly overlooked, frontline service: our prisons' (Neill, 2020). This chapter focuses on the impact of the first two waves of the COVID-19 pandemic on the prison system in England and Wales. Through an analysis of epidemiological and criminological evidence alongside policy literature, it highlights the impact of the pandemic itself on prison residents and the ways in which COVID-19 policy and practice affected prison life. From here, it identifies a series of lessons around the ways pandemics are managed in the prison system and provides recommendations for how future pandemics might be managed. In doing so, the chapter provides a detailed account of pandemic management within the prison system itself and considers the dichotomy that exists between populist penal politics and public health more generally.

The problem: pandemics in prison

The first two cases of COVID-19 in the prison system in England and Wales were reported by HMP Manchester in early March 2020, and as happened with transmission in the general population, the virus spread quickly throughout the prison estate (Jarvis, 2020). Figures from the Prison Reform Trust (PRT) show that roughly one month after the identification of the first two cases, there were over 500 confirmed cases, both prison staff and residents, spread over 67 prisons (PRT, 2020). This figure is likely to be a significant underrepresentation given that only symptomatic infection was being tested at the time (Rice et al, 2021), and that was largely dependent on the availability of testing facilities. Indeed, such was the variability of access to testing across the estate that by April 2020 there were 227 laboratory-confirmed cases among residents, but 1,385 'possible/probable cases' (O'Moore, 2020: 3).

The introduction of COVID-19 into the prison system was potentially disastrous. Early modelling from the UK Health Security Agency (formerly Public Health England) estimated that without any regime changes, there could be up to 2,700 deaths (based on a population of 81,000) across the prison estate (O'Moore, 2020: 6). More conservative estimates were produced in modelling undertaken by UCL, which predicted a rate of up to 1 per cent, or 800 deaths, from a similar population (Townsend et al, 2020). Criminal justice researchers, epidemiologists and public health experts were clear in their concerns surrounding the potential impact of COVID-19 in the prison system, suggesting that 'the risk of exposure of COVID-19 to prisoners and staff ... is far, far greater than the risk to individuals in the wider community' (Coker, 2020: 2). Indeed, when writing in 2011 about influenza, the Health Protection Agency noted that 'prisons run the risk of significant and potentially more serious outbreaks, with large[r] numbers of cases than the community' (2011: 153). There are multiple reasons for this, relating to the virology of COVID-19 itself but also the broader contextual realities of the prison service in England and Wales before the pandemic hit.

There is a significant body of evidence demonstrating that while COVID-19 is highly contagious and can spread quickly (World Health Organization – WHO, 2020a), with symptomatic and asymptomatic transmission more likely to occur through prolonged close contact (Li et al, 2020), this is particularly the case in closed environments. Nishiura et al (2020) note that 'the odds that a primary case transmitted COVID-19 in a closed environment was 18.7 times greater compared to an open-air environment' (see also Coker, 2020; Leclerc et al, 2020). Infection can also occur through contact with contaminated surfaces (Kaur et al, 2021). Research has also identified that 'poor ventilation in confined indoor spaces is associated with increased transmission of respiratory infections and COVID-19 in particular' (European Centre for Disease Prevention and Control, 2020a).

The contagiousness of a disease is represented in the form of a basic reproduction value, commonly given as 'R_0' (WHO, 2020a). This value suggests how many people an infected individual is likely to pass the virus on to. An R_0 of 1, for example, suggests that each infected individual will pass the virus on to one more person, who will infect one more person and so on. During the early stages of the first wave of the pandemic, the R_0 was between 2 and 2.5 in England and Wales,[1] meaning that every infected person would transmit the virus to another 2 to 2.5 people. In an attempt to reduce the levels of transmission within the community, there was a need for stringent social distancing measures to be implemented, with research demonstrating that '[s]ocial distancing measures reduce the value of the effective reproduction number R' (Anderson et al, 2020: 932; see also Kaur et al, 2021). Implementing social distancing practices in a prison environment, however, is at best difficult.

In order to provide context to this discussion, we first have to recognize the fact that long before the COVID-19 pandemic, prisons were considered to be 'epidemiological pumps' (Coker, 2020) and 'potential hotbed[s] for viral transmission' (Neill, 2020). The Prison Service could be seen to be in a state of crisis long before the introduction of COVID-19. It was experiencing 'mass incarceration, overcrowding, underfunding and growing concerns over the substandard conditions within prisons' (Brennan, 2020: 1215). In December 2019, the prison population stood at 82,300, 'equating to 98% of the useable operational capacity of the estate', with the most overcrowded prisons operating at between 147 per cent and 163 per cent of their operational capacity (National Audit Office, 2020: 18). While this may perhaps seem like a relatively abstract figure, a 2018 inspection report from the House of Commons Health Committee brings the nature of such overcrowding into stark relief:

> We were shown a three-bed cell, consisting of a bunk bed on the left-hand side and another bed up against the opposite wall. The gap between the two beds appeared to be about a metre wide. Room to move around the cell was limited; if all three men were standing there was not enough space for them to pass each other without touching. (House of Commons Health Committee, 2018; see also Brennan, 2020).

Such overcrowding was further compacted by the levels of disrepair to be found across the prison estate as a result of underinvestment and budget cuts. A 2020 report from the National Audit Office states that 'as at April 2019, there was [sic] 63,200 outstanding maintenance jobs and, as at November 2019, MPPS estimates it could cost £916m to address the major works backlog' (National Audit Office, 2020: 7). The report goes on to state that in the ten years from 2009–10 to 2019–20, 1,730 cells had been permanently decommissioned across the estate for 'failing to meet ... legislative and prison standards for space, light, heating and ventilation, as well as statutory obligations for health, safety and fire prevention' (National Audit Office,

2020: 18). This rate of cell attrition was expected to continue, with HM Prison & Probation Service (HMPPS) expecting to lose a further 500 cells annually, 'owing to the scale of disrepair, based on recent trends' (National Audit Office, 2020: 18).

Even without such levels of overcrowding, underinvestment and poor prison conditions, the frenetic nature of prison life and the constantly fluctuating population make it exceptionally difficult to control the transmission of communicable disease within a prison environment – especially a virus as transmissible as COVID-19. Before the first identified cases of COVID-19 in the prison estate and for a short while afterwards, the movement of and interaction between residents was common. They would move between blocks for education, employment, gym time and recreation, and to eat, sleep and so on. Movement between prisons was also common for a range of reasons, such as changing risk categories or to support reintegration post release. There is also a constant stream of residents entering and leaving the prison system each year. A recent report from the Sage EMG Transmission Group (2021: 8–9) notes that 'in a normal year there are c. 37k transfers between prisons, 55k releases, 100k hospital appointments, 53k people received from courts, 99k people received from community/police and 65k court appearances'. This fluctuation or 'churn' coupled with the constant influx of people into the prison environment from outside, such as prison service staff, service providers, visitors and so on, makes it difficult to prevent the introduction of viruses into a prison and even more difficult to control them once they're inside.

This became evident once COVID-19 entered the prison estate. Infection rates within the prison population were considerably higher than in the community, with 7.6 confirmed cases per 1,000 people in prisons compared to 4.9 per 1,000 in the general population during the first wave of the pandemic. While such numbers were cause for concern on their own, this was compounded further with the realization that the prison population closely matched the profile of people who were most likely to contract severe disease or even die as a result of infection.

It was identified early in the pandemic that those who were at the highest risk of severe disease and death from COVID-19 were those 'aged over 60 years and those with underlying [health] conditions' (WHO, 2020c: 12). Data from the Office for National Statistics (ONS) at the start of the pandemic showed that the majority of early deaths associated with COVID-19 were among those aged 65 and over, with nearly 40 per cent of all deaths within the first four months of the pandemic occurring in the 85 and over age group (Kay, 2020; ONS, 2020). Indeed, an early study by Guan et al (2020: 1710) found that 'patients with severe disease were older than those with non-severe disease by a median of 7 years'. While it is important to acknowledge broader contextual factors relating to the case fatality rates

(CFRs) of COVID-19, those over 60 present a higher risk of contracting severe disease as a result of infection than those under 60.

Alongside this, the available research has also demonstrated a link between underlying health concerns, or 'comorbidities', and an increased CFR linked to COVID-19 infection (WHO, 2020c). Studies into COVID-19 mortality rates found that 'the presence of any coexisting illness was more common among patients with severe disease than among those with nonsevere disease' (Guan et al, 2020: 1710). Unfortunately, as a patient's age increases, so too does the likelihood of an increased number of comorbidities. An analysis of the epidemiology of COVID-19 by Rice et al (2021: 2185–6) argues that '[o]lder age groups also experience a high burden of noncommunicable diseases, putting them at increased risk for more severe infection'.

Both age and underlying conditions are of significance when it comes to the prison population at the start of the pandemic. It is generally accepted that the prison population is ageing, with the 60 and over category being the fastest growing across the prison estate. In 2020 there were 3,281 people over the age of 60 in prison, with 1,638 aged 70 or over. This figure jumps to 13,038 for those aged 50 and over (PRT, 2021a). Not only this, but the general health of prisoners was (and remains) a cause for concern. Beard (2020: 1) notes that 'the physical health of the prison population, across a broad range of conditions, is much poorer than that of the general population'. Levels of respiratory conditions among people in prison is higher than that found in the general population, as is the prevalence of immunosuppression (as a result of HIV infection; Health Protection Agency, 2011). When COVID-19 hit, the poor health of the prison population, combined with their age levels and the problems with prison sanitary conditions, discussed previously, created a perfect storm for viral transmission, severe disease and death across the prison estate. What was clear was that in order to reduce the rates of transmission and death across the prison estate, the prison service needed to act quickly. Coker (2020: 15, emphasis added) warned that '[h]ours matter if transmission is to be stopped. Without *timely* and *effective* containment steps, a prison would result in transmission and climbing of cases until a peak was reached in terms of new cases occurring on a daily basis' and an increased CFR along with it.

The response: plugging the 'epidemiological pump'

The potential for transmission of infectious disease within the prison estate is significant. A recent report by the Department of Health (2011: 153) notes that 'prisons run the risk of significant and potentially more serious outbreaks' of communicable disease than in the community, owing to not only the architecture of the prison system but also the demographic of its population so much so that, as already mentioned, prisons have widely been considered 'epidemiological pumps' for a range of communicable diseases (Coker, 2020). While there is considerable international evidence documenting the spread of infectious disease within prisons (Baillargeon et al, 2004; Dolan et al, 2007; Department of Health, 2011), the epidemiological profile of COVID-19 combined with the realities of incarceration in England and Wales meant that rapid action was required in order to contain the spread of the virus across the estate. The epidemiological pump needed to be plugged, and quickly.

It should be noted that the Prison Service responded promptly to the threat posed by COVID-19. In March 2020, the entire prison estate was placed into 'command mode', meaning all prisons under a single national command structure that was overseen by the COVID-19 Gold Commander. While command mode was usually only implemented in a single site, the introduction of a national command mode allowed for decisions to be made quickly and consistently across the entire estate. In addition to the implementation of command mode nationally, the Prison Service introduced a COVID-19 strategy which was targeted at reducing the introduction and transmission of the virus across the prison estate. The strategy was centred around three distinct elements (HMPPS, 2020: 1):

- the introduction of the Exceptional Regime Management Plan;
- a temporary Population Management Strategy; and
- a cohorting strategy separating symptomatic, newly arrived and most vulnerable prisoners.

These were introduced alongside an increase in personal protective equipment distribution, routine testing of prison *staff* and increased hand sanitization facilities.

The Exceptional Regime Management Plan

Before going into detail about the nature of the Exceptional Regime Management Plan (ERMP), a brief note on regime management pre COVID-19: Under the national Regime Management Planning strategy, each prison adopts a regime plan from one of four categories: Green, Green/Amber, Amber/Red, Red. These are largely dependent on resources and staffing levels at any given time. Prisons aim to deliver Green regimes as long as staffing levels allow, but as resources and staffing reduce, so too does the level of activity that can be undertaken, and the regime category is adjusted accordingly. Red is the lowest standard of regime that a prison 'can ever achieve' (HMPPS, 2020: 3). This is reserved for 'periods when staff resources have fallen below the locally agreed Minimum Staffing Level ... and only basic regime can be achieved' (HMPPS, 2020: 3). This is important to note because the ERMP introduced to combat the transmission of COVID-19 across the prison estate sat '*below* red regime' activity (HMPPS, 2020: 7, emphasis added). The ERMP identified four key principles that were to be maintained at all times:

1. Provision of meals;
2. Provision of medication and essential healthcare services;
3. Provision of safety and welfare services such as suicide prevention support for vulnerable prisoners
4. Provision of access to family contact (via in-cell phones or other temporary measures) (HMPPS, 2020: 3)

The ERMP was initially conceived to combat potential reductions in staff levels due to COVID-19 infection. However, the rapid spread of the virus in the community (and the potential for even faster spread throughout the prison estate) prompted its introduction in April 2020 in an attempt to reduce transmission among residents. The implementation of the ERMP resulted in residents spending significantly longer periods of time in cells (up to 23 hours a day), with all nonessential activity (accessing the gym, education, employment and so on) suspended. Residents were grouped into smaller cohorts that were unlocked separately for meals in order to reduce contact between residents en masse. But there remained a limit to the extent to which interaction between residents could be controlled given the level of overcrowding across the estate at the start of the pandemic. In order to effectively control the risk of transmission among residents, the prison population needed to be reduced.

Population Management Strategy

It was widely recognized by public health experts (Coker, 2020; Edge et al, 2021), social scientists (Kay, 2020) and policy makers alike that a reduction in the prison population was necessary to reduce the potential for COVID-19 transmission across the prison estate. The population management strategy was introduced shortly after the ERMP and consisted of two main components. The first was a new model for inter-prison transfers (IPTs). When the ERMP was implemented, all prison transfers were immediately suspended in order to reduce the likelihood of residents with COVID-19 transmitting the virus to a new site. The new IPT strategy allowed for transfers between prison, but only in exceptional circumstances, such as exceptional compassionate, legal or operational circumstances, or for transfers to and from secure mental health facilities or between the prison and immigration removal estates (HMPPS, 2020: 5).

The second, and arguably more contentious, component of the population management strategy was the (short-lived) early release scheme for suitable residents who were nearing their planned release date. The scheme was part of a drive towards single cell occupancy, which would reduce the potential for transmission between residents sharing accommodation. The implementation of the early release scheme would bring England and Wales in line with Scotland, Ireland and other international jurisdictions that had already launched such schemes (Kay, 2020). The scheme was initially earmarked for pregnant women and those in mother and baby units, but it was extended in April 2020 to include those in male prisons who were within two months of their automatic release date. It was estimated that around 4,000 residents would be eligible for the early release scheme (Beard, 2020) and that this would create the headroom needed to implement effective social distancing and cohorting strategies (discussed in the next section) within the prison estate.

The implementation of the scheme, however, was fraught with problems and subject to criticism from multiple avenues. While there was agreement that early release was an efficient way to create space across the prison estate, the initial rollout of the scheme was slow. For instance, on 31 March 2020, it was announced that 70 pregnant women were to be released as part of the early release scheme, yet only 6 had been released by 7 April, and only 18 residents across male and female prisons had been released (Howard League for Penal Reform, 2020). Criticism also came in the form of questions surrounding the target number of residents to be released under the scheme. Modelling from Public Health England indicated that the prison population would need a significant reduction in order to achieve single cell occupancy, estimating that about 15,000 people would need to be released (O'Moore, 2020). The Prison Governors Association was also critical of the proposed scheme, arguing that 'following application of the stringent criteria and risk assessment, the number eligible would be far less [than the 4,000 residents considered eligible by the HMPPS], possibly as low as 2,000' (2020: 1–2). A far cry from the 15,000 releases deemed necessary to create space across the estate.

Such debates, however, quickly became irrelevant as the early release scheme failed to be successfully implemented. The scheme was briefly suspended after six Category D residents were incorrectly released and needed to be recalled (Grierson, 2020). It was subsequently relaunched at the end of April, before being shelved indefinitely shortly after. The automatic release of residents coupled with fewer people being sentenced to custody as a result of the increasing backlog of cases going through the courts (see Chapter 3) meant that the prison population had dipped below the numbers hoped for had the scheme been successful. In total, 33 residents were released during this period (BBC, 2020).

Cohorting strategy

'Cohorting', in this context, refers to grouping residents together in order to maintain a degree of control over transmission risk within a prison and to protect those at high risk of contracting severe disease from the virus. The cohorting strategy implemented by the HMPPS in relation to COVID-19 sought to achieve three key aims:

> to protect those most susceptible to the virus, ... to isolate those who are *symptomatic* ... and ... to hold newly received prisoners separated from the main population until enough time has passed for COVID-19 infection to be *expressed in symptoms if they are infected*. (HMPPS, 2020: 6, emphasis added)

In order to achieve this, three separate cohorting units were created within each prison, and these were, ideally, held separate from the general prison population (Table 5.1).

A similar cohorting strategy had been used in 2010 to reduce the impact of influenza on the prison system. Residents with suspected influenza were assessed and either isolated on their own (if there was space to do so) or cohorted with other positive cases (Health Protection Agency, 2011). While this was an effective strategy for combatting the spread of influenza, it's use in relation to COVID-19, particularly early in the pandemic, was problematic. A caution from the WHO highlights this issue:

> Building scenarios and strategies only on the basis of well-known pathogens risks failing to exploit all possible measures to slow transmission of the COVID-19 virus, reduce disease and save lives.
> COVID-19 is not SARS and it is not influenza. (WHO, 2020c: 18)

Table 5.1: Cohorting units

Name	Description
Reverse Cohort Unit (RCU)	Temporary separation of newly received residents for 14 days each
Protective Isolation Unit (PIU)	Temporary isolation for *symptomatic residents* for up to seven days each; to be used if isolation within current cellular location is deemed inappropriate
Shielding Unit (SU)	Temporary isolation for those residents in the NHS England vulnerable persons cohort until the government advises shielding is no longer necessary

Source: Adapted from HMPPS (2020)

One of the major concerns surrounding the cohorting strategy was the fact that it was based solely on symptomatic cases. With the exception of shielding vulnerable residents, the other aims of the strategy focused on isolating symptomatic residents or cohorting new residents long enough for them to become symptomatic if they were in fact infected. The problem here is that the available epidemiological evidence shows that COVID-19 can result in both symptomatic and asymptomatic infection (Li et al, 2020; Zhou et al, 2020), meaning that some cases will not express any symptoms but remain just as infectious as those who do. There were also question marks over the time in isolation for residents in the Protective Isolation Units (PIUs). Initial guidance from the WHO (2020b) 'required a patient to be clinically recovered and to have two negative RT-PCR [reverse transcription–polymerase chain reaction] results on sequential samples taken at least 24 hours apart' before terminating isolation. In May 2020, this changed to ten days after the onset of symptoms plus three days without symptoms (for symptomatic cases). The seven-day isolation period in the PIU, then, not only seemingly went against this guidance but also risked releasing infectious residents early.

It does have to be remembered that the testing infrastructure and capacity at the start of the pandemic was limited, so focusing testing efforts on prison staff, who spent time both in the community and the prison estate and were potentially asymptomatic, makes sense. This is especially true if the strategy to minimize transmission within the prison was robust enough to offer protection from community transmission. The problem is that it wasn't, and so the implementation of a cohorting strategy based on symptomatic infection meant that there was potential for a significant body of positive cases to be missed, thereby limiting the ability of the strategy to control the spread of the virus. The organization required to implement a cohorting strategy also takes time. Davies et al (2020: 60) note that 'by 21 April – a month after the lockdown strategy was launched – only a quarter of prisons had been able to fully implement compartmentalization'.

Creating space

Alongside the cohorting strategy, there was a need to create space across the prison estate to allow for easier facilitation of social distancing measures in each prison. The early release scheme (mentioned earlier and discussed in more detail in the section headed 'Early release schemes') was one way of creating space, but a number of other strategies were also used to achieve this aim. First, the HMPPS announced that 500 single-occupancy 'temporary accommodation' units would be installed in seven category C and D prisons in England and Wales (Ministry of Justice and HMPPS, 2020c). This would allow residents who were currently sharing cells to move to single cell occupancy, thereby reducing the risk of transmission between residents. Given what we know about the transmission of COVID-19 in overcrowded environments with poor ventilation, increasing the amount of accommodation within a prison in order to allow for greater distancing between residents made sense; even so, there were criticisms of this approach.

In order for the strategy to be successful, space needed to be created quickly. As we have seen, 'hours matter' in reducing COVID-19 transmission (Coker, 2020: 15). But building new accommodation within the prison estate takes time, so compromises had to be made. Garside (2020) notes that '[b]ehind the euphemisms lies a stark reality. The "temporary, single occupancy cells" are adapted shipping containers' (see Figure 5.1). The use of adapted shipping containers in this way is not a new phenomenon, as containers have been used as '"quick fix" solutions for prison accommodation' in many countries worldwide (Grant, 2013: 36). However, they are far from the ideal solution, for several reasons. The available research on the use of such containers as makeshift prison accommodation has suggested that the design and positioning, along with the increased capacity resulting in reduced levels of interaction between prisoners and staff, can increase the potential for prison violence (Wright and Goodstein, 1991; Grant, 2013). Moreover, the composition of shipping containers can cause considerable environmental issues, such as interstitial and surface condensation (Smith, 2005), and there are also issues of sound reverberation and noise disruption (Grant, 2013).

Alongside the introduction of temporary accommodation in existing sites, the HMPPS announced the reopening of the former Medway Secure Training Centre as an annex to HMP Rochester, which would temporarily house 70 Category D residents during the pandemic (Ministry of Justice and HMPPS, 2020b).

Each of these approaches to creating space meant the prison service could distribute the prison population more broadly, thereby allowing for the implementation of social distancing, which could prevent the transmission of COVID-19 throughout the estate. While the efficiency with which this was done should be recognized, critics were mindful of the potential problems associated with such a response. For instance, expanding the levels of accommodation across the estate also expanded the surface area which needed to be covered in each prison. While this is great for social distancing measures, we have to remember that the prison system was facing a staffing crisis *before* the pandemic (PRT, 2019; Davies et al, 2020), which was only exacerbated with COVID-19 being transmitted through the estate. By mid-2020 it was estimated that nearly a quarter of all prison staff were self-isolating as a result of COVID-19 infection (Beard, 2020), severely reducing the ability of each prison to successfully implement even the most basic regime under the ERMP. On top of this, the word 'temporary' should be treated with caution when it is used in this context, with previous attempts

Figure 5.1: Shipping containers used as temporary prison accommodation

to close 'temporary prison accommodation' not being particularly successful. For instance, HMP Weare, a prison ship berthed at Portland Harbour in Dorset, was 'temporarily' utilized to relieve pressure on the prison system in 1997. It remained open for eight years before finally being closed in 2005 (see Garside, 2020).

The lessons: successes and areas for improvement

The policy discussed in this chapter laid the groundwork for what has turned out to be a long-term pandemic strategy within the prison estate. As in the community, the prison service has (at the time of writing) had to deal with three waves of COVID-19, with the intensity of transmission and subsequent risks of outbreaks and mortality being 'substantially higher' in the second wave than the first (Sage EMG Transmission Group, 2021: 10). Once again, this impacted on the prison estate to a greater extent than the community, with the standardized mortality rates in prisons being '1.7 fold higher than the general population in the first wave and 4.5 fold higher in the second wave' (Sage EMG Transmission Group, 2021: 10).[2] But with each wave, the service was able to learn and adapt. The testing infrastructure improved, with reception testing for new residents being introduced in September 2020 along with increased routine testing of prison staff, the provision for mass testing during outbreaks and the introduction of a wastewater testing pilot (Sage EMG Transmission Group, 2021: 2). Residents were also vaccinated in line with the priority groups established in the community vaccination drive.

By June 2020, the service was looking to safely remove the restrictions implemented across the estate with the introduction of the National Framework for Prison Regimes and Services (Ministry of Justice and HMPPS, 2020a). The framework allowed for individual prisons to move between regime stages, from Stage 5, 'complete lockdown', for sites experiencing an active and large-scale outbreak, to Stage 1, 'prepare', for sites with no or very low rates of infection. The level of restriction decreases from Stage 5 to Stage 1, with the reintroduction at Stage 3 of social visits with limited capacity and the reintroduction of education at Stage 2. Movement between stages is determined by national and local conditions, such as the imposition of national or local lockdowns, and is based on assessment of each site individually.

The result of these efforts is that the prison service was able to avoid the worst-case scenarios predicted in the early modelling by Public Health England and UCL. As of January 2022, across the prison estate, there have been 32,823 confirmed cases of COVID-19 among residents and 159 deaths confirmed or suspected to be from COVID-19 (Ministry of Justice and HMPPS, 2022).[3] A far cry from the 77,800 cases and 2,700 deaths predicted by Public Health England and even the conservative estimates from UCL's modelling. There are multiple reasons for this.

A key factor is that the prison service reacted quickly in order to reduce the transmission of the virus. The first national lockdown in England and Wales was imposed on 23 March 2020, and the prison service implemented their own lockdown the following day and introduced the ERMP in April 2020 (Hardwick, 2020). When the second national lockdown was announced on 5 November 2020, the prison service implemented its second lockdown on 6 November. The speed at which the restrictions were implemented in prisons reduced the potential for transmission between residents (HM Inspectorate of Prisons – HMIP, 2020b) and the available evidence shows that 'the prompt imposition of [lockdown measures] saved lives' (Hardwick, 2020: 12). The swift imposition of a central command structure has also been recognized as being beneficial in controlling the spread of the virus, as it allowed for decisive and consistent action to be taken quickly across the entire estate (Davies et al, 2020). It has been noted that 'strict central control appears to have contributed to limiting local outbreaks of the virus and its transmission from prison to prison' (Hardwick, 2020: 15).

The available evidence also demonstrates that levels of communication between prison staff and residents were effective in obtaining support for the stringent lockdown measures being implemented (HMIP, 2020b), particularly during the early stages of the pandemic. A summary of short scrutiny visits conducted by HM Inspectorate of Prisons (2020a: 6) states:

> While many of these limitations were extreme, there was a high level of acceptance and cooperation among [residents], supported by generally good communication about the reasons for such actions by most prison managers. For some weeks, there was a sense of [residents] … and staff 'being in this together'.

The service was also seen to react with technological advancements, both in relation to testing and maintaining links with the community. As previously mentioned, the development of the testing infrastructure enabled mass testing at outbreak sites and the revision of guidance for reverse cohorting so that time in the Reverse Cohort Unit (RCU) could be cut from 14 days to 7 days with two negative lateral flow tests (SAGE EMG Transmission Group, 2021). This allowed for greater use of the RCU as residents were able to be released into the main prison sooner, freeing up space for other residents within the unit. Existing projects aiming to implement video call facilities in all prisons were also accelerated (HMIP, 2020a).

It is important to remember that the facilitation of COVID-19 restrictions, which has saved lives across the prison estate, could not have been undertaken without the cooperation of a dedicated workforce and an understanding prison population. The available reviews of the response to the pandemic in prisons highlight staff dedication and resident compliance as key factors allowing the prison system to remain operational. Hardwick (2020: 16) notes that '[p]rison service managers and staff and [residents] themselves have not had the credit they deserve for the way in which they responded to the […] COVID-19 epidemic' (see also HMIP, 2020b).

It can be argued, therefore, that there have been successes within the prison estate during this time. The measures introduced to reduce the transmission of the virus, and subsequent hospitalizations and deaths, have been seen to work. The number of confirmed cases and deaths, while still tragic, have remained considerably lower than even conservative estimates put forward at the start of the pandemic. However, as Hewson et al (2020: 570) note, while these measures were 'implemented to reduce disease within prisons … these measures are not cost free'.

These costs relate to the impact of prolonged lockdown measures on residents and staff. While it was seemingly the case that residents understood and accepted the need for stringent lockdown measures at the start of the pandemic, support began to wane as weeks turned into months and years, and with prisons moving between lockdown conditions. A recent survey of service users found that with prolonged periods of 'being contained within small cells (often shared) and [with] limited contact with prison staff, healthcare, civilian staff and peers, the sense of goodwill is dissipating and resilience is waning' (Wainwright and Gipson, nd: 22). This was compounded by poor prison conditions, discussed earlier, with HMIP referring to the living conditions in some prisons as 'unacceptable and degrading' (HMIP, 2020a: 13).

Research undertaken with prison staff has also highlighted the negative impact of centrally imposed lockdown measures, as they were seen to curtail the autonomy of individual prison governors. Prison staff reported frustration at not being able to make adjustments to regimes without permission from the HMPPS, resulting in delays to the relaxation of restrictions in individual prisons. This added to the frustration felt by residents as staff were unable to provide any indication of when lockdown measures would be lifted (HMIP, 2020a), particularly when residents could see that the restrictions in the community, outside the prison walls, were slowly being lifted, yet the ones inside remained (HMIP, 2021).

Perhaps the largest cost, however, is the impact of the measures on the mental and physical well-being of residents. In a study undertaken by a service user charity, 'around half of all respondents found their mental health had deteriorated since the start of the pandemic' (Wainwright and Gipson, nd: 3). The extended time in cells as a result of the ERMP, along with reduced exercise/recreation time, social contact with other residents and prison staff, and the cancellation of social visits (Ministry of Justice, 2020), meant that residents found themselves effectively warehoused for up to 23 hours a day with little purposeful activity to keep them occupied (HMIP, 2020a; PRT 2022). The prison service introduced in-cell activity and education packs, but these could not cater to the diverse range of learning needs among residents so were, at best, a stopgap measure (HMIP, 2021). The cumulative effect of prolonged lockdown measures on the mental health and well-being of residents has been considerable. A recent report from HMIP (2021: 24) highlights the significant impact of these measures on residents, noting: '[p]risoners we interviewed described feeling drained, depleted, lacking in purpose and were sometimes resigned to the situation. Some felt their lives were going to waste. They often felt lonely and unsupported. They were frustrated and sometimes angry.'

The PRT found that the impact of lockdown on the mental health of residents could be categorized into themes surrounding 'aggravation of diagnosed mental health conditions; anger, frustration, irritability; anxiety, fear, uncertainty, confusion and depression, low self-worth [and] suicidal thinking' (PRT, 2021b: 29). This was exacerbated by the fact that the majority of specialist services which offered structured support around mental health were either running at a reduced capacity or simply unavailable when needed (HMIP, 2020a; Sage EMG Transmission Group, 2021).

One of the largest contributing factors to declining mental health among residents, however, was the lack of contact with family as a result of the lockdown restrictions imposed across the estate. Surveys with residents have shown that lack of social contact with family members was considered the 'biggest cause [of] declining mental health' (Wainwright and Gipson, nd: 7). Not only was there an impact on residents' mental health as a result of lack of family contact, but research has also demonstrated a broader impact in relation to the mental health of children and family members. It has recently been recognized that children's relationships with imprisoned parents have suffered during the pandemic. It has been estimated that each year more than 300,000 children have a parent in prison (Crest Advisory, 2019), and a recent study found that by the end of the first lockdown, many of these children had not had face-to-face contact with their imprisoned parent since March 2020 (Minson, 2021). Not only does this have significant implications in relation to the mental and physical well-being of these children (Minson, 2021), but also it has the potential for long-term impact on both socialization and intergenerational offending (discussed in more detail in the section headed 'Supporting rehabilitation for the COVID-19 generation'; Farmer, 2017). While the Prison Service did accelerate the project of installing video call facilities within prisons, it has been noted that 'the roll-out has been too slow to relieve the frustration of not having visits and this delay has been very keenly felt' (HMIP, 2020a: 16).

While there remain concerns about the immediate health and well-being of residents as a result of restricted regimes, there are also longer-term issues which need to be considered. The HMIP, in an aggregate report of their short scrutiny visits early in the pandemic, note: 'there is now a real risk of psychological decline among [residents], which needs to be addressed urgently, so that [residents], children and detainees do not suffer long term damage to their mental health and well-being, and prisons can fulfil their rehabilitative goals' (2020a: 7). Almost two years after this report was published, and with the prison system beginning to emerge from its third wave of COVID-19, it is important that we consider the long-term impact of COVID-19 on the prison system and the legacy it will leave behind.

The legacy of COVID-19 on the prison system

As seen throughout this collection, the impact of the pandemic on the criminal justice system has been significant in a number of ways. The prison service is affected by broader systemic and policy issues to do with the pandemic alongside those within its own walls. It is therefore vital to consider the long-term costs of strict criminal justice interventions on this COVID-19 generation of residents if we are to successfully move on.

Delaying sentencing and release

The pandemic has seen both extensions and delays in sentencing, resulting in existing residents potentially staying in prison for longer. As noted in Chapter 3 in this collection, as a result of the pandemic, the vast majority of trials and court hearings were suspended or significantly reduced in March 2020, adding to the backlog of cases waiting to be heard. Indeed, it has been estimated that at the peak, there were more than 500,000 cases awaiting hearings across England and Wales (Brennan, 2020). While this allowed for a reduction in the number of people being sent to prison, it also meant that the time spent in prison by people awaiting trial was significantly extended. Legislation was introduced to extend the time a person could be held in custody on remand while awaiting trial at Crown Court from 182 to 238 days (PRT, 2022). The imposition of this legislation has resulted in the highest number of people on remand since 2010 (PRT, 2022: 21). This is significant in a number of ways. First, as already mentioned, there are significant physical and mental health implications for those spending time in prison. Time on remand has been found to be particularly precarious for residents, with research noting that '[r]emand is a period in which [residents] are especially vulnerable and often ruminate about legal outcomes and have distress, uncertainty, and anxiety about their future' (Hewson et al, 2020: 568). This is evidenced by the rates of self-harm and self-inflicted deaths by residents on remand, with over a quarter of all self-inflicted deaths in prison in 2020 being committed by people on remand (PRT, 2022: 16). Such concerns can only have been exacerbated by the introduction of COVID-19 in the estate, for all the reasons discussed throughout this chapter.

It also needs to be noted that the increased periods on remand as a result of the backlog of cases going through the courts have disproportionately impacted Black and minority ethnic communities. A report into Black, Asian and minority ethnic disproportionality in the criminal justice system found that 'black, mixed ethnic and other ethnic men were more than 20% more likely than white men to be remanded in custody' (Uhrig, 2016: 19). The same population were over 50 per cent more likely to plead not guilty than White men when the case was heard at Crown Court. The imposition of longer remand periods will have significantly impacted Black, mixed ethnic and minority ethnic communities to a greater extent than others. It is also important to remember at this point that Black and minority ethnic groups have been shown to have poorer health outcomes related to COVID-19 infection than other groups (Sage EMG Transmission Group, 2021).

Alongside these issues, perhaps even compounding them, is the fact that the use of remand while awaiting trial does not necessarily translate to the receipt of custodial sentences once a case reaches court. The available data demonstrates that 11 per cent of people remanded in custody awaiting trial are found not guilty, with an additional 14 per cent being given non-custodial sentences (PRT, 2022: 16). These individuals would have experienced longer periods on remand than they would have had the pandemic not happened. In-person parole hearings were also suspended as a result of the pandemic, which, arguably, resulted in 'the denial of consideration of early release for some [residents] (Brennan, 2020: 1222), thereby extending sentences for residents who may otherwise have been released sooner. The denial of early release seemingly typified the policy response to COVID-19 in prisons in England and Wales.

Early release schemes: populist politics vs public health

The available epidemiological evidence demonstrates that aside from vaccination, one of the most effective ways of reducing the transmission of COVID-19 is through social distancing measures. As we have seen in this chapter, an overcrowded prison estate does not allow for levels of social distancing sufficient to reduce transmission of the virus. It was noted earlier on that one of the policies designed to create the necessary headroom for single cell occupancy was the use of an early release scheme for residents nearing the end of their sentence. According to estimates from Public Health England, close to 15,000 residents would have needed to be released to achieve the required headroom (O'Moore, 2020), though the target was cut to 4,000 by the Ministry of Justice in 2020 (Beard, 2020). The scheme would have brought England and Wales in line with many other jurisdictions around the world. A recent global analysis of prisoner release schemes in response to COVID-19 found estimated that 53 national jurisdictions had utilized early release schemes to 'decongest their prison systems' (DLA Piper, 2020: 4). It was estimated that at least 475,000 residents were released internationally between March and July 2020, and that the schemes have been largely successful, with many jurisdictions reporting high numbers of residents released and low reconviction rates in the short term (DLA Piper, 2020: 3). The implementation of the scheme in England and Wales was a failure, however, with only 262 residents released before the scheme was shelved indefinitely. An investigation of why this was the case provides some illuminating insights into not only the scheme itself and the impact of COVID-19 on the criminal justice system, but also the penal policy and the use of imprisonment more generally.

The scheme was suspended in late April 2020 as it was no longer deemed necessary. The combination of fewer people being sentenced to prison, owing to the backlog of cases going through the court system, and existing residents reaching their automatic release points meant the prison population reduced below the Ministry of Justice's targets without the need for early release (Davies et al, 2020). Between 28 February and 17

April 2020, the prison population fell by 2,400, and it continued to decline steadily for a short while afterwards (O'Moore, 2020). It could be argued, as it has been in this volume, that this is simply due to the holistic nature of criminal justice: anything that impacts on one branch of the system will naturally impact on the others, sometimes to their benefit and other times to their detriment. There is certainly an argument that the prison service unintentionally benefited from the backlog of cases going through the court system. A closer examination of policy decisions at the time, however, suggests an alternative interpretation concerning the suspension of the early release scheme.

While a number of international jurisdictions were beginning to report considerable numbers released under their own early release schemes, policy officials in England and Wales were much more hesitant in declaring how many residents would be eligible for the scheme and much slower in rolling it out. In a meeting of the House of Commons Justice Committee on 7 April 2020, then Secretary of State for Justice Robert Buckland QC MP stated that it was 'difficult to be precise or to estimate ahead' as to how many residents will be released under the scheme, noting that 'at any time, prisoners were automatically released from custody, and thousands left custody over any period of months in a normal way' (Justice Committee, 2020). Around the same time, the head of the HMPPS, Jo Farrar, stated to the House of Commons that 'the temporary release of prisoners was not the only strategy that had been considered to manage the prison population' (Brennan, 2020: 1225). While these statements are true to a degree, there remained a sense of uncertainty, and at times unease, from policy makers surrounding the use of a temporary release scheme at all. One potential explanation for this, according to Davies and colleagues (2020: 50), is that while such schemes theoretically allowed for social distancing across the prison estate, there had been 'little consideration to the limited political appetite for releasing prisoners early'. The problem with the currently available discussions surrounding the approach to early release in England and Wales is that they tend to view such policies from a public health perspective. As such, the reluctance to release residents early makes little sense, with discussions suggesting that the prison service almost unintentionally benefited from backlogs further up the chain. Once we consider the unease surrounding early release within the broader context of penal populism and the rise of populist politics (Pratt and Miao, 2019), the approach to the early release scheme, and the management of people in custody during the pandemic more generally, arguably makes more sense.

It has to be remembered that the pandemic began in the context of an increasingly punitive political climate. The Conservative Party manifesto for the 2019 general election made a strong commitment to tougher sentencing and promised another 10,000 prison places. Indeed, one of the core tenets of penal populism that made it an attractive option to the Conservative Party is that appearing to be 'tough on crime' placed them 'on the side of "the people" and their expectations and understandings', thereby improving 'their credentials with the electorate' (Pratt and Miao, 2019: 29). Having been elected, if the Conservative government had been seen to release residents 'early', it ran the risk of jeopardizing its reputation. This was evidenced shortly after the announcement of the early release scheme in 2020 when *The Sun* newspaper ran the headline 'LET OFF: Up to 4000 "low risk" criminals to be released early in bid to stop coronavirus tearing through prisons' (Brown, 2020).

Thus, the approach to early release in England and Wales makes much more sense from a political perspective than from a public health one. The overtly punitive tones surrounding the initial scheme, which even suggested the use of electronic monitoring of all residents released under it, to the objection of the Prison Governors Association (2020), are indicative of this. With the growing backlog of cases going through the courts alongside the natural outflow from the estate of residents at the end of their sentence, the prison population was falling on its own. With a little patience and without the potential fallout, inaction would bring about the same headroom as action. As a consequence, the message of the vast majority of the public health literature surrounding the transmission of COVID-19 within prison settings – that speed is of the essence in order to reduce the potential for explosive transmission and save lives (Coker, 2020) – was not heeded. As such, the limited use of the early release scheme is a clear example of the tension between public health and populist politics in criminal justice, with one seemingly obvious winner.

Supporting rehabilitation for the COVID-19 generation

At the time of writing, as we begin to emerge from another wave of COVID-19 across the prison estate, attention must turn to the long-term impact of public health measures on the rehabilitation of residents. The suspension of all meaningful activity and family visits as a result of the ERMP and later lockdown measures will have had a significant effect on residents but, left unchecked, could send ripples of impact through generations.

The available evidence demonstrates a clear link between access to education and involvement in crime. Exclusion from school remains a significant predictor of later engagement with the criminal justice system, as do higher truancy levels, limited (or no) qualifications and high levels of unemployment (PRT, 2021a). If, as a recent review of prison education suggests, 'education is the engine of social mobility, it is also the engine of prisoner rehabilitation' (Coates, 2016: i). Education has often been considered 'one of the key elements in the process of change and transformation' for people in prison (Behan, 2014: 21; see also Wright, 2008). There is a significant body of evidence that demonstrates a link between engaging in meaningful activity in prison and increased rehabilitative potential. Vacca (2004) found that participation in prison education programmes reduces the likelihood of return to prison after release. The Coates (2016) review found that those who have completed education programmes during their sentence are 25 per cent less likely to be reconvicted and 26 per cent more likely to find employment within a year of release. The impact of COVID-19 on the delivery of education within the prison estate has had multiple impacts which need to be considered.

A direct impact of suspension of education programmes relates to residents' employability and levels of literacy. Perhaps of more concern, however, is the legacy of suspending education in terms of what it means for residents and the longer-term impact on their rehabilitation. As discussed earlier, the HMIP found that residents were 'chronically bored and exhausted by spending hours locked in their cells'; they 'frequently compared themselves to caged animals' (2021: 4). The lack of prison education provision, in addition to limiting the potential for educational attainment and subsequent employment on release, has a broader social impact. There is a body of evidence demonstrating that '[s]olitary confinement is not conducive to building self-confidence and self-worth, breaking down barriers and encountering stimulation for self-reflection' (O'Brien et al, 2021: 697) – something which engaging in meaningful activity, such as education, allows for. Finally, education represents an escape from the realities of everyday prison life, and research has demonstrated that with the loss of education provision because of COVID-19, 'the practice of education as freedom has been quashed' (O'Brien et al, 2021: 696).

When considering the impact of lockdown measures on rehabilitation efforts, the effect on family dynamics must also be taken into consideration. Alongside education and employment opportunities, family work, to quote Lord Farmer (2017: 5), represents the 'third leg of the stool that brings stability and structure to [residents'] lives, particularly when they leave prison'. As such, in order to recognize the full impact of COVID-19 measures on the rehabilitation of residents, we must consider the impact of the loss of social visits on rehabilitation efforts. As previously noted, the suspension of social visits due to the imposition of the ERMP and later lockdown measures had a deleterious impact on the mental health of residents. However, there are longer-term impacts of these measures that also need to be considered. There is a significant body of evidence that demonstrates the importance of maintaining prosocial familial relationships in supporting desistance and rehabilitation efforts for people with convictions (Kay, 2020). Research has shown that a common theme in desistance narratives relates to support from families acting as a catalyst for change and supporting transitional processes (Maruna, 2001; Cid and Marti, 2012). Family ties have been found to be an important source of prosocial capital (Farrall, 2004; Kay, 2020) and were identified as a key dimension in supporting desistance efforts. Research has shown a link between family contact while in custody and improved outcomes on release, with data suggesting that reoffending rates are 39 per cent lower for residents who received regular family visits compared to those who did not (Farmer, 2017). The suspension of in-person visits and the limited access to other forms of communication as a result of regime restrictions and limited resources, therefore, runs the risk of not only increasing the isolation felt by residents, but also weakening the bonds with family members which are known to be fundamental in supporting the change process (Minson, 2021). As in-person visits begin to return, it is important to ensure that efforts to re-establish connections between residents and families are consistent and carefully managed.

Alongside the impact on residents of prolonged COVID-19 restrictions in the prison estate, ripples of impact are sent out into the broader community. There is a real concern that reduced interaction between residents and family members will have a significant impact on familial relationships and the potential for intergenerational offending. We know that the impact of parental imprisonment on children is considerable. Research has demonstrated that children with a parent in prison face disruption to their home lives and education alongside increased poverty (Minson, 2019). They are also more likely to suffer from poor mental health and report higher levels of problematic substance use and addiction in later life (Miller, 2014). Evidence also suggests that children who experience parental imprisonment are less likely to be in education, training or employment as adults (Mears and Siennick, 2016; see also Minson, 2021), all of which are indicators of later involvement with the criminal justice system.[4] Family visits have been shown to mitigate against the impact of parental imprisonment (Cranmer et al, 2017), and the reduction of contact due to COVID-19 is already showing a negative impact on relationships between residents and their children. Minson (2021) found that the removal of in-person social visits and limited access to other forms of communication negatively impacted on these relationships. The limited in-cell telephone equipment and access to video calls meant that, at times, residents were having to choose between calling family members and having a shower in the time they had out of their cells. The children in the study took the loss of contact to mean parents did not want to get in touch with them, and this distress further impacted on the mental health of residents (Minson, 2021).

To begin to move on from COVID-19 and mitigate the impact of prolonged isolation on residents and their families, the rapid return of meaningful activity and social visits is of vital importance. This, however, will be a difficult undertaking as long as there is still a need to maintain social distancing measures across the prison estate, with HMPPS (2020: 2) suggesting that 'it may never be possible to provide the same standards in prisons while public health restrictions remain necessary'.

Conclusion

It is important to remember at this point that while the pandemic did create new issues within the prison system (setting up a robust testing infrastructure, for example), the vast majority of the issues that needed to be addressed during this time were not new. It has been argued that 'the pandemic aggravated many problems that existed for years in prison in England and Wales and exposed the poor living conditions of those profoundly isolated behind prison walls' (Brennan, 2020: 1229). Overcrowding, underfunding and poorly maintained buildings meant that when COVID-19 hit, the prison system was almost the ideal place for it to spread. The response to the pandemic within prisons, however, has been illuminating and has provided multiple lessons that we must take forward to continue to mitigate against the impact of the virus in the estate as we begin to 'live with covid' (HM Government, 2022), but also to consider the ways in which prison policy operates, and who it operates on.

Recommendation 1: ensure continued investment in prison staff levels and appropriate training

Recognition needs to be given to prison staff who responded rapidly to the imposition of the ERMP and who demonstrated the importance of communication with residents in fostering support for the measures. As has been shown throughout this chapter, cooperation between staff and residents allowed for measures to be implemented with speed and efficiency (HMIP, 2020a). The Prisons Strategy White Paper indicates there is to be significant investment in both new prison officers and improving the health and well-being of existing prison staff. The pandemic has again demonstrated the vital role that prison staff play in not only implementing HMPPS policy but also facilitating such policy through effective communication and relationships with residents. As the prison population begins to climb and activity starts to resume, these relationships will be more important than ever.

Recommendation 2: reduce the prison population to allow for the effective implementation of health/well-being/rehabilitation strategies

Perhaps of most importance, we now know that the prison population can be reduced and that there are significant benefits of doing so. Reducing the population can not only help reduce the transmission of communicable diseases such as COVID-19 across the prison system but also reduce the broader impacts of overcrowding on the health and well-being of residents (MacDonald, 2018). The concern here is that currently the opposite is occurring. The backlog through the court system is diminishing, and this will raise the number of residents; also new legislation in the form of the Police, Crime, Sentencing and Courts Bill 2021, which looks to impose minimum terms for specific offences and increase sentencing tariffs for a range of others, will see a significant rise in the prison population. An impact assessment of these sentencing proposals found that the Bill would result in 'a total increase in the adult prison population of around 1,050 offenders in steady state by 2029/30 although this impact will begin to be felt from 2022/23 with just over 300 additional prisoners' (Ministry of Justice, 2021b: 13). Taking this and the court backlog into account, it is estimated that the prison population in England and Wales could approach 100,000 buy 2026 (Ministry of Justice, 2021b). Attempts have been made to mitigate against the impact of overcrowding in the form of a considerable expansion of the prison estate, with the 2021 *Prisons Strategy White Paper* promising the delivery of 18,000 new prison places by the mid-2020s (Ministry of Justice, 2021a). However, international research suggests that such attempts rarely impact on overcrowding levels; rather, they serve to increase prison populations. As Guetzkow and Schoon (2015: 401) concisely argue, 'if you build it, they will fill it'. The pandemic has clearly demonstrated the need for a drastic reduction in the prison population, and it is to this aim that we should now be working.

Recommendation 3: ensure effective rollout of telecommunication infrastructure across all sites

A further lesson from the pandemic is that communication technology can be used safely and effectively within the prison system. While there were delays in implementation of this technology, which caused significant frustration, the value of video calls, in-cell telephony and virtual visits has been recognized in the available research (HMIP, 2020a). The use of such systems in future could supplement in-person visits, thereby allowing more residents to be in contact with family on a regular basis, mitigating against some the pains of imprisonment that have been documented throughout the literature (Sykes, 1958; Crewe, 2011).

Concerns remain, however, with regard to the predominant epistemology within criminal justice policy that is seeing an expansion of prison building and an increase in the prison population while the pandemic continues to surge. The Sage EMG Transmission Group (2021: 67) notes that 'outbreaks in prison only require the importation of a single infection' to take hold.

As the prison service begins to move towards post-pandemic regimes, caution is still needed to prevent a return to the strict lockdown measures that we have seen since 2020. For a multitude of reasons, the prison service is in a much stronger position to deal with COVID-19 outbreaks now than it was two years ago, but the evidence base remains clear that the best ways to prevent transmission and explosive outbreaks are a broad vaccination strategy and the implementation of social distancing measures, the latter of which relies on strict control of the prison population. COVID-19 will not be the last pandemic that the prison service will need to survive. The lessons we have learned in relation to testing infrastructures, cohorting strategies and vaccination rollouts, as well as the long-term impact of lockdown measures on residents, can be taken forward to inform strategies for any pandemics that follow, but a balance must be struck between public health knowledge and political appetite for punishment if we are to maximize their benefit.

Notes

[1] It is important to note at this point that the R_0 value is determined across the general population and was likely, for the reasons previously mentioned, to be larger in the prison population.
[2] At the time of writing, the prison service is still dealing with the third wave of COVID-19, caused by the omicron variant, so mortality data for this wave remains incomplete.
[3] Note that deaths 'confirmed or suspected to be from COVID-19' is distinct from deaths 'related to COVID-19', as the latter includes all deaths within 60 days of a positive test *regardless of the cause of death*.
[4] While such factors are indicators of involvement with the criminal justice system in later life, the evidence base suggesting a direct causal link between parental offending and offending in children over the life course is less well established (Flynn, 2013).

References

Anderson, R.M., Heesterbeek, H., Klinkenberg, D. and Hollingsworth, T.D. (2020) 'How will country-based mitigation measures influence the course of the COVID-19 epidemic?', *The Lancet*, 395(10228): 931–4.

Baillargeon, J., Black, S.A., Leach, C.T., Jenson, H., Pulvino, J., Bradshaw, P. and Murray, O. (2004) 'The infectious disease profile of Texas prison inmates', *Preventive Medicine*, 38(5): 607–12.

BBC (2020) 'Plans for prisoner early release shelved by government', [online] 10 May, Available from: www.bbc.co.uk/news/uk-politics-52607618

Beard, J. (2020) *Coronavirus: Prisons (England and Wales)*, House of Commons, Briefing Paper 8892, London: House of Commons Library.

Behan, C. (2014) 'Learning to escape: prison education, rehabilitation and the potential for transformation', *Journal of Prison Education and Reentry*, 1(1): 20–31.

Brennan, P.K. (2020) 'Responses taken to mitigate COVID-19 in prisons in England and Wales', *Victims & Offenders*, 15(7–8): 1215–33.

Brown, A. (2020) 'LET OFF: Up to 4000 "low risk" criminals to be released early in bid to stop coronavirus tearing through prisons', *The Sun*, [online] 4 April, Available from: www.thesun.co.uk/news/11326606/criminals-released-prison-coronavirus/

Cid, J. and Martí, J. (2012) 'Turning points and returning points: understanding the role of family ties in the process of desistance', *European Journal of Criminology*, 9(6): 603–620.

Coates, S. (2016) *Unlocking Potential: A Review of Education in Prison*, London: Ministry of Justice.

Coker, R. (2020) *Expert Report: Covid-19 and Prisons in England and Wales*, Howard League for Penal Reform, Prison Reform Trust, [online] Available from: https://howardleague.org/wp-content/uploads/2020/04/2020_04_01_COKER_Report_HL_PRT.pdf

Cranmer, L., Goff, M., Peterson, B. and Sandstrom, H. (2017) *Parent–Child Visiting Practices in Prisons and Jails: A Synthesis of Research and Practice Research Report*, Washington D.C: Urban Institute.

Crest Advisory (2019) 'Prisons and COVID19: what went right?', [online] Available from: https://www.crestadvisory.com/post/prisons-and-covid-19-what-went-right

Crewe, B. (2011) 'Depth, weight, tightness: revisiting the pains of imprisonment', *Punishment & Society*, 13(5): 509–529.

Davies, N., Atkins, G., Guerin, B. and Sodhi, S. (2020) *How Fit Were Public Services for Coronavirus?* London: Institute for Government.

Department of Health (2011) *Prevention of Infection and Communicable Disease Control in Prisons and Places of Detention: A Manual for Healthcare Workers and Other Staff*, London: Department of Health.

DLA Piper (2020) *A Global Analysis of Prisoner Releases in the Response to COVID-19*, DLA Piper.

Dolan, K., Kite, B., Black, E., Aceijas, C. and Stimson, G.V. (2007) 'HIV in prison in low-income and middle-income countries', *The Lancet Infectious Diseases*, 7(1): 32–41.

Edge, C., Hard, J., Wainwright, L., Gipson, D., Wainwright, V., and Shaw, J., et al (2021) *COVID-19 and the Prison Population*, Working Paper 8, Health Foundation.

European Centre for Disease Prevention and Control (2020a) 'Heating, ventilation and air conditioning systems in the context of COVID19', [online] Available from: https://www.ecdc.europa.eu/en/publications-data/heating-ventilation-air-conditioning-systems-covid-19

European Centre for Disease Prevention and Control (2020b) 'COVID-19', [online] Available from: https://www.ecdc.europa.eu/en/covid-19/latest-evidence/transmission

Farmer, M. (2017) *The Importance of Strengthening Prisoners' Family Ties to Prevent Reoffending and Reduce Intergenerational Crime*, [online] Available from: https://assets.publishing.service.gov.uk/government/uploads/system/uploads/attachment_data/file/642244/farmer-review-report.pdf

Farrall, S. (2004) 'Social capital and offender reintegration: making probation desistance focussed,' in Maruna, S. and Immarigeon, R. (eds) *After Crime and Punishment: Pathways to Offender Reintegration*, Devon: Willan Publishing.

Flynn, C. (2013) 'Understanding the risk of offending for the children of imprisoned parents: a review of the evidence', *Children and Youth Services Review*, 35(2): 213–217.

Garside, R. (2020) 'Prisons need to emerge from the lockdown', *Centre for Crime and Justice Studies*, [online] 1 May, Available from: www.crimeandjustice.org.uk/resources/prisons-need-emerge-lockdown

Grant, E. (2013) '"Pack 'em, rack 'em and stack 'em": the appropriateness of the use and reuse of shipping containers for prison accommodation', *Australasian Journal of Construction Economics and Building*, 13(2): 35–44.

Grierson, J. (2020) 'UK coronavirus prison plan on hold after six inmates freed in error', *The Guardian*, [online] 18 April, Available from: www.theguardian.com/society/2020/apr/18/uk-coronavirus-prison-plan-suspended-after-six-mistakenly-released

Guan, W., Ni, Z., Hu, Y., Liang, W., Ou, C., and He, J., et al (2020) 'Clinical characteristics of coronavirus disease 2019 in China', *The New England Journal of Medicine*, 382(18): 1708–20.

Guetzkow, J. and Schoon, E. (2015) 'If you build it, they will fill it: the consequences of prison overcrowding litigation', *Law and Society Review*, 49(2): 401–32.

Hardwick, N. (2020) 'Prisons and Covid-19: what went right?', *Crest*, [online] Available from: www.crestadvisory.com/post/prisons-and-covid-19-what-went-right

Health Protection Agency (2011) *Prevention of Infection and Communicable Disease Control in Prisons and Places of Detention: A Manual for Healthcare Workers and Other Staff*, London: Department of Health.

Hewson, T., Shepherd, A., Hard, J. and Shaw, J. (2020) 'Effects of the COVID-19 pandemic on the mental health of prisoners', *The Lancet Psychiatry*, 7(7): 568–70.

HM Government (2022), 'COVID-19 response: living with COVID-19', [online] Available from: https://www.gov.uk/government/publications/covid-19-response-living-with-covid-19

HMIP (HM Inspectorate of Prisons) (2020a) *Aggregate Report on Short Scrutiny Visits by HM Chief Inspector of Prisons*, London: HMIP.

HMIP (2020b) *Report on Short Scrutiny Visits to Local Prisons by HM Chief Inspector of Prisons*, London: HMIP.

HMIP (2021) *What Happens to Prisoners in a Pandemic: A Thematic Review by HM Inspectorate of Prisons*, London: HMIP.

HMPPS (HM Prison & Probation Service) (2020) *HMPPS Prison Regime Management During COVID-19*, [online] Available from: https://ep2022-dev.tunaweb.com/wp-content/uploads/2020/06/HMPPS-Regime-Management-Planning-during-COVID-19-Final-for-Sharing1.pdf

House of Commons Health Committee (2018) 'Prison health, Annex 1: visit to Greenwich cluster', [online] Available from: https://publications.parliament.uk/pa/cm201719/cmselect/cmhealth/963/96302.htm

Howard League for Penal Reform (2020) 'Prisons', [online] Available from: https://howardleague.org/prisons-information

Jarvis, J. (2020) 'First UK prisoner with coronavirus confirmed at HMP Manchester', *Evening Standard*, [online] 18 March, Available from: www.standard.co.uk/news/health/uk-prisoncoronavirus-case-confirmed-hmp-manchester-a4390981.html

Justice Committee (2020) Justice Committee Meeting, Tuesday 7th April 2020, [online] Available from: https://publications.parliament.uk/pa/cm5801/cmselect/cmjust/correspondence/200407-Justice-Committee-meeting-Robert-Buckland-note1.pdf

Kaur, S., Bherwani, H., Gulia, S., Vijay, R. and Kumar, R. (2021) 'Understanding COVID-19 transmission, health impacts and mitigation: timely social distancing is the key', *Environment, Development and Sustainability*, 23(5): 6681–97.

Kay, C. (2020) 'COVID-19 in custody: responding to pandemics in prisons in England and Wales', *British Journal of Community Justice*, [online] Available from: https://mmuperu.co.uk/bjcj/wp-content/uploads/sites/2/2020/09/BJCJ_Kay_2020.pdf

Leclerc, Q.J., Fuller, N.M., Knight, L.E., Funk, S. and Knight, G.M. (2020) 'What settings have been linked to SARS-CoV-2 transmission clusters?', *Wellcome Open Research*, [online] Available from: wellcomeopenresearch.org/articles/5-83/v2

Li, C., Ji, F., Wang, L., Wang, L., Hao, J., and Dai, M., et al (2020) 'Asymptomatic and human-to-human transmission of SARS-CoV-2 in a 2-family cluster, Xuzhou, China', *Emerging Infectious Diseases*, 26(7): 1626–8.

MacDonald, M. (2018), 'Overcrowding and its impact on prison conditions and health', *International Journal of Prisoner Health*, 14(2): 65–68.

Maruna, S. (2001) 'Making good: how ex-convicts reform and rebuild their lives', [online] Available from: https://psycnet.apa.org/record/2001-18143-000

Mears, D.P. and Siennick, S.E. (2016) 'Young adult outcomes and the life-course penalties of parental incarceration', *Journal of Research in Crime and Delinquency*, 53(1): 3–35.

Miller, K.M. (2014) 'Maternal criminal justice involvement and co-occurring mental health and substance abuse problems: examining moderation of sex and race on children's mental health', *Children and Youth Services Review*, 37: 71–80.

Ministry of Justice (2020) 'Press release. Prison visits cancelled', [online] 24 March, Available from: www.gov.uk/government/news/prison-visits-cancelled

Ministry of Justice (2021a) 'Prison population projections 2021–2026', [online] Available from: https://assets.publishing.service.gov.uk/government/uploads/system/uploads/attachment_data/file/1035682/Prison_Population_Projections_2021_to_2026.pdf

Ministry of Justice (2021b) *Prisons Strategy White Paper*, CP 581, [online] Available from: https://assets.publishing.service.gov.uk/government/uploads/system/uploads/attachment_data/file/1038765/prisons-strategy-white-paper.pdf

Ministry of Justice and HMPPS (2020a) *COVID-19: National Framework for Prison Regimes and Services*, Ministry of Justice and HMPPS.

Ministry of Justice and HMPPS (2020b) 'Press release. Further expansion of prison estate to protect NHS', [online] 29 April, Available from: www.gov.uk/government/news/further-expansion-of-prison-estate-to-protect-nhs

Ministry of Justice and HMPPS (2020c) 'Press release. Prison estate expanded to protect NHS from coronavirus risk', [online] 9 April, Available from: www.gov.uk/government/news/prison-estate-expanded-to-protect-nhs-from-coronavirus-risk

Ministry of Justice and HMPPS (2022) 'HMPPS COVID-19 statistics: January 2022', [online] 11 February, Available from: www.gov.uk/government/statistics/hmpps-covid-19-statistics-january-2022

Minson, S. (2019) *Maternal Sentencing and the Rights of the Child*, London: Palgrave.

Minson, S. (2021) *The Impact of COVID-19 Prison Lockdowns on Children with a Parent in Prison*, Oxford: Centre for Criminology, University of Oxford.

National Audit Office (2020) *Improving the Prison Estate*, Session 2019–20, HC 41, Available from: www.nao.org.uk/wp-content/uploads/2020/02/Improving-the-prison-estate.pdf

Neill, R. (2020) 'We must help our prisons in the fight against coronavirus', *The House*, [online] 19 March, Available from: www.politicshome.com/thehouse/article/bob-neill-mp-we-must-help-our-prisons-in-the-fight-against-coronavirus

Nishiura, H., Ositani, H., Kobayashi, T., Saito, T., Sunagawa, T., Matusi, T. and Wakita, T. (2020) 'Closed environments facilitate the secondary transmission of coronavirus disease 2019 (COVID-19)', [online] Preprint ahead of peer review, *medRxiv*. doi: 10.1101/2020.02.28.20029272.

O'Brien, K., King, H., Phillips, J., Dalton, K. and Phoenix (2021) '"Education as the practice of freedom?" – prison education and the pandemic', *Educational Review*, 74(3): 685–703.

O'Moore, E. (2020) *Briefing Paper: Interim Assessment of Impact of Various Population Management Strategies in Prisons in Response to COVID-19 Pandemic in England*, Her Majesty's Prison and Probation Service, [online] Available from: https://assets.publishing.service.gov.uk/government/uploads/system/uploads/attachment_data/file/882622/covid-19-population-management-strategy-prisons.pdf

ONS (Office for National Statistics) (2020) 'Coronavirus (COVID-19) Roundup', [online] 26 March, Available from: https://www.ons.gov.uk/peoplepopulationandcommunity/healthandsocialcare/conditionsanddiseases/articles/coronaviruscovid19roundup23to27march2020/2020-03-27

Pratt, J. and Miao, M. (2019) 'The end of penal populism: the rise of populist politics', *Archiwum Kryminologii*, XLI/2: 15–40.

Prison Governors' Association (2020) *Prison Governors' Association (PGA) Evidence to Justice Committee on COVID-19*, [online] 6 April, Available from: https://committees.parliament.uk/publications/617/documents/2593/default/

PRT (Prison Reform Trust) (2019) *Prison: The Facts. Bromley Briefings Summer 2019*, London: Prison Reform Trust.

PRT (2020) *Tackling the Spread of Coronavirus in Prison* [online] Available from: www.prisonreformtrust.org.uk/PressPolicy/News/Coronavirus/PageIndex/2

PRT (2021a) *Prison: The Facts. Bromley Briefings Summer 2021*, London: Prison Reform Trust.

PRT (2021b) *Covid-19 Action Prisons Project: Tracking Innovation, Valuing Experience: How Prisons are Responding to Covid-19 Briefing #3*, London: Prison Reform Trust.

PRT (2022) *Bromley Briefings Prison Factfile: Winter 2022*, London: Prison Reform Trust.

Public Health England (2020) 'Number of coronavirus (COVID-19) cases and risk in the UK' [online] Available from: www.gov.uk/guidance/coronavirus-covid-19-information-for-the-public

Rice, W.M., Chudasama, D.Y., Lewis, J., Senyah, F., Florence, I., Thelwall, S., Glaser, L., Czachorowski, M., Plugge, E., Kirkbride, H. et al (2021) 'Epidemiology of COVID-19 in prisons, England, 2020', *Emerging Infectious Diseases*, 27(8): 2183–6.

Sage EMG Transmission Group (2021) *COVID-19 Transmission in Prison Settings*, [online] Available from: https://assets.publishing.service.gov.uk/government/uploads/system/uploads/attachment_data/file/979807/S1166_EMG_transmission_in_prisons.pdf

Smith, J. (2005) *Shipping Containers as Building Components*, Brighton: University of Brighton.

Sykes, G. (1958) *The Society of Captives: A Study of a Maximum-Security Prison*, Princeton, NJ: Princeton University Press.

Townsend, M., Savage, M. and Doward, J. (2020) 'Prisons "could see 800 deaths" from coronavirus without protective measures', *The Guardian*, [online] 21 March, Available from: www.theguardian.com/uk-news/2020/mar/21/prisons-could-see-800-deaths-from-coronavirus-without-protective-measures

Uhrig, N. (2016) 'Black, Asian and Minority Ethnic disproportionality in the Criminal Justice System in England and Wales', [online] Available from: https://www.gov.uk/government/publications/black-asian-and-minority-ethnic-disproportionality-in-the-criminal-justice-system-in-england-and-wales

Vacca, J.S. (2004) 'Educated prisoners are less likely to return to prison', *Journal of Correctional Education*, 55(4): 297–305.

Wainwright, L. and Gipson, D. (nd) *The Impact of Lockdown to Mental Health: A Summary of Patient Views*, EP:IC.

WHO (World Health Organization) (2020a) 'Coronavirus disease (COVID-19) pandemic', [online] Available from: www.euro.who.int/en/healthtopics/health-emergencies/coronavirus-covid-19/novel-coronavirus-2019-ncov

WHO (2020b) 'Criteria for releasing COVID-19 patients from isolation: scientific brief', [online] 17 June, Available from: www.who.int/news-room/commentaries/detail/criteria-for-releasing-covid-19-patients-from-isolation

WHO (2020c) *Report of the WHO-China Joint Mission on Coronavirus Disease 2019 (COVID-19)*, [online] Available from: www.who.int/publications/i/item/report-of-the-who-china-joint-mission-on-coronavirus-disease-2019-(covid-19)

Wright, K. and Goodstein, L. (1991) 'Correctional environments', in J. Thompson and L. Mays (eds) *American Jails: Public Policy Issues*, New York: Plenum Press, pp 181–94.

Wright, R. (ed) (2008) *In the Borderlands: Learning to Teach in Prisons and Alternative Settings* (2nd edn), San Bernadino, CA: California State University.

Zhou, F., Yu, T., Du, R., Fan, G., Liu, Y., and Liu, Z., et al (2020) 'Clinical course and risk factors for mortality of adult inpatients with COVID-19 in Wuhan, China: a retrospective cohort study', *The Lancet*, 395(10229): 1054–62.

6

Youth Justice and COVID-19: Courts, Community and Custody

Kathy Hampson and Stephen Case

Introduction

Despite being a hub of medical and scientific innovation and an economic and political big hitter, the United Kingdom (UK) appears to have fared particularly badly in the COVID-19 pandemic, with nearly 8.5 million people testing positive, more than half a million resultant hospital admissions and nearly 161,800 deaths (giving COVID-19 on the death certificate) since it began (UK Government, 2021a). This has meant that for every aspect of life, sweeping changes have been made, backed by legislation, to try to limit damage to public health and enable essential services to continue. Youth justice is one such area. It has seen enormous restrictions imposed on it, but also, consequently, a disproportionately damaging effect on already-vulnerable justice-involved children. This chapter explores the effect of these impositions on the youth justice system (YJS) in England and Wales, analyzing the 'pains' and 'gains' of COVID-19, repurposing Sykes's (1958) 'pains of imprisonment' thesis and echoing Bateman's (2020) application of this to the effects of COVID-19 on children in custody, but developing this to apply across the whole gamut of children's justice experience (from pre-court prevention right through to custody and resettlement).

In this chapter, employing the dual lenses of children's rights and 'Child First' as the guiding principle for a YJS which (at least in rhetoric) sees children as *children* (rather than 'offenders'; cf Case and Browning, 2021), we examine how engagement (both practitioner and system engagement with children and vice versa) has been adversely affected (pains) throughout all levels of involvement from prevention work to custody and resettlement, damaging support to vulnerable children, foregrounding them as offenders and eroding their vital rights as children (as enshrined in the United Nations Convention on the Rights of the Child (UNCRC; United Nations – UN, 1989) to which the UK is a signatory state), and we also consider where there have been gains through rapidly developing practice and innovation. The subthemes of innovation, contact, access, safeguarding and engagement are applied to actions of the courts, community contact with children and the custodial environment. Informing this chapter are policy and legislative changes affecting youth justice in England and Wales, inspections of practice which took place at various stages of the pandemic 'lockdowns' and informal conversations held with youth justice practitioners and managers to gain insight into how this was being felt at the coalface with justice-involved children.

Youth justice in England and Wales

In order to contextualize the arguments around the pains and gains of COVID-19 in English and Welsh youth justice, it is important to outline the particular systems, structures, processes, organizations and guiding principles which background our analytical framework. Youth justice in the UK is a complex affair. The UK is made up of four 'home nations': England, Wales, Scotland and Northern Ireland. Two of these nations – Scotland and Northern Ireland – have separate devolved responsibility for the justice sector. However, England and Wales still have one conjoined system, with the same legislation covering both home nations under the purview of the Ministry of Justice, although local policies diverge in some respects (Case, 2014). The YJS of England and Wales, therefore, is legislated out of Westminster (England) and was largely borne out of the Crime and Disorder Act 1998. This Act brought into being the current constituent agencies of the YJS, namely the Youth Justice Board (YJB), responsible for guiding youth justice policies/strategies nationally and providing practice support locally,[1] and Youth Offending Teams (YOTs), responsible for coalface working with justice-involved children. YOTs are multiagency teams in every local authority area, comprising workers from the statutory agencies of probation, education, social services, health and the police, who, along with voluntary and charitable services (where appropriate and available locally), work with both statutory cases (children given court orders after conviction of criminal offences) and prevention cases (children thought to be vulnerable to involvement in criminal behaviour, though not yet convicted). As the minimum age of criminal responsibility in England and Wales is (unacceptably) low, at 10 years of age, the YJS is required to meet the needs of a wide age range of children, up to the age of criminal majority (18 years of age), when they enter the adult criminal justice system.

As is the case in many other anglophone countries, the YJS of England and Wales was predicated on principles privileging the identification and amelioration of 'risk factors' (that is, the Risk Factor Prevention Paradigm), as originally identified by the positivistic and deterministic Cambridge Study (West and Farrington, 1973; Farrington, 2000; see Case and Haines, 2009, for a comprehensive methodological, conceptual, evidential and ethical critique). Two decades on, while there has been some softening of this approach and acknowledgement that the YJS is an inherently damaging environment for children (McAra and McVie, 2007), the parlance of 'risk' (seeing children as 'risky' rather than vulnerable and 'at risk') still permeates much of the rhetoric and policy surrounding youth justice. A major challenge to the tenacity of risk as a guiding principle for youth justice was provided by the youth justice review, undertaken in 2016 by educationalist Charlie Taylor, who advocated for 'a new system in which young people are treated as children first and offenders second' (Taylor, 2016: 48). Subsequently, Taylor was able to turn the strategic aims of the YJB towards 'Child First, Offender Second' youth justice (now Child First) when he became chair in 2017.

Child First justice

From 2018, one of the YJB's stated values was 'we see children first and offenders second' (2019: 7), and by 2021, this had developed into a 'strategic approach and central guiding principle' of a 'Child First approach' (2021: 10). Child First has been developed into the four interrelated tenets detailed in Table 6.1.

Child First justice, while a new direction for the YJB in England and Wales, is actually rooted in *pre*-Crime and Disorder Act Welsh theorizing by Haines and Drakeford (1998), who were already seeing the potential disadvantaging and damaging effects of treating children as risky offenders. Wales tried to break away from the risk straightjacket, despite being part of the English jurisdiction, through the slightly different funding arrangements in Wales and the involvement of the Welsh Assembly Government. The *All-Wales Youth Offending Strategy* (Welsh Assembly Government and YJB, 2004: 3) stated that 'Young people should be treated as children first and offenders second' while also firmly centralizing children's rights as a principle for all policy concerning children, all of which was reaffirmed in the updated youth justice strategy for Wales 'Children and Young People First' (Welsh Government and YJB, 2014). While the principle of 'Child First' has therefore been a guiding principle within Wales for well over a decade, its translation into practice has been more difficult (Thomas, 2015), possibly due to the joint jurisdiction and the reluctance of Westminster to shape policy affecting children according to their rights as articulated in the UNCRC (UN, 1989).

Table 6.1: The four tenets of Child First justice

Tenet	Description	Criteria for operationalization
Seeing children as children	Prioritize the best interests of children and recognize their particular needs, capacities, rights and potential	All work is child-focused, developmentally informed, acknowledges structural barriers and meets responsibilities towards children
Developing prosocial identity for positive child outcomes	Promote children's individual strengths and capacities to develop their prosocial identity for sustainable desistance, leading to safer communities and fewer victims	All work is constructive and future-focused, built on supportive relationships that empower children to fulfil their potential and make positive contributions to society
Collaboration with children	Encourage children's active participation, engagement and wider social inclusion	All work is meaningful collaboration with children and their carers
Promotion of diversion	Promote a childhood removed from the justice system, using pre-emptive prevention, diversion and minimal intervention	All work minimizes criminogenic stigma from contact with the system

Source: YJB (2021); see also Case and Browning (2021)

The adoption of Child First justice by the YJB was therefore timely in terms of centre-staging children's best interests in the teeth of the COVID-19 pandemic. However, it was not enough to insulate justice-involved children from the worst effects of COVID-19-related policies, which brought significant challenges to the operationalization of the Child First tenets (see Table 6.1). The children who come into contact with the YJS are among the most vulnerable in our society, disadvantaged by a disproportionate level of adverse childhood experiences and trauma and by such structural disadvantages as child poverty (Yates, 2010). The double disadvantage of then being criminalized, possibly partly as a result of these factors which are entirely beyond their control, has been turned into *triple* disadvantage through ill-thought-out policy responses to the COVID-19 pandemic, causing these children further problems (pains) and effectively putting on hold any real operationalization of Child First justice in practice.

Initial COVID-19 restrictions affecting the YJS

In March 2020, the UK entered the first of what would become several national 'lockdowns' severely restricting the activities of citizens[2] (BBC, 2020).

The Ministry of Justice[3] set out a range of policy changes, restrictions and support strategies to facilitate the operation of the whole criminal justice system (including the YJS) during lockdown. Despite Wales having control of its own COVID-19 policies, youth justice in Wales was subject to Westminster's regulations as a non-devolved nation for (in)justice. As a first response, all but essential court activity was suspended, all justice- and education-related inspections were halted, no visits were allowed into custody (including legal visits) and a new scheme for early release from custody was introduced to try to reduce custody numbers at this time (Ministry of Justice, 2020a, 2020b).

The YJB then developed strategies and policies specifically relating to the YJS, provided localized support mechanisms and gave guidance to YOTs on day-to-day practice (YJB, 2020c, 2020d). YOT workers were classified as 'key workers' so they could continue to work outside the home, which enabled the most vulnerable children to receive face-to-face contact, albeit with restrictions. Children in custody had their education provision replaced by 'in-room' activities and were given additional access to telephones and usage credit to help mitigate the damage of isolation. The YJB promised to advocate for all justice-involved children (in custody and in the community) with the government to ensure no additional disadvantage (pains) from lockdown policies or the effects of the pandemic more generally, and to defend their rights. Part of this was actively seeking to reduce the number of children entering the (damaging) justice system, reducing numbers of children in custody by promoting use of the new early release scheme, and further developing the YJB's resource hub[4] so that good COVID-19-related practice (potential gains and mitigation of pains) could be easily disseminated (YJB, 2020e).

The YJB clearly wanted to protect justice-involved children during the pandemic, but unfortunately, perhaps betraying their lack of power in places, the practice realities have not lived up to the policy/strategy rhetoric. The pandemic and its resultant policies have highlighted and exacerbated disadvantage (UN, 2020; Harris and Goodfellow, 2021) and also caused severe disruption in social relationships through widespread isolation, especially damaging for adolescents, who are still in a developmental stage of their socialization (Gayer-Anderson et al, 2020). Therefore, justice-involved children, already disproportionately affected by social disadvantage, by being caught in a criminal and criminalizing system and at (or near) adolescence, are suffering triple disadvantage – the so-called 'pains' of COVID-19 (Bateman, 2020).

The pains and gains of COVID-19

The lockdown policies affecting youth justice in England and Wales have affected different aspects of the system in a variety of ways. In some senses there have been innovations developed in order to mitigate the worst of the effects, representing the gains of COVID-19, but inevitably, given the double disadvantage of justice-involved children, adding a layer of COVID-19-specific restrictions has exacerbated to a disproportionate extent the difficulties these children already face. We now, through the dual lenses of Child First justice and children's rights, consider three different stages of system intervention – courts, community (YOT) supervision and custody – and how the pains and gains of COVID-19 might be experienced within these contexts.

The pains and gains of COVID-19 in courts

As discussed, most court activity ceased as soon as the first UK 'lockdown' was introduced, meaning that only certain types of case could be heard – remand/bail hearings being one example. This necessarily caused huge backlogs in court listings, with many individuals facing trials or conviction hearings without any indication of when they might be listed. Taylor's review of the YJS identified system delay as a significant and particularly damaging issue for children: 'Children have reported being frustrated by lengthy court processes and feeling that their life is on hold until proceedings have concluded. A significant delay before a trial begins not only harms victims, it also undermines the impact on the child of the court process and the sentence they receive' (2016: 30). This not only accepts that 'justice delayed is justice denied' (Sleight, 2020), but also identifies additional issues this might cause specifically to justice-involved children who have difficulties with envisaging future trajectories and with joining up long-past actions with future consequences. The YJB had made a commitment to try to reduce the delays caused to children through justice system processes, recognizing that extended periods on bail might cause stress and even, effectively, system-precipitated offending (YJB, 2003). However, court business cessation put a very firm stop on this, with children in limbo regarding the progress of their cases.

The continuance of 'urgent and important cases' included bail/remand hearings (HMCTS, 2020: 3), which had the unfortunate effect of *increasing* custody levels rather than decreasing them (the YJB's indicated aim). This occurred because children could be remanded to custody (and appeared more likely to be remanded than bailed when heard through virtual courts; Harris and Goodfellow, 2021), but the case for which they were being held could not be tabled, extending their remand period disproportionately (even more likely for Black and minority ethnic children, who have a higher tendency to be remanded; YJB and Ministry of Justice, 2021). For the majority of cases which have been suspended, defendants have no indication of when their cases might be heard, which might cause distress to anyone in this situation. However, it risks real loss of justice for children on the cusp of 18, who may find that delayed court hearings see them convicted as adults should they turn 18 before the first hearing – with the consequential loss of safeguards like anonymity, application of juvenile sentencing options, less time before sentences are considered 'spent' and loss of 'appropriate adult' support. All this loss comes, of course, despite having committed the crime as a child under the age of 18 (Just for Kids Law, 2020). Lack of court activity also means that children who would normally have had their court order revoked early for good progress (a practice often used by YOTs to reward good engagement) would not benefit from this. Consequently, having to stay on a court order for longer not only increases the time with an inherently damaging system (McAra and McVie, 2007), but also extends the period in which they must declare their conviction in such vital life processes as job application, further prejudicing their chances of advancement in prosocial non-offending society[5] (UK Government, 2019).

One of the innovations which has been either precipitated by COVID-19 or at the very least speeded up by it in terms of uptake is the use of 'virtual courts' to hear cases remotely. This innovation could benefit children if it speeds up their access to justice, especially given current delays and suspensions, thus becoming a *gain* of COVID-19. However, it could also be something of a double-edged sword given some of the misgivings which have been identified previously and emphasized in guidance, particularly around engagement with the process and difficulties with effectively communicating in a virtual setting, potentially turning it into a *pain* of COVID-19 (Harris and Goodfellow, 2021). There are particular concerns that welfare issues might arise from using virtual courts to sentence children. However, judicial guidance on this continues to suggest that sentencing when a child is already in custody may be appropriately done virtually (Royal Courts of Justice, 2017), which negates research on the deleterious effects of incarceration more generally on children's mental health (cf Goldson, 2005), as they may not get adequate support (otherwise offered by an attending YOT worker who knows the child) at that point of sentencing, suggesting safeguarding concerns. This directly contradicts the YJB's (2016: 1) opinion that '[f]or trial, sentencing and appeal hearings, children and young people must appear at court in person'. Indeed, the Standing Committee for Youth Justice (now the Alliance for Youth Justice) flagged concerns around difficulties children might have with concentration and understanding, also citing frequent technical difficulties as interfering with the clarity of proceedings (Harris, 2018). The YJB was clear in its response to court digitization proposals that 'a digital by default position is not suitable for young people' (YJB, 2016: 21). YOT workers have also reported that virtual proceedings effectively remove their input because they lose the visual support they would normally give to the child (the child cannot see them), and their ability to conduct post-court interviews may even be entirely lost because of the way video links are arranged, losing a further vital point of contact to support the children and also help them in understanding what happened in their hearing (Harris, 2018; Harris and Goodfellow, 2021).

A key concern with, and pain of, virtual youth justice is the almost inevitable erosion of children's rights as enshrined in the UNCRC (UN, 1989). Article 6 identifies a child's right to a fair trial, but this requires and assumes their ability to fully participate in proceedings (also specified in Article 12 and a major tenet of Child First justice), implying a good level of understanding throughout, alongside effective legal representation and advice. However, this cannot be assumed of children who as a group have higher-than-average levels of communication difficulties and whose emotional maturity levels might limit their ability to fully take seriously what may present like a television programme or video game (YJB, 2016; Harris, 2018). Such deficits can result in 'inappropriate' behaviour or responses garnering censure and even a possibility of higher sentencing or increased likelihood of custodial remand rather than bail, indicating additional safeguarding concerns and threats to the right to a fair trial (Harris, 2018). Contrastingly, concerns have also been expressed that lack of understanding can often result in children becoming detached from court proceedings and unresponsive in terms of their input (or giving verbal compliance in the face of incomprehensible questions; Wigzell et al, 2015), effectively denying their right to be heard by not facilitating their voice (Arthur, 2016). Difficulties with concentration (this group has a higher-than-average incidence of such conditions as attention deficit hyperactivity disorder [ADHD; Fazel, 2008]) also significantly impede a child's ability to meaningfully participate in face-to-face court proceedings (Arthur, 2016), something which a virtual court environment potentially only serves to exacerbate. These concerns regarding rights erosion also extend to Article 3 of the UNCRC (UN, 1989), which requires that the child's best interests be paramount. The considered opinion of the YJB seems to indicate that this may not be possible in virtual contexts (YJB, 2016), but in any case, before this methodology is adopted for child defendants, exploration of necessary safeguards should ensure that they are protected from the difficulties outlined earlier (Lewis and Manson, 2020). Somewhat worryingly, although there is no evidence of clear investigation into their use with children. HM Courts & Tribunals Service states: 'Remote hearings that have allowed justice to continue throughout the pandemic will continue to play an important role in the future. ... By 2022, it'll be the default service, replacing the systems we currently use' (HMCTS, 2021). This means remote hearings will potentially be a continuing pain post COVID-19 for justice-involved children.[6]

The pains and gains of COVID-19 in community YOT supervision

YOTs work in a number of different ways with children in the community and at different stages of their youth justice journey. Children whose activities or behaviours cause concern may be referred to YOTs for prevention work (to prevent them from becoming involved with offending behaviour). However, when children do commit crimes, the first system response is to try to divert them from formal (court) action by offering them voluntary programmes of support or by giving them pre-court outcomes (like a Youth Caution[7]). After this, the child will be taken to court and if convicted, can be given either a community sentence (supervised by the YOT), whereby the child will meet their worker at an agreed level of frequency, often with a range of requirements to fulfil, or a custodial sentence, during which the YOT will maintain contact with the child through (at least) monthly visits and review meetings (to which they will often take parents/carers who would find visiting the child difficult otherwise). YOTs then supervise a child leaving custody, overseeing their resettlement back into the community. The roles which YOT workers play, therefore, are many and varied, depending on the stage of youth justice journey and the needs of each child.

In order to effectively support children at any stage of this journey, good engagement is key, both in terms of YOT workers engaging with children and children engaging with their YOT workers. Effective engagement from the child to the YOT worker has been defined as needing to touch on all three areas of behaviour, emotion and cognition, which facilitates the child to 'reflect ... on the person that he or she would like to be' (Wright et al, 2014: 2). Little appears to be known about what is needed for effective engagement from the YOT worker to the child, but a constructive relationship is key to any YOT intervention (Johns et al, 2017; Case and Browning, 2021). However, it is this relationship which is potentially very much at risk when COVID-19 restrictions limit the amount and type of contact between workers and children. Children on statutory orders who are not engaging with the YOT (in the sense of attending appointments) are at risk of being returned to court for noncompliance (breach), which could lead to further, more punitive (possibly custody) punishments being applied. If engagement is threatened by COVID-19 restrictions, then the pandemic might directly cause harsher sentencing for children.

Being aware of the importance of relationships, YOTs adapted quickly to the imposition of restrictions with the development of innovative practice (gains) aimed at maintaining relationships between children and workers and enabling the work of supervision to continue, even if the parties were not able to meet face to face. This is well evidenced through a plethora of good practice sharing on the YJB Resource Hub.[8] Examples of good practice include suggesting ideas for 'remote reparation' (including instructions and materials for making face masks), setting up a range of digital media to facilitate virtual contact via phone or laptop (conducting supervision sessions through What's App, Skype or similar), posting of board games and other resources to children, organizing online quizzes and group catch-ups, setting challenges, delivering food parcels and other necessities, setting up restorative activities in which the child supports vulnerable others (like painting stones to give to care homes), delivering lessons via online videos (for example, guitar, exercise, basic skills, cookery – with ingredients provided) and participating in 'walk and talk' sessions (YJB, 2021).

The aforementioned 'constructive innovations' might become enduring gains from COVID-19, enabling YOTs to continue to develop in a virtual age. Informal consultations with YOT workers on their experiences of COVID-19 developments revealed that they felt many children benefited from digital contacts, as they seemed to engage better, perhaps being more comfortable with this than having to travel to a YOT office. However, workers could also see that other children took this as an opportunity to become difficult to track down, something with which some parents colluded. This clearly puts these children at risk of being breached for noncompliance. Another potential pain of phone-based contact is that there is less opportunity to disclose abuse, especially if the child is within earshot of an abusive adult or has to access the call through that adult's handset. This has clear safeguarding implications (see Harris and Goodfellow, 2021), increasing vulnerability, which is only exacerbated by not being able to escape their home environment due to the 'stay at home' order accompanying lockdown restrictions. Laudably, YOTs have tried to mitigate these issues by maintaining face-to-face contact with the children deemed most vulnerable, meaning that some YOT workers had to continue to meet children despite the risks of infection (YJB and YOT Managers Cymru, 2020). And the minimum requirements for any contact – social distancing (maintaining a distance of two metres from others) and face masks – are bound to have affected the abilities of both children and workers to effectively engage with each other.

Pandemic policies could also increase 'child criminalization' through increased pressure on familial relationships caused by the stress of the situation combined with the necessity to 'stay at home', effectively halting coping mechanisms like being able to go and stay with other family members for a while, all of which could increase the risk of interfamilial violence, including child-to-adult violence (YJB, 2020a; cf Condry and Miles, 2012). Justice-involved children might find it more difficult than other children to maintain adherence to the tight restrictions imposed, like staying at home and not meeting people from other households (for example, friends), especially given the high levels of ADHD or conduct disorder diagnoses among the former (Silva et al, 2014). This puts them at a higher risk of COVID-19-related police action, possibly resulting in fines for families who are more likely to be experiencing poverty (Nugent, 2015).

While for some children, using 'digital technology' to facilitate supervision might be working well, the same cannot be said for all, and the pandemic has highlighted unprecedented levels of deprivation and division in our society between those who have and those who do not. Digital poverty has meant that not everyone has the same level of access to digital resources (whether that is because they do not have access to Wi-Fi, credit for mobile internet is extremely limited or competed for by the whole family, or there is a lack of hardware for children to access digital services), an issue particularly highlighted for justice-involved children in a COVID-19-themed inspection of YOT work (HMIP, 2020). YOTs have attempted to mitigate these issues by lending out laptops and phones, but this does not address issues of Wi-Fi internet access, especially at a time when other potential sources of access (cafes, pubs, libraries) are all closed. School closures also enforced at this time have exacerbated the issue, with children in digital poverty often unable to access work which has been provided digitally, meaning that their access to education (required both by law and in respect of their rights as children – see Article 28 of the UNCRC; UN, 1989) have been effectively curtailed by COVID-19 policies. While the government gave children deemed 'vulnerable' access to school even through lockdown, this label was (inexplicably) not extended as a matter of course to justice-involved children (HMIP, 2020), so they had no automatic right to access education, despite their very evident vulnerabilities.

The evolution of 'digital online working' within YOTs during the pandemic has extended also to other aspects of their work, potentially facilitating greater communication between agencies (professionals may have found it easier to attend meetings held virtually rather than in person), but potentially restricting the effectiveness or even the availability of some important functions, especially for children at the lower end of system response (most notably, prevention work and diversion from court orders). Prior to the pandemic, prevention work by YOTs (aiming to prevent children who have not yet been convicted of any crimes but may be causing concern regarding their vulnerability in this respect) had been enjoying an increasing profile as research showed that children were more likely to remain embroiled in the YJS once they entered it, rather than the system response effectively helping them to escape (Case and Haines, 2015). However, once the pandemic restrictions began, prevention work (a nonstatutory aspect of YOT work, yet the primary aim of the YJS) ceased entirely, as YOTs retracted to minimum service in an attempt to maintain basic contact with children on statutory orders, which had clearly become a much more time-consuming and complex proposition (cf Wrexham Youth Justice Service, 2020). Given the importance of prevention work in keeping children from ever entering the YJS, this could potentially have a devastating effect on numbers of first-time entrants to the system over the coming months and years, thus becoming a continuing pain of COVID-19.

In order to promote the 'diversion' of children from court and into out-of-court systems and alternative support services, several processes have developed in England and Wales as ways to offer alternatives to prosecution to children arrested for low-level offences. In England, this has tended to be 'triage', where a YOT worker is either based in the police station or visits when a child is arrested; they then negotiate with police for a response that doesn't require the child to go to court – usually a Youth Caution or a Youth Conditional Caution (Home Office, 2012). In Wales, the model used tends to be the Bureau, whereby an eligible child (low-level offending and no previous convictions) is taken through a process involving a clinic offering outcomes such as a noncriminal disposal, or Youth Caution or Youth Conditional Caution. It is unclear how the triage system has been affected by the pandemic, although there is some evidence to suggest that YOT workers still attended police stations in person (cf Hillingdon Youth Justice Service, 2020). However, it has been identified as 'good practice' that Bureaus have continued, facilitated by videoconferencing or telephone (YOT Managers Cymru and YJB, 2020). Although it is positive that diversion options are still available, given the concerns highlighted earlier in relation to virtual courts, holding Bureau clinics remotely risks riding roughshod over children's rights in ways similar to those previously discussed.

Where diversion has not been possible and children are prosecuted in court for the first time (if pleading guilty), a Referral Order tends to be imposed[9] (UK Government, 2018). A Referral Order is unique in that it begins with a Referral Panel meeting comprising community representatives, the child and their parent/carer, a YOT worker and the victim (or their representative), where a contract will be agreed as to what the child will do while on the order. This is reviewed at three-month intervals and at the order's finish, again by a panel similarly comprised. During the pandemic, Referral Order Panels either consisted of multiple-way phone calls (Lancashire Child and Youth Justice Service, 2020) or went online through videoconferencing (YOT Managers Cymru and YJB, 2020). Some review and end panels even ceased to occur, with children being sent a letter remarking on their progress instead, thus losing a vital opportunity to offer real encouragement to a child who has done well (HMIP, 2020a). There is a risk that holding panel meetings online could reduce the ability or opportunity for the child to make meaningful input into their own plan, thereby letting it become something of a fait accompli before they even see it. Panel members have expressed concerns themselves about the virtual platform, telling HMIP (2020a: 20) that they 'couldn't really get a sense of the child and too much was lost in not being able to see the non-verbal communication and dynamics between children and their parents and carers'.

In summary, while it is undeniable that YOTs have shown remarkable ability to be innovative, flexible and creative during the COVID-19 pandemic, clearly maintaining a view that justice-involved children are vulnerable and need consistent support, thus demonstrating Child First thinking, the sheer reliance on online solutions to maintaining contact is clearly problematic given issues of digital poverty and loss of effectiveness, for all the reasons already discussed. In addition, those services for which face-to-face contact is surely vital, like appointments relating to substance misuse and physical and mental health, appeared often to be managed entirely through phone contact, raising concerns about safeguarding and effectiveness, especially at a time of heightened concern and anxiety in the general population (cf Ealing YJS, 2020; Wrexham Youth Justice Service, 2020).

The pains and gains of COVID-19 in custody

The imprisonment of children has long been an area of contention in youth justice, with the UNCRC stating that it should be 'used only as a measure of last resort and for the shortest appropriate period of time' (UN, 1989: Article 37). In England and Wales, numbers of children in custody have plummeted in recent years, with the average number (860 in March 2019) indicating a reduction of 70 per cent over the previous decade (YJB and Ministry of Justice, 2021). However, this apparent good news hides more disturbing trends on longer sentences (a breach of Article 37) and more use of remand instead of bail. Resettlement back into the community after custody also poses particular challenges, since this group constitute the highest reoffending rate for all disposal types (YJB and Ministry of Justice, 2021). This has resulted in a sustained (and yet seemingly still ineffective) focus by the YJB on resettlement over the past few years (Hampson, 2016), given that reoffending rates for custody leavers remain stubbornly high.

Children in custody[10] during the pandemic are at risk of further difficulties compounding those already caused by the deleterious effects of imprisonment (Goldson, 2005), which illustrates the triple disadvantage visited on children by the pandemic and presumably underpins the YJB's stated aim of custody reduction. Further to this, the engagement (and avoidance of deleterious disengagement) of children in custody is crucial for effective practice in the pursuit of positive behaviours/outcomes (for example, consistent and meaningful participation in education, other prosocial activities, rehabilitation, therapy) evidenced to promote desistence and reduced reoffending, both in custody and following release (Stephenson and Jamieson, 2006; Case and Haines, 2021). However, COVID-19 policies and practice have *increased* isolation (both within the institution, with children locked up for vast periods in the day, and in terms of reduced contact with the outside, with all visits from family and professionals suspended) and thus caused further disengagement from support services, detachment from entitlements like health and education (both conducted remotely) and rights breaches (for example, UNCRC Article 39 – recovery and reintegration after neglect, exploitation or abuse; UN, 1989). It could be argued, therefore, that the difficulties (pains) of lockdown for children in custody are different and potentially even more deleterious than for convicted children supervised in the community, but because they are 'out of sight, out of mind' they are more easily neglected and ignored.

While the success of the YJB's stated aim to reduce custody numbers during the pandemic is borne out in recent figures indicating a 24 per cent fall in custody from March to July 2020 (from 737 to 563 children), albeit with a minor increase in August to 571 children (YCS, 2021), this hides more worrying concerns. The drop in custodial numbers during COVID-19 is not attributable to the government's temporary early release scheme (Ministry of Justice, 2020c), despite this being part of the YJB's stated protections. In fact, no children were released through this programme. This alarming fact was admitted in evidence given to the House of Commons Justice Committee on 2 June 2020 and confirmed as still true in a freedom of information request by the authors as the scheme expired. A possible explanation for this total neglect by the early release scheme is children's continued ineligibility – for children to be eligible, they need to be within 61 days of the end of their licence, the offence cannot be one of a list of excluded 'violent' offences, and suitable accommodation has to be available in advance. This sustained ineligibility, the apparent lack of will to relax the tight stipulations in such an exceptional time, and the consequent neglect both by the early release scheme and of the health, well-being and rights of children in custody (so breaching several articles of the UNCRC; UN, 1989) are contrary to the YJB's stated strategic aims for mitigating the impact of the COVID-19 crisis. This specifically included '[m]aximising children granted bail (including those currently remanded in prison)' (YJB, 2020e: 1), but despite reductions in overall custody numbers, the proportion of children in custody on remand increased significantly through lockdown from 33 per cent of children in custody in March 2020 to 39 per cent by August (YCS, 2021). These figures highlight the abject failure of the YJB to prevent children being remanded during this time and the delays in justice which court cessation caused to children already waiting (many unnecessarily) on remand before the lockdown. That most children remanded do not go on to receive a custodial sentence (66 per cent, according to the House of Commons Justice Committee, 2020) shows that the principles of 'best interests of the child' and custody as 'last resort' (UNCRC Article 37b; UN, 1989) do not appear to be applied in remand decisions, resulting in serious over-remanding, which is particularly damaging during the COVID-19 crisis (Howard League for Penal Reform, 2020). The reduction in custody figures for children during this time would appear to be entirely due to natural release at the end of sentence, as little new sentencing was taking place during lockdown, and this was completely unaided by any use of the government's early release scheme.

For children trapped in custody over the pandemic period (sentenced and unsentenced), particularly those in YOIs (which hold five times the custody numbers of SCHs and STCs combined; YCS, 2021), little provision was put in place to allay their inevitable fears regarding, for example, whether life will ever return to some kind of normality, whether they would see older family members again and whether they or their loved ones would experience much-feared symptoms seen in news reports. Children in custody in the YJS of England and Wales were left without any face-to-face visits and no suitable replacement for some considerable time, meaning that reassurance offered through family contact was severely stymied. The concurrent suspension of professional visits, especially for children on remand, constituted a further loss of rights in terms of being able to access legal advice (breaching UNCRC Article 37d – the right to legal advice; UN, 1989; see Harris and Goodfellow, 2021).

In relation to the facilitation of virtual contact in custody, despite there having been a trial by one YOI prior to the pandemic on the use of Skype to expand online child–family visitation (Thomas and Haines, 2016), the learning from this project was not utilized to facilitate a quick rollout of such a vital potential point of contact for children with the outside world at the point of lockdown. A short scrutiny inspection of three YOIs in April 2020 noted that only one of them had managed to facilitate the use of video calls within the prison (coincidentally, the same one that was involved in the earlier Skype project), but even then, the first video call only happened on the day of the inspection (HM Chief Inspector of Prisons, 2020a). The apparent explanation for this serious delay, when the rest of the world was developing skills in video calling apace, was the necessity for an initial pilot to be held in an adult facility (HMP Berwyn). This requirement immediately calls into question the loss of previously evaluated projects which could have quickly been applied to the YOIs in this situation. In contrast, the SCHs appeared to have taken up video calling quickly and frequently (indicative of pain experienced in YOIs, yet gains experienced in SCHs), with one worker commenting that the children had 'constant' family contact to help them cope. There was some development in the use of video calling by the time of a second short scrutiny inspection in July, as the two (different) YOIs involved in this had introduced 'purple visits' – video calls via a laptop (HM Chief Inspector of Prisons, 2020b). However, the inspection noted the relatively low take-up of this opportunity by the children and mused on whether this was due to the perceived necessity of the institutions to have a member of staff present with the child, which could have been off-putting for normal child–family interactions – something which the previous Skype project evaluation pointed out as a weakness (Thomas and Haines, 2016). This is another clear indication of missed learning. The inspection also highlighted issues with families being unable to provide the required ID to be eligible, which again layers disadvantage on disadvantage (HM Chief Inspector of Prisons, 2020b).

Engagement with custodial education is another acute concern, particularly as it has been identified as central to the development of positive, trusting relationships, constructive interactions with adults and enhanced capacity for children to manage their own behaviour (Taylor, 2016; Case and Hazel, 2020). Regulations in 'normal times' require that children receive a minimum of 25 to 30 hours of education each week, depending on the type of custodial provision (Houses of Parliament, 2016), and this also equates to out-of-cell time. Even in 'normal times', education in custody, while stated as being at 'the heart of youth custody' (Parliamentary Office of Science & Technology, 2016: 1), seems to fall short of that aim, being generic, un/disengaging and isolationist (Case and Hazel, 2020). However, the second short scrutiny visit found that although other types of custody, particularly SCHs, had swiftly restarted face-to-face education following lockdown, YOIs were still only providing additional 'in-room activities' (YJB, 2020e), resulting in children routinely spending in excess of 22 hours a day in their cell alone, and in the worst cases, only being out of the cell for 40 minutes (HM Chief Inspector of Prisons, 2020b). In fact, for STCs, the way was paved for this kind of isolation to continue well into 2022 (Grant, 2020), with legislation facilitating the practice, which is extremely damaging to children's development and well-being (cf Bateman, 2020; Orben et al, 2020).

It is helpful, given these extreme restrictive practices of increasing in-cell time, cessation of visits and lack of face-to-face services like education and health (all of which breaches the children's rights set out in the UNCRC; UN, 1989), that concessions have been given to children to increase their access to telecommunications within the cell, with most having an in-cell telephone. Increased access (in terms of time – children are not able to use their phones at any time) has been allowed, free access to a range of helplines for children to be able to talk through their worries (for example, Childline) has been permitted, and increased telephone credit has been instigated. However, while this is all to be applauded, there are significant limitations still present. All YOIs have increased telephone credit, but to such a varying degree that it is become something of a postcode lottery – the most generous increase being £20 per week and the least generous, £5 (HM Chief Inspector of Prisons, 2020a). However, it must be questioned why children are having to pay at all to make valuable calls to family at such a distressing time. Given that children's need may not correlate with their institution's generosity or their family's finances, surely arrangements could be made for free access or at least a significant period when access is free?

Taking the issues examined into account, it can be seen that children in custody have not been protected from being incarcerated during the pandemic and that neither they nor their rights have been well protected while in custody during this time. When the rest of the world has switched to online communications through increasing use of videoconferencing and other online platforms (facilitating, for example, homeworking and a variety of social/faith groups; Ofcom, 2020), this route has been largely unavailable or severely delayed for children in custody, underlining the isolation caused both by being locked up for the vast majority of each day and the cessation of face-to-face visits, surely breaching their right to their best interests being a 'primary consideration' (UNCRC Article 3; UN, 1989).

Youth justice after the initial lockdown

Since these initial (reactive) policies and practice developments to mitigate the problems caused by COVID-19 for justice-involved children, agencies have published 'recovery' plans to enable a return to more 'normal' operations (cf HMCTS, 2020; YJB, 2020b). However, some 20 months into the pandemic, working practices were certainly still far from their pre-COVID-19 status, exacerbated by second and third waves of the virus causing reversal back into previously relaxed lockdown policies (Iacobucci, 2021). Indeed, recovery plans written in 2020 seem rather optimistic in the teeth of these continuing infection waves throughout 2021, despite a remarkably successful UK vaccination programme which saw nearly 80 per cent of the population over 12 years old receive at two doses by October 2021 (UK Government, 2021a; although using age as a prioritizer, children will not yet have benefited from this). Reacting to increasing infections over the winter of 2020–21, all the home nations of the UK (the governments of England, Wales, Scotland and Northern Ireland each being responsible for their own jurisdiction in this) reinstituted lockdowns similar to that of March 2020, but with some interesting differences, perhaps demonstrating lessons learned from the initial, and highly reactive, almost-total lockdown of society. Although visits to *adults* in custodial institutions in England and Wales were again halted, this was not the case for children, whose facility to receive visits was never again completely curtailed (adults began lockdown at Stage 4 and children at Stage 3 of the national framework; Ministry of Justice and HMPPS, 2020), 'balancing the need to ensure the safety of staff and children, while also providing key aspects of regime delivery to children such as "face to face" education and social visits' (Ministry of Justice stakeholder update, February 2021). While measures to address digital poverty (provision of such equipment as laptops, wireless routers, SIM cards with digital credit for those identified as 'disadvantaged') began in 2020, these were slow to become effective (Sibieta and Cottell, 2020), though much more was made available in both jurisdictions as the second lockdown began in January 2021. For example, in England this scheme did not even begin until May 2020 and by mid-June it had seen 137,000 items distributed (Department for Education, 2020); by mid-July this had increased to over 1.3 million (UK Government, 2021b). While it is unclear how far justice-involved children have benefited from this, criteria like being a care leaver, having no household access to Wi-Fi or having a social worker, and the facility for local authorities (rather than just schools) to be distributors, potentially widens out eligibility beyond simply school pupils, as this restricted eligibility could preclude many justice-involved children due to the high prevalence of school exclusion and being, for other reasons, 'off-roll'.

Restrictions put in place in January 2021 are being eased in the summer (July for England and August for Wales) despite rising COVID-19 case numbers, which brings with it concern about the potential for further lockdowns going into the winter. However clearly *some* lessons have been learned regarding protection of justice-involved children in these circumstances. This continuing situation makes it very difficult to see how practice is set to change within the sector as a result of the pandemic – it might revert back or develop differently for the future, producing more enduring pains and gains.

Enduring pains and gains of COVID-19?

It is clear that some COVID-19-related policy and practice changes were only ever meant to be short term and that they may well have posed a risk to both the development of Child First justice and ensuring children access to their rights. The changes have either been discontinued already (like the suspension of prison visits) or will be very soon as the UK opens up again (this includes the majority of 'virtual' YOT work, notwithstanding the potential need for further protective measures). Conversely, there are some changes which are likely to be adopted going forward into a post-COVID-19 world. This could be very positive for practice development that has creatively explored other ways to work with children, which YOTs have been quick to adopt and develop (like use of 'walk and talk' sessions, allotments and other outside contacts). However, certain changes, as discussed, were not in the child's 'best interests' (UNCRC Article 3; UN, 1989) and will have lasting consequences because the child will continue to be adversely affected well after practice reverts back or because the changes have become the new normal – these then become the enduring pains and gains of COVID-19. In terms of Child First justice in practice, all the tenets which characterize (see Table 6.1) this have been, and continue to be, affected for children pre court, those going to court, those sentenced to community orders and those sentenced to custody.

Tenet 1, 'seeing children as children', is not simply a matter of the attitudes of staff (many YOT workers demonstrate clear understanding of this tenet) but also of how the whole system treats a child. Virtual courts are clearly an innovation that is here to stay, but concerns around children's ability to interact appropriately with them (given difficulties with comprehension, communication and lack of support) suggest that they risk eroding a child's right to a fair trial (UNCRC Article 40; UN, 1989), and in failing to take into account children's developmental needs and capabilities, they do not appropriately 'see children as children'. Where cases have been delayed due to the pandemic and individuals end up being sentenced as an adult despite being under 18 at the time of the offence, these individuals have clearly not been seen as children by the system. This surely also applies to children in custody, many of whom may never have spent a night away from home before their incarceration yet suddenly have to cope with isolation that an adult might struggle with. During the pandemic, access to telephone communications was extended for children in custody, but it is unclear whether these facilities will remain open to children after regimes return to a more 'normal' state. It is an opportunity to provide vital support to children in an unsupportive situation, possibly increasing the likelihood of more effective resettlement after release due to children being able to communicate more freely with family as and when they need to; this would therefore also potentially reduce reoffending post release (a gain). The potential benefits of giving children free (in terms of not needing to pay for the phone call) access to calls at any time should be thoroughly explored. Given the high cost of custody as it stands (in excess of £210,000 per year per child for SCHs and £76,000 per child per year for YOIs; UK Parliament, 2018), this would surely be a negligible amount to bring incalculable benefits.

Tenet 2, 'developing prosocial identity for positive child outcomes', requires relationship to be at the heart of all work with children, but relationships have been severely limited by virtual-only contact. YOT workers, when they are able to meet their clients once more face to face, will need to work to build up rapport again. Some children may have spent a very isolated period in custody without even the support of their worker (let alone their families). Lack of educational provision – whether because the child is not currently 'on roll' anywhere or because they lack the requisite support or equipment for home-schooling and were not considered 'vulnerable' and therefore eligible for a precious school place during lockdown – may have seriously hampered children's ability to develop to their potential. The soaring youth unemployment rate will make it even more challenging for justice-involved children to move towards prosocial independence given the disadvantaging effects of a criminal record (ONS, 2021). Whether this means they return to the 'system' through further criminalization (or through difficulties in realizing 'desistance' due to lack of opportunity and/or support) remains to be seen.

Tenet 3, 'collaboration with children', may also have been adversely affected by lack of face-to-face contact, as children's ability to provide meaningful input into intervention plans is likely to have been damaged. Referral Order Panel members commented on the disconnect they felt with children they only saw on screen, and it is difficult to see how children in that situation can provide any real voice in their plan through a video conference with largely unknown adults. This is reflected throughout the YJS in the lack of human contact at every level (for example, virtual appointments in the community and virtual visits in custody). This risks children's disengagement and detachment from intervention plans in the community and resettlement plans for those in custody. Communication difficulties and power imbalances make true participation even more challenging when the facility to talk face to face, and therefore pick up vital nonverbal cues, is not available, further disenfranchising the very children the plans are meant to help.

Tenet 4, 'promotion of diversion', refers to limiting children's involvement with the (damaging) justice system. This applies to all levels in the system, from stopping children ever entering the system, through prevention work, to reducing use of custody. That YOTs felt the need to withdraw almost entirely from any prevention work clearly impacts on the development of this tenet in practice, but wider than this, the increased risk of (further and re-) criminalization due to COVID-19 policies may potentially reverse the reductions in system numbers which have been the trend over the past decade at most levels of youth justice operations. Notably, children most at risk of COVID-19-related prosecutions may have been disproportionately involved in criminal exploitation by others (due, for example, to having nothing to occupy them during lockdown as well as the absence of supportive, court-ordered interventions) and may otherwise have been free of justice agencies. In addition, the commencement of Knife Crime Prevention Orders in London (Home Office and Malthouse, 2020) as a response to knife crime (rather than the less criminalizing public health model demonstrated in Glasgow; see Scottish Government, nd), paused during the pandemic, may well see the criminalizing of children at an unprecedented level. A system which increases the criminalization of children cannot be considered Child First.

Conclusion

We have demonstrated that while there have been some interesting innovations due to efforts by agents of youth justice to mitigate the effects of the pandemic restrictions on justice-involved children, which have effectively become gains of COVID-19 for these children, there have been many more ways in which justice-involved children have suffered triple disadvantage (being normally doubly disadvantaged) – the pains of COVID-19. Clearly, the trajectory of Child First practice development has been severely affected (a pain), as many of the changes made have directly and adversely impacted on the four tenets, outlined in Table 6.1. The enduring nature of some of these pains makes it more difficult to see Child First developing as a 'strategic approach and central guiding principle' (YJB, 2021: 10) for youth justice in a world recovering from COVID-19.

Notes
1. When originally set up, the YJB's responsibility covered both community youth justice and the secure estate, but following evidence of mismanagement of custodial establishments and neglect of custodial objectives by the YJB, the Youth Custody Service (YCS) was established with overall responsibility for youth custody in England and Wales (Youth Custody Improvement Board, 2017).
2. For example, all but essential shops and services closed (including schools), citizens generally had to stay at home and only key workers could work outside the home.
3. The Ministry of Justice is a department of the UK government with responsibility for the whole justice system (adult and child); ultimately both the YJB and the YCS answer to the ministry.
4. One of the YJB's aims is to support effective practice, and their web-based Youth Justice Resource Hub showcases YOT innovations and good practice; see https://yjresourcehub.uk/
5. The Rehabilitation of Offenders Act 1974 (with subsequent revisions) provides that a criminal conviction can be considered 'spent' after a certain period of time (dependent on the offence/age of the person) and therefore no longer needs to be declared as a matter of course on most applications.
6. However, it was not possible to ascertain the extent to which virtual courts were actually used during the pandemic with children in the youth court environment, as this does not appear to have been recorded anywhere (Lewis and Manson, 2020; Harris and Goodfellow, 2021).
7. The Legal Aid, Sentencing and Punishment of Offenders Act 2012 created two pre-court cautions for children, which could be applied at any point in a child's youth justice journey for minor crimes – the Youth Caution and the Youth Conditional Caution (conditional on the child engaging with a three-month intervention) – which, in many YOTs, are administered by a police officer seconded to the YOT.
8. The YJB have set up an online repository of evidenced good practice put forward by YOTs – the Resource Hub (see https://yjresourcehub.uk/).
9. For a first court appearance, the court has the option of issuing a Referral Order or placing the child in custody, so unless the offence is very serious a Referral Order is the most likely outcome; since the Legal Aid, Sentencing and Punishment of Offenders Act 2012, Referral Orders are now available on an unlimited basis for low-level, but prosecuted, offences (UK Government, 2018).
10. Children given custody in England and Wales are sent to one of three types of institution: Secure Children's Homes (SCHs; generally small units for younger and more vulnerable children, run by local authorities), Secure Training Centres (STCs; large units for somewhat less vulnerable children up to 17, generally privately run) and Young Offender Institutions (YOIs; large, more prison-like units for boys between 15 and 18, generally run by the YCS – these hold the vast majority of children in custody).

References

Arthur, R. (2016) 'Giving effect to young people's right to participate effectively in criminal proceedings', *Child and Family Law Quarterly*, 28(3): 223–38.

Bateman, T. (2020) 'Unjust pains: the impact of COVID-19 on children in prison', *Journal of Children's Services*. doi: 10.1108/JCS-07-2020-0045.

BBC (2020) 'Coronavirus: strict new curbs on life in UK announced by PM', *BBC*, [online] 24 March, Available from: www.bbc.co.uk/news/uk-52012432

Case, S. (2014) 'Strategic complexities and opportunities in Welsh youth justice: exploring YJB Cymru', *Safer Communities*, 13(3): 109–19.

Case, S. and Browning, A. (2021) *Child First Justice: The Research Evidence-base*, Loughborough University, [online] Available from: https://repository.lboro.ac.uk/ndownloader/files/26748341/1

Case, S. and Haines, K. (2009) *Understanding Youth Offending Risk Factor Research, Policy and Practice*, Abingdon: Routledge.

Case, S. and Haines, K. (2015) '*Children First, Offenders Second* positive promotion: reframing the prevention debate', *Youth Justice*, 15(3): 226–39.

Case, S. and Haines, K. (2021) 'Abolishing youth justice systems: Children First, offenders nowhere', *Youth Justice*, 21(1): 3–17.

Case, S. and Hazel, N. (2020) 'Child First, Offender Second – a progressive model for education in custody', *International Journal of Educational Development*, 77: 102244. doi: 10.1016/j.ijedudev.2020.102244.

Condry, R. and Miles, C. (2012) 'Adolescent to parent violence and youth justice in England and Wales', *Social Policy and Society*, 11(2): 241–50.

Department for Education (2020) *Devices and 4G Wireless Routers Data*, [online] Available from: https://assets.publishing.service.gov.uk/government/uploads/system/uploads/attachment_data/file/921211/Devices_and_4G_wireless_routers_data_ad_hoc_stats.pdf

Ealing YJS (2020) *YJS Contingency Plan*, [online] Available from: https://yjresourcehub.uk/covid-19-resources-for-youth-justice/item/download/885_8c5a20f873ff99d201bfca9c043fd92b.html

Farrington, D.P. (2000) 'Explaining and preventing crime: the globalization of knowledge', *Criminology*, 38(1): 1–24.

Fazel, D.A. (2008) 'Mental disorders among adolescents in juvenile detention and correctional facilities: a systematic review and metaregression analysis of 25 surveys', *Journal of American Academy*, 47(9): 1010–19.

Gayer-Anderson, C., Latham, R., El Zerbi, C., Strang, L., Moxham Hall, V., and Knowles, G., et al (2020) *Impacts of Social Isolation among Disadvantaged and Vulnerable Groups during Public Health Crises*, ESRC/UKRI Research Briefing, London: Centre for Society and Mental Health, King's College London.

Goldson, B. (2005) 'Child imprisonment: a case for abolition', *Youth Justice*, 5(2): 77–90.

Grant, H. (2020) '"It's just too long": children in detention may face Covid-19 restrictions until 2022', *The Guardian*, [online] 21 July, Available from: www.theguardian.com/global-development/2020/jul/21/its-just-too-long-children-in-detention-may-face-covid-19-restrictions-until-2022

Haines, K. and Drakeford, M. (1998) *Young People and Youth Justice*, London: Palgrave.

Hampson, K.S. (2016) 'From the mouths of dragons: how does the resettlement of young people from North Wales measure up … in their own words?', *Youth Justice*, 16(3): 246–62.

Harris, M. (2018) *'They Just Don't Understand What's Happened or Why': A Report on Child Defendants and Video Links*, Standing Committee for Youth Justice, [online] Available from: www.basw.co.uk/system/files/resources/basw_35104-3.pdf

Harris, M. and Goodfellow, P. (2021) *The Youth Justice System's Response to the COVID-19 Pandemic*, [online] Available from: www.mmu.ac.uk/media/mmuacuk/content/documents/mcys/Impact-of-COVID---Literature-Review.pdf

Hillingdon Youth Justice Service (2020) *COVID-19 Impact Assessment and Initial Recovery Planning*, [online] Available from: https://yjresourcehub.uk/covid-19-resources-for-youth-justice/item/722-impact-assessment-and-initial-recovery-planning-hillingdon-yot-april-2020.html

HM Chief Inspector of Prisons (2020a) *Report on Short Scrutiny Visits to Young Offender Institutions Holding Children*, [online] 21 April, Available from: www.justiceinspectorates.gov.uk/hmiprisons/wp-content/uploads/sites/4/2020/05/YOIs-SSV-Web-2020.pdf

HM Chief Inspector of Prisons (2020b) *Report on Short Scrutiny Visits to Young Offender Institutions Holding Children*, [online] 7 July, Available from: www.justiceinspectorates.gov.uk/hmiprisons/wp-content/uploads/sites/4/2020/07/YOI-SSV-2.pdf

HMCTS (HM Courts & Tribunals Service) (2020) *COVID-19: Update on the HMCTS Response for Criminal Courts in England & Wales*, [online] Available from: https://assets.publishing.service.gov.uk/government/uploads/system/uploads/attachment_data/file/915493/HMCTS401_recovery_overview_for_crime_WEB.pdf

HMCTS (2021) 'Building for the future at HMCTS', [online] 24 June, Available from: https://insidehmcts.blog.gov.uk/2021/06/24/building-for-the-future-at-hmcts/

HMIP (HM Inspectorate of Probation) (2020) *A Thematic Review of the Work of Youth Offending Services during the COVID-19 Pandemic*, [online] Available from: www.justiceinspectorates.gov.uk/hmiprobation/wp- content/uploads/sites/5/2020/11/201110-A-thematic-review-of-the-work-of-youth-offending-services-during-the-COVID-19-pandemic.pdf

Home Office (2012) *Assessing Young People in Police Custody: An Examination of the Operation of Triage Schemes*, Occasional paper 106, [online] Available from: https://assets.publishing.service.gov.uk/government/uploads/system/uploads/attachment_data/file/116265/occ106.pdf

Home Office and Malthouse, K. (2020) 'Introduction of knife crime prevention orders', [online] 4 March, Available from: www.gov.uk/government/news/introduction-of-knife-crime-prevention-orders

House of Commons Justice Committee (2020) *Coronavirus (COVID-19): The Impact on Courts*, Sixth Report of Session 2019–21, HC 519, [online] Available from: https://committees.parliament.uk/publications/2188/documents/20351/default

House of Parliament (2016) 'Education in youth custody', [online] Available from: https://post.parliament.uk/research-briefings/post-pn-0524/

Howard League for Penal Reform (2020) *Ending the Detention of Unsentenced Children during the Covid-19 Pandemic: A Guide for Practitioners*, [online] Available from: https://howardleague.org/wp-content/uploads/2020/11/Ending-the-detention-of-unsentenced-children-during-the-Covid-19-pandemic.pdf

Iacobucci, G. (2021) 'Covid-19: prepare for a third wave, warns England's chief medical officer', *British Medical Journal*, 373: n1577. doi: 10.1136/bmj.n1577.

Johns, D.F., Williams, K. and Haines, K. (2017) 'Ecological youth justice: understanding the social ecology of young people's prolific offending', *Youth Justice*, 17(1): 3–21.

Just For Kids Law (2020) *Timely Justice: Turning 18: A Briefing on the Impact of Turning 18 in the Criminal Justice System*, [online] Available from: https://justforkidslaw.org/sites/default/files/upload/YJLC%20Turning%2018%20briefing%20(June%202020).pdf

Lancashire Child and Youth Justice Service (2020) *Referral Order Panel Process for Staff (Initial, Review and Final) – During Covid 19 Restrictions*, [online] Available from: https://yjresourcehub.uk/covid-19-resources-for-youth-justice/item/771

Lewis, A. and Manson, D. (2020) *The Implications of Video Link Hearings on the Effective Participation of Child Defendants and How Best to Manage Them*, Garden Court Chambers, [online] 5 May, Available from: www.gardencourtchambers.co.uk/resources/download/164/video-link-hearings-and-children-presentation-slides-5-may-2020.pdf

McAra, L. and McVie, S. (2007) 'Youth justice? The impact of system contact on patterns of desistance from offending', *European Journal of Criminology*, 4(3): 315–45.

Ministry of Justice (2020a) 'Coronavirus (COVID-19) and prisons', [online] Available from: www.gov.uk/guidance/coronavirus-covid-19-and-prisons

Ministry of Justice (2020b) 'Coronavirus (COVID-19): courts and tribunals planning and preparation', [online] Available from: www.gov.uk/guidance/coronavirus-covid-19-courts-and-tribunals-planning-and-preparation#history

Ministry of Justice (2020c) 'End of custody temporary release', [online] Available from: https://assets.publishing.service.gov.uk/government/uploads/system/uploads/attachment_data/file/881061/end-custody-temporary-release.pdf

Ministry of Justice and HMPPS (2020) *COVID-19: National Framework for Prison Regimes and Services*, London: Ministry of Justice and HMPPS.

Nugent, B. (2015) 'The view from unbroken windows', *Scottish Justice Matters*, 3(3): 14.

Ofcom (2020) *Online Nation: 2020 Summary Report*, [online] Available from: www.ofcom.org.uk/__data/assets/pdf_file/0028/196408/online-nation-2020-summary.pdf

ONS (Office for National Statistics) (2021) 'Labour market overview, UK: April 2021', [online] 20 April, Available from: www.ons.gov.uk/employmentandlabourmarket/peopleinwork/employmentandemployeetypes/bulletins/uklabourmarket/april2021#measuring-the-data

Orben, A., Tomova, L. and Blakemore, S. (2020) 'The effects of social deprivation on adolescent development and mental health', *The Lancet Child & Adolescent Health*, 4(8): 634–640.

Parliamentary Office of Science & Technology (2016) *Education in Youth Custody*, POSTNOTE 524, [online], Available from: http://researchbriefings.files.parliament.uk/documents/POST-PN-0524/POST-PN-0524.pdf

Royal Courts of Justice (2017) *Amendment No. 3 to the Criminal Practice Directions 2015*, [online] Available from: www.judiciary.uk/wp-content/uploads/2017/01/amendment-no-3-cpd-jan-2017-final.pdf

Scottish Government (nd) 'Crime prevention', [online] Available from: www.gov.scot/policies/crime-prevention-and-reduction/violence-knife-crime/

Sibieta, L. and Cottell, J. (2020) 'Education policy response across the UK to the pandemic', [online] Available from: https://epi.org.uk/publications-and-research/education-responses-uk-pandemic/

Silva, D., Colvin, L., Glauert, R. and Bower, C. (2014) 'Contact with the juvenile justice system in children treated with stimulant medication for attention deficit hyperactivity disorder: a population study', *The Lancet Psychiatry*, 1(4): 278–85.

Sleight, D. (2020) 'Justice delayed is justice denied for clients in lockdown limbo', *The Law Society Gazette*, [online] 13 November, Available from: www.lawgazette.co.uk/commentary-and-opinion/justice-delayed-is-justice-denied-for-clients-in-lockdown-limbo/5106414.article

Stephenson, M. and Jamieson, J. (2006) *Barriers to Engagement in Education, Training and Employment*, London: Youth Justice Board.

Sykes, G.M. (1958) *The Society of Captives: A Study of a Maximum Security Prison*, Princeton, NJ: Princeton University Press.

Taylor, C. (2016) *Review of the Youth Justice System in England and Wales*, Cm 9298, Ministry of Justice, [online] Available from: https://assets.publishing.service.gov.uk/government/uploads/system/uploads/attachment_data/file/577103/youth-justice-review-final-report.pdf

Thomas, S. (2015) *Children First, Offenders Second: An Aspiration or a Reality for Youth Justice in Wales*, Doctoral thesis, University of Bedfordshire, [online] Available from: https://uobrep.openrepository.com/bitstream/handle/10547/622111/Children%20First%20Offender%20Second%20Sue%20Thomas%20%202015.pdf?sequence=1&isAllowed=y

Thomas, S. and Haines, K. (2016) *Skype Project – Parc Young Offender Institution. Findings from the Pilot (May 2015 to April 2016)*, Youth Justice Board and Swansea University.

UK Government (2018) *Criminal Justice and Courts Bill: Referral Orders*, [online] Available from: https://assets.publishing.service.gov.uk/government/uploads/system/uploads/attachment_data/file/322209/fact-sheet-youth-referral-orders.pdf

UK Government (2019) *Telling People about Your Criminal Record*, [online] Available from: https://www.gov.uk/tell-employer-or-college-about-criminal-record/check-your-conviction-caution

UK Government (2021a) 'Coronavirus (COVID-19) in the UK', [online] Available from: https://coronavirus-staging.data.gov.uk/

UK Government (2021b) 'Laptops and tablets data', [online] Available from: https://explore-education-statistics.service.gov.uk/find-statistics/laptops-and-tablets-data

UK Parliament (2018) 'Youth custody: costs. Question for Ministry of Justice', [online] 15 May, Available from: https://questions-statements.parliament.uk/written-questions/detail/2018-05-15/144303

UN (United Nations) (1989) *United Nations Convention on the Rights of the Child*, [online] Available from: www.ohchr.org/sites/default/files/crc.pdf

UN (2020) *COVID-19 and Human Rights: We Are All in this Together*, [online] Available from: www.un.org/victimsofterrorism/sites/www.un.org.victimsofterrorism/files/un_-_human_rights_and_covid_april_2020.pdf

Welsh Assembly Government and YJB (Youth Justice Board) (2004) *All-Wales Youth Offending Strategy*, [online] Available from: http://dera.ioe.ac.uk/10864/1/strategye%3Flang%3Den

Welsh Government and YJB (2014) *Children and Young People First*, [online] Available from: https://assets.publishing.service.gov.uk/government/uploads/system/uploads/attachment_data/file/374572/Youth_Justice_Strategy_English.PDF

West, D.J. and Farrington, D.P. (1973) *Who Becomes Delinquent?* London: Heinemann.

Wigzell, A., Kirby, A. and Jacobson, J. (2015) *The Youth Proceedings Advocacy Review: Final Report*, London: Bar Standards Board.

Wrexham Youth Justice Service (2020) *COVID-19 Contingency Plan – Wrexham Youth Justice Service*, [online] Available from: https://yjresource hub.uk/covid-19-resources-for-youth-justice/item/download/874_94798 2a74714454e97d7756ceba45829.html on 10 November 2020

Wright S, Bateman T and Hazel N (2014) *Engaging Young People in Resettlement*. London: Beyond Youth Custody.

Yates, J. (2010) 'Structural disadvantage: youth, class, crime and poverty', in W. Taylor, R. Earle and R. Hester (eds) *Youth Justice Handbook: Theory, Policy and Practice*, Abingdon: Routledge, pp 5–22.

YJB (Youth Justice Board) (2003) *Swift Administration of Justice (KEEP)*, London: Youth Justice Board.

YJB (2016) YJB *Position Statement on Young People Appearing in Court Via Video Link*, [online] Available from: https://youthjusticeboard.newswea ver.co.uk/icfiles/1/1861/11612/5475544/1edb16998b2fd5187bfea092/ yjb%20position%20statement%20on%20video%20link%20hearings.pdf

YJB (2019) *Youth Justice Board for England and Wales:* Strategic Plan 2019–2022, [online] Available from: https://assets.publishing.service.gov.uk/gov ernment/uploads/system/uploads/attachment_data/file/802702/YJB_Stra tegic_Plan_2019_to_2022.pdf

YJB (2020a) 'Child to parent violence – summary of resources and services', [online] Available from: https://yjresourcehub.uk/covid-19-resources-for-youth-justice/item/688-child-to-parent-violence.html

YJB (2020b) *COVID-19 Recovery Plans: Guidance for Youth Offending Teams*, [online] Available from: https://assets.publishing.service.gov.uk/governm ent/uploads/system/uploads/attachment_data/file/899450/COVID-19_ YJB_Recovery_Guidance_for_YOTs.pdf

YJB (2020c) 'Youth Justice Board update on COVID-19' [online] Available from: www.gov.uk/government/news/youth-justice-board-upd ate-on-covid-19

YJB (2020d) *Youth Justice Partner COVID-19 Update*, [online] Available from: https://yjresourcehub.uk/covid-19-resources-for-youth-justice/ item/download/852_458b6afb3bcb42adcbfbf1ef0592940e.html

YJB (2021) *Strategic Plan 2021 - 2024*, [online] Available from: https://ass ets.publishing.service.gov.uk/government/uploads/system/uploads/atta chment_data/file/966200/YJB_Strategic_Plan_2021_-_2024.pdf

YJB and Ministry of Justice (2021) *Youth Justice Statistics 2019–2020*, [online] 28 January, Available from: https://assets.publishing.service.gov.uk/gov ernment/uploads/system/uploads/attachment_data/file/956621/youth-justice-statistics-2019-2020.pdf

YJB and YOT Managers Cymru (2020) 'Good practice in youth justice during the COVID-19 pandemic in Wales', [online] Available from: https://yjresourcehub.uk/covid-19-resources-for-youth-justice/item/download/933_5acf0a5bffe72aea68e11d79d772593d.html

YOT Managers Cymru and YJB (Youth Justice Board) (2020) *A Summary Highlighting Good Practice in Youth Justice during the COVID-19 Pandemic in Wales (July 2020)*, [online] Available from: https://yjresourcehub.uk/images/YJB/YJB_YOT_Managers_Cymru_COVID19_Good_Practice_Summary_Report_July_2020.pdf

Youth Custody and Improvement Board (2017) 'Youth Custody Improvement Board: findings and recommendations', [online] Available from: https://www.gov.uk/government/publications/youth-custody-improvement-board-findings-and-recommendations

Youth Custody Service (2021) 'Monthly Youth Custody Report – February 2021', [online] Available from: https://assets.publishing.service.gov.uk/government/uploads/system/uploads/attachment_data/file/1122610/youth-custody-report-october-2022.xlsx

PART II

Crime, Justice and COVID-19: Critical Issues

7

Racism, Policing and the Pandemic

Scarlet Harris, Remi Joseph-Salisbury, Patrick Williams and Lisa White

Introduction

While in the United Kingdom, the government was initially slow to recognize the profound dangers of the COVID-19 pandemic, soon after Prime Minister Boris Johnson's initial plea to the public to 'stay at home', in March 2021, emergency legislation was rushed through parliament. On 25 March, the 350-page Coronavirus Act 2020 received royal assent, bringing the biggest restrictions on civil liberties in a generation into law the following day. Overnight, the Coronavirus Act, along with the broader raft of legal restrictions under The Health Protection (Coronavirus) Regulations 2020, made it unlawful to undertake a wide range of hitherto economically essential, prosocial and noncriminal activities. Even as the Act was rushed through parliament, civil liberties organizations were alerting parliamentarians to its dangers (Gidda, 2020).

As antiracist commentators and academics forewarned (Frazer-Carroll, 2020; Khan, 2020), racial disproportionality in policing has endured and often increased through the pandemic. As the first 'lockdown' came into effect, stop and search practices 'surged' despite the steep drop in crime rates (Grierson, 2020). Limited and prone to undercounting as they may be, Home Office data show that in the year ending March 2021, stop and search practices (under Section 1 of the Police and Criminal Evidence Act 1984) increased significantly to reach their highest level in seven years, impacting most on racially minoritized men (Home Office, 2022). Home Office data (2021) also show an increase in use of force for the year ending March 2021. This was racially disproportionate too, with Black people accounting for 16 per cent of those affected (though they make up just 3 per cent of the population according to the 2011 Census), and Asian people accounting for 8 per cent (7 per cent of the population according to the

2011 Census). In the summer of 2020, these patterns coalesced with mass global protests against racist police violence. The police murder of George Floyd in the United States catalyzed millions to march under the banner of Black Lives Matter (BLM) and spoke to the ongoing police brutality faced by racially minoritized people in Britain (Joseph-Salisbury et al, 2020).

With this unprecedented context in mind, this chapter addresses the qualitative experiences of policing during the pandemic from the perspective of racially minoritized people and communities – in other words, the overpoliced (Elliott-Cooper, 2021) and those most impacted by lockdown restrictions (Katikireddi et al, 2021). The discussion is based on 22 in-depth research conversations that took place over Zoom between December 2020 and April 2021. Participants were racially minoritized individuals who had had at least one encounter with the police during the COVID-19 pandemic (beginning in March 2020 and ongoing at the time of the research). The sample reflected a range of ethnic identifications, and there was an expansive conceptualization of policing as an *encounter*. Participants were recruited from geographical locations across England, including London, the Home Counties, the East Midlands, Yorkshire, Greater Manchester and the North East. The sample consisted of 8 people who identified as women and 14 who identified as men, and participants were between the ages of 19 and 62.

In the following three sections, we foreground the accounts of participants to offer insight into the ways policing in the pandemic has been experienced by those most subject to it. First, we address how lockdown conditions, in combination with new police powers, build on and further enable long-standing patterns of racialized policing. Second, we consider police contact amid the dangers of virus transmission and the associated trauma arising from such encounters. Third, we highlight how those subject to policing navigate and manage police encounters in an attempt to mitigate the risk of police violence and criminalization.

The theme of safety runs throughout the chapter: crucially, participants were seeking safety not only from the threat of an infectious (and sometimes deadly) disease, but also from the (also potentially lethal) violence and harassment of the police. As this short account demonstrates, then, rather than contributing to public safety, policing during the pandemic has (re)produced profound harms for those from racially minoritized groups and communities.

"It's almost giving like a golden ticket": new police powers and discriminatory policing

Discussions with participants underscored the significance of long-standing problems that did not begin with, but have been intensified by, the context of the COVID-19 pandemic. In this section, we aim to highlight histories of economic inequality, police violence and racism, which often profoundly shaped the accounts given by participants, while also teasing out the specificities of racialized (and classed) overpolicing during periods of pandemic-related restrictions.

Some individuals felt that in relation to the unjust policing of racially minoritized and working-class communities, the behaviour of the police during the pandemic had not substantially changed. As Kieran quipped, "a leopard is not going to change its spots because there's a disease outside". More generally, participants' historical accounts pointed to the legacies and intergenerational trauma of racist police violence, with participants identifying long histories of police racism faced by individuals and communities that well predate the onset of the pandemic. Nevertheless, the vast majority of participants felt that forms of racist and classed overpolicing had been *exacerbated* in the context of the pandemic.

Kalifa witnessed and experienced police violence when her relative was unjustly arrested while dropping off food for an elderly relative during the first lockdown. Reflecting on the particular context of the pandemic in relation to the incident, she said:

> 'it's almost giving like a golden ticket to kind of go out there in Black communities and just ridicule us. You know? To me, there's like something that triggers the police with Black people … they manhandle us, they verbally attack us, they treat us like animals, and then they go home and are dead nice to their wife and kids. How does that work?'

Relatedly, a number of participants recognized that those more likely to be out in public during periods of heightened restrictions were those already most vulnerable to being targeted by the police. The uneven impact of lockdown-type conditions, noted in academic research and by human rights groups (Amnesty International, 2021; Nazroo and Bécares, 2021; Whitehead, 2021), demonstrates how the pandemic interacts with existing social and economic inequalities, including structural racism and poverty. As participants reflected, these conditions also determine who becomes the target of policing during periods of lockdown, where – for a multitude of reasons – not everybody is able to 'stay at home'.

In addition, many of those we spoke to expressed serious concerns about the specific use of new and unprecedented police powers granted via the Health Protection (Coronavirus) Regulations 2020 and the Coronavirus Act 2020 (Spurrier, 2020). A number of accounts echoed Kalifa's description of the police being granted a "golden ticket", new powers providing a ready excuse to stop, question and harass people for simply being outside of their home. There was a sense that these powers helped to extend the already-overwhelming presence of policing in the lives of those we spoke to.

We also heard multiple accounts which suggested police were invoking or using coronavirus regulations imprecisely and inconsistently. Often new regulations were used in conjunction with other mechanisms of racist overpolicing, most notably drug-related stops/searches, to further target racially minoritized individuals (see Eastwood et al, 2013; Shiner et al, 2018; Koram, 2019). For instance, Sara described an interaction where a police stop predicated on possession of drugs was quickly reframed and justified with a nod to coronavirus regulations:

'I asked him [police officer] how come you're stopping me? And then he said you smell like you was in possession of cannabis, or I have smelled a strong smell of cannabis coming from you. So I said, well, it's funny that you say that, because I don't actually smoke and I don't have any cannabis on me. So then I'm saying, can I just ask you why don't you just search me and get it over with, like, I literally don't have anything on me, so you'll know I'm innocent when you search me. He said to me, I don't have grounds to do that, or I don't need to do that, or something along them lines. So I said, well, if you don't have grounds to do that or you don't need to do that, why are you stopping me? He said, well, you and your mates are breaking COVID rules. We're in a Tier 4 lockdown and you was with them in Sainsbury's, wasn't you? So I said, I don't know who they are. I don't know how many times I have to tell you, but I don't know these people, do you know what I mean? You're only stopping me because I'm Black and you're racially profiling me. And I don't even want to play the race card, but some people would be acting a lot worse than I am right now.'

Such accounts demonstrate how the policing of the pandemic has overlapped with existing (over)policing patterns which rely on and reproduce myths of Black criminality – morphing from the spectre of the drug dealer to the virus spreader – demonstrating the elasticity of racism as they do so.

"One rule for you, one rule for us": police contact, COVID-19 risk and related trauma

Both face coverings and social distancing have been identified in scientific research as key non-pharmaceutical interventions to reduce transmission and contraction of the virus (Aljayyoussi, 2020; Blackburn, 2020). They have been central to the government's public guidance in response to the pandemic (Henriquez et al, 2021) as well as guidance issued by the Police Federation (2020, nd; National Police Chiefs' Council et al, nd-a, nd-b). However, in addition to fundamental questions about the non-necessity of many police encounters, a key concern of participants was the failure of police officers to maintain adequate social distancing and wear face coverings in their encounters with members of the public (cf Kempton, 2020). This stark contradiction was captured by one participant: "you're [police officer] not wearing any mask. It's like one rule for you, one rule for us." Participants recounted feeling that police failures in these areas had put them at undue risk and described how this was a source of stress and trauma, once again casting serious doubt on the extent to which the policing of the pandemic can be considered to have been in the interests of public health.

The BLM protests of 2020 were a high-profile site – in concert with institutionally racist policing – in which police demonstrated an abject failure to maintain COVID-related safety measures. In a report by Netpol, testimonies from protestors and legal observers revealed how a lack of social distancing and personal protective equipment (PPE) coalesced with aggressive policing tactics such as kettling and the targeting of Black protestors (Elliott-Cooper, 2020). Reflecting these reports, Hafsa, a legal observer who took part in our research, commented: "at BLM last year, we noticed that the police weren't wearing PPE at all. They weren't wearing masks." Hafsa went on to consider the subsequent Kill the Bill protests in 2021, unpacking the contradictions in the police's approach:

> 'the whole irony of it and the whole illogic of it is the fact that obviously breach of COVID regs is inherently meant to be a public health response, and it's just completely illogical that for them … a public health response involves sending like 40 to 100 police officers into an area, kettling people, using PAVA spray and then putting loads of people in police stations and in custody where obviously the risk of transmission is going to be higher … so, it's just so obvious to us, this has got nothing to do with public health. This is just about the police being able to shut down protests. That's the reality of it, because if it was a genuine public health response, then what they're doing right now wouldn't make sense.'

Beyond the protests that took place during the pandemic, participants in our research shared a range of other experiences that spoke to the multilayered trauma of being exposed to the virus via encounters with police. Reflecting wider concerns about the risks of stop and search practices in the context of COVID-19 (see Aljayyoussi, 2020), a number of these experiences related to street or traffic stops.

Sara, for example, recalled having had two police encounters during the pandemic while heavily pregnant. The National Health Service has categorized pregnant women as clinically vulnerable, and research since has indicated a range of negative pregnancy outcomes from severe COVID-19 infection (National Perinatal Epidemiology Unit, 2021; NHS, nd). Recalling her first encounter with police while pregnant, Sara said:

> 'I was heavily, maybe seven months pregnant at this point ... they were all uniformed, no masks ... nobody had [a mask on], they weren't mindful of distance between us ... they were literally up by the window and ... don't have social distance.'

Sara also noted how, given her pregnancy and that "they were quite close to the window", her partner, in a bid to remind the officers of the associated risks, had asked "can you move or wear masks?" This was met with a blunt "no". In both encounters Sara recalled, she felt that police officers had put her at an increased risk of harm, not just through the unnecessary stop and hostile interaction, but also through the lack of care for social distancing and mask wearing. These encounters were therefore a source of stress, trauma and fear even beyond that which often accompanies experiences of policing for racially minoritized people.

Becoming "the hostage negotiator": navigating and managing police encounters

Many participants were concerned about the dangers of police encounters escalating into more serious incidents. Several participants recalled encounters in which police officers took combative and confrontational approaches, appearing to escalate rather than de-escalate interactions. This marks a stark contrast between approaches to policing set out in police guidance and the realities of being policed as a racially minoritized person. Police guidance issued during the pandemic suggested that forces implement COVID-19 regulations by following 'the 4 Es', with efforts to 'Engage. Explain. Encourage' all coming before (and in an attempt to reduce) 'Enforcement' – an apparent last resort. Yet, as Fola explained, this approach rarely matched the experiences of racially minoritized people:

> 'They're trained in de-escalation *apparently* ... like, you don't de-escalate, you just bring more violence and harm. You drag [the] community across the floor, you're dragging young people, you're punching young people. Like what are you doing?'

In the context of aggressive and escalatory policing, many participants spoke of how the responsibility to de-escalate police encounters fell on them. Outlining what is at stake when the polic*ed* carry the burden of managing such encounters, Kieran made clear that "some people are going to frequently have that interaction where they have to become a lawyer, they have to become the hostage negotiator". At the same time, he pointed out that "they still have to just be themselves, the hostage ... Essentially that's what you are, you know, and if you amplify it in a certain way, you'll be a real hostage because they'll put you in a cell."

In addition to different modes of self-presentation (such as articulating oneself in a certain way), participants discussed drawing on professional status in attempts to de-escalate encounters with police. Clara was out running in her local neighbourhood – an overwhelmingly White suburban area – when she was pursued by a male stranger in a van. She fled to a local train station to seek help, where she was told by a police officer that the man who had followed her had accused her of attempting to steal his car. Clara explained how, as discussions with the police officer became increasingly hostile, she appealed to her high-profile job and "the situation changed". She went on to say: "I had to show how I'm one of you or I'm acceptable ... in order for it to change. Whereas had it [been] somebody else ... it may not have been able to take that course as quickly as it did."

Along with other participants, Clara revealed an acute awareness of who might be particularly vulnerable to police violence and who might be in a position to successfully de-escalate an encounter and reduce the risk of harm:

'If this was my 20-year-old son or my 16-year-old son that that man said tried to steal his car, what could have happened? Anything could have happened, anything from them being brought into the criminal justice system to them being harmed. A number of things could have happened just by them not having that same ability to articulate themselves and not having the profile that I have to be able to turn things around.'

Indeed, a number of participants who were mothers underscored similar fears in relation to the vulnerability of their Black sons, and this was echoed by others (men and women) who expressed concern for younger racially minoritized people in their families and communities. These accounts push us to consider those situations in which the polic*ed* are unwilling or unable to de-escalate police encounters. Barriers to de-escalating police encounters may be particularly acute for some groups. Racialized and gendered stereotypes ascribed to Black men (as threatening, for example) can increase the risk of escalation, and those experiencing mental health crises and autistic crises can face particular difficulties during police encounters (Crane et al, 2016; Anonymous, 2020; Resistance Lab, 2020; Haas and Gibbs, 2021; Panchal, 2021). Official statistics already attest to the disproportionate overpolicing of young Black men, and a growing body of research is highlighting the often-fatal consequences for young Black men with mental health issues (Bourne, 2021; Bruce-Jones, 2021; Thompson, 2021).

Against this context, it is no surprise that a recurring theme in discussions was participants' use of mobile phones to record police encounters. In addition, mobile phone footage of George Floyd's murder at the hands of a police officer had sparked the global BLM protests just months before interviews for this research took place, amplifying and amplified by viral footage of police violence against Black people in the UK.[1] Underscored by a lack of faith in police body-worn cameras, participants offered several reasons for opting to record police encounters on their phones. Taking out a phone was seen to have the potential to change the power dynamics of an encounter and ensure that officers acted appropriately: "when they see that camera, they try their best to behave", said Omar.

Beyond the encounter itself, recordings were understood to offer an 'evidence base' that could challenge police constructions of reality where it was felt that the testimonies of those subject to unjust policing would not be believed. As Omar described:

'I approach it as, record it. One of these days, one of these officers are going to cross the line as I am recording and, on that day, I don't want to miss it. I want to have it on tape, because no one is going to believe me when I tell them ... at the end of the day, it is the officer's word against my word, and their word holds a significantly more amount of weight than mine does.'

Video footage was seen to be useful in seeking accountability and raising awareness about police racism, harassment and violence through various channels. Some participants shared footage on social media, others with the 'Independent' Office for Police Conduct or with police forces themselves.

However, a number of participants highlighted the risks of recording police encounters, feeling that it could "aggravate the situation", and many felt resigned to the fact that even with video evidence, justice and accountability were incredibly unlikely outcomes. There is also the risk, in our highly networked and digitized age, that video footage takes on a life of its own. Kalifa explained her fears when a video of her police encounter went 'viral':

'When our video went out, I was trying to get it off, and my reason why I was trying to get it off was because I was frightened that a riot might start, and I didn't want it to be at the hands of me and my son. ... I was begging so many people to take it down, because it was sent viral and we were getting calls from Africa and the Caribbean ... our phones were like ringing solid for two days.'

There are no straightforward answers regarding de-escalating police encounters.[2] Accounts from participants do, however, reveal the ways in which an awareness of vulnerability to (potentially fatal) police violence permeates everyday life for racially minoritized people, adding a further layer of trauma to ongoing racist police violence.

Conclusion

Before the onset of the COVID-19 pandemic, British society was already on a trajectory towards an increasingly punitive social order, with policing at its heart. The pandemic became a vehicle through which this trajectory was articulated and accelerated as the British state placed policing at the centre of its response (Bhattacharyya et al, 2021). As this chapter has argued, such punitive responses have severe consequences that are distributed and felt highly unevenly. The accounts that make up this chapter detail experiences of harassment, intimidation, provocation, confrontation and violence, puncturing the myth of policing for the public good. Far from keeping people safe, increased police powers reproduce racial injustice, further entrench existing structural inequalities and pose a threat to the safety and well-being of racially minoritized and working-class communities.

But emergency-style powers are rarely time-limited or exceptional. Rather, they pave the way for longer-standing forms of state control. As we 'learn to live' with the virus, attention should be paid to the impact of the draconian Police, Crime, Sentencing and Courts Act 2022, which grants police drastically more power and protection in a range of areas (see Liberty, 2021). The need to develop alternative responses to the multiple crises we currently face – ones which do not rely on policing and carcerality – could not be more urgent. And, particularly for those at the sharp end of racist policing, there is much at stake.

Notes

[1] For instance, in March 2020, video footage circulated of Desmond Ziggy Mombeyarara being tasered in front of his 5-year-old son (Walker, 2020). Just months later, on 9 June and in the midst of the BLM demonstrations, the rapper Wretch 32 shared a video of his father, 62-year-old Millard Scott, being tasered, which rendered him unconscious and caused him to fall down the stairs in his own home (PA Media, 2020).

[2] As Y-Stop, a stop and search project for young people, note, while there 'are potential benefits to recording stop and search', there is also a risk of aggravating officers, and therefore no easy answer about 'the pros and cons of filming'. They suggest that those experiencing policing may have to assess the particular situation and use 'common sense' (Y-Stop, nd).

References

Aljayyoussi, G. (2020) 'Is stop and search contributing to the spread of COVID-19 in the UK?', *The Conversation*, [online] 9 July, Available from: https://theconversation.com/is-stop-and-search-contributing-to-the-spread-of-covid-19-in-the-uk-141835

Amnesty International (2021) 'COVID-19 hits those shackled by oppression hardest thanks to decades of inequalities, neglect and abuse', [online] 7 April, Available from: www.amnesty.org/en/latest/news/2021/04/annual-report-COVID-19-decades-of-oppression-inequality-abuse/

Anonymous (2020) 'The police pointed a taser at my 12-year-old autistic son', *The Metro*, [online] 8 December, Available from: https://metro.co.uk/2020/12/08/the-police-pointed-a-taser-at-my-12-year-old-autistic-son-13639348/?ito=cbshare

Bhattacharyya, G., Elliott-Cooper, A., Balani, S., Nisancioglu, K., Koram, K., and Gebrial, D., et al (2021) *Empire's Endgame: Racism and the British State*, London: Pluto Press.

Blackburn, P. (2020) 'Government makes wearing face masks mandatory', *The British Medical Association*, [online] Available from: www.bma.org.uk/news-and-opinion/government-makes-wearing-face-masks-mandatory

Bourne, J. (2021) 'Mental health and black deaths in police custody', *Institute of Race Relations*, [online] 28 January, Available from: https://irr.org.uk/article/mental-health-police-deaths/

Bruce-Jones, E. (2021) 'Mental health and death in custody: the Angiolini review', *Race & Class*, 62(3): 7–17.

Crane, L., Maras, K.L., Hawken, T., Mulcahy, S. and Memon, A. (2016) 'Experiences of autism spectrum disorder and policing in England and Wales: surveying police and the autism community', *Community, Journal of Autism Developmental Disorders*, 46(6): 2028–41.

Eastwood, N., Shiner, M. and Bear, D. (2013) 'The numbers in black and white: ethnic disparities in the policing and prosecution of drugs offences in England and Wales', *Release*, [online] Available from: www.release.org.uk/sites/default/files/pdf/publications/Release%20-%20Race%20Disparity%20Report%20final%20version.pdf

Elliott-Cooper, A. (2020) *Britain Is Not Innocent: A Netpol Report on the Policing of Black Lives Matter Protests in Britain's Towns and Cities in 2020*, [online] Available from: https://netpol.org/wp-content/uploads/2020/11/Britain-is-not-innocent-web-version.pdf

Elliott-Cooper, A. (2021) *Black Resistance to British Policing*, Manchester: Manchester University Press.

Frazer-Carroll, M. (2020) 'From stop and search to coronavirus – increased police powers will always harm people of colour', *Gal-dem*, [online] 25 March, Available from: https://gal-dem.com/from-stop-and-search-to-coronavirus-increased-police-powers-will-always-harm-people-of-colour/

Gidda, M. (2020) 'Revealed: surge in police use of force during height of lockdown', *Liberty Investigates*, [online] 29 October, Available from: https://libertyinvestigates.org.uk/articles/revealed-surge-in-police-use-of-force-during-height-of-lockdown/

Grierson, J. (2020) 'Met carried out 22,000 searches on young black men during lockdown', *The Guardian*, [online] 8 July, Available from: www.theguardian.com/law/2020/jul/08/one-in-10-of-londons-young-black-males-stopped-by-police-in-may

Haas, K. and Gibbs, V. (2021) 'Does a person's autism play a role in their interactions with police: the perceptions of autistic adults and parent/carers', *Journal of Autism and Developmental Disorders*, 51(5): 1628–40.

Henriquez, F., Burleigh, M.C. and MacKay, W. (2021) 'Is your mask effective against COVID-19? Three questions you should ask yourself', *The Conversation*, [online] 3 February, Available from: https://theconversation.com/is-your-mask-effective-against-covid-19-three-questions-you-should-ask-yourself-153839

Home Office (2021) 'Police use of force statistics, England and Wales: April 2020 to March 2021', [online] 16 December, Available from: www.gov.uk/government/statistics/police-use-of-force-statistics-england-and-wales-april-2020-to-march-2021/police-use-of-force-statistics-england-and-wales-april-2020-to-march-2021#use-of-force-by-age-gender-ethnicity-and-health-condition-of-individuals

Home Office (2022) 'Police powers and procedures: stop and search and arrests, England and Wales, year ending 31 March 2021 second edition', [online] 5 May, Available from: www.gov.uk/government/statistics/police-powers-and-procedures-stop-and-search-and-arrests-england-and-wales-year-ending-31-march-2021/police-powers-and-procedures-stop-and-search-and-arrests-england-and-wales-year-ending-31-march-2021#stop-and-search

Joseph-Salisbury, R., Connelly, L. and Wangari-Jones, P. (2020) '"The UK is not innocent": Black Lives Matter, policing and abolition in the UK', *Equality, Diversity and Inclusion*, 40(1): 21–8.

Katikireddi, S.V., Lal, S., Carrol, E.D., Niedzwiedz, C.L., Khunti, K., and Dundas, R., et al (2021) 'Unequal impact of the COVID-19 crisis on minority ethnic groups: a framework for understanding and addressing inequalities', *Journal of Epidemiology & Community Health*, 7: 970–4.

Kempton, S. (2020) 'Blog: Cover up to keep you and your family safe', *Police Fedeeration*, [online] 13 July, Available from: www.polfed.org/news/latest-news/2020/blog-cover-up-to-keep-you-and-your-family-safe

Khan, A. (2020) 'Many black communities have poor experiences at hands of police', *Al Jazeeral*, [online] 9 April, Available from: www.aljazeera.com/news/2020/4/9/many-black-communities-have-poor-experiences-at-hands-of-police

Koram, K. (ed) (2019) *The War on Drugs and the Global Colour Line*, London: Pluto Press.

Liberty (2021) *Liberty's Briefing on the Police, Crime, Sentencing and Courts Bill for Second Reading in the House of Commons*, [online] Available from: www.libertyhumanrights.org.uk/wp-content/uploads/2021/03/Libertys-Briefing-on-the-Police-Crime-Sentencing-and-Courts-Bill-HoC-2nd-reading-March-2021-1.pdf

National Perinatal Epidemiology Unit (2021) 'Pregnant women now a priority group for COVID-19 vaccination', [online] 16 December, Available from: www.npeu.ox.ac.uk/news/2194-pregnant-women-now-a-priority-group-for-covid-19-vaccination

National Police Chiefs' Council, College of Policing and National Police Coordination Centre (nd-a) *Face Coverings: Briefing for Forces – England*, [online] Available from: www.polfed.org/media/15965/npocc-face-covering-guidance-1.pdf

National Police Chiefs' Council, College of Policing and National Police Coordination Centre (nd-b) *Personal Protective Equipment (PPE) Operational Guidance*, [online] Available from: www.polfed.org/avonsom/media/1502/seventh-guidance-document.pdf

Nazroo, J. and Bécares, L. (2021) *Ethnic Inequalities in COVID-19 Mortality: A Consequence of Persistent Racism*, Runnymede/CoDE briefings, [online] Available from: www.runnymedetrust.org/publications/ethnic-inequalities-in-covid-19-mortality-a-consequence-of-persistent-racism

NHS (nd) 'Pregnancy and coronavirus (COVID-19)', [online] Available from: www.nhs.uk/conditions/coronavirus-covid-19/people-at-higher-risk/pregnancy-and-coronavirus/

PA Media (2020) 'Rapper Wretch 32 shares video of police tasering his father', *The Guardian*, [online] 10 June, Available from: www.theguardian.com/uk-news/2020/jun/10/rapper-wretch-32-shares-video-of-police-tasering-his-father

Panchal, d. (2021) 'Policing: an intersectional analysis of race and neurodivergence', *Intersectional Approaches to Disability and Race*, [online] 9 July, Available from: https://intersect-nd-dis-rg.wixsite.com/rg-site/panchal-policing-intersectional-analysis-of-race-and-neurodivergence

Police Federation (nd) 'Covid-19 face coverings', [online] Available from: www.polfed.org/support/covid-19/covid-19-face-coverings/

Police Federation (2020) 'National Vice-Chair urges officers to wear face coverings', [online] 11 July, Available from: www.polfed.org/news/latest-news/2020/national-vice-chair-urges-officers-to-wear-face-coverings/

Resistance Lab (2020) 'A growing threat to life: taser usage by Greater Manchester Police', [online] Available from: https://resistancelab.network/our-work/taser-report/index.html

Shiner, M., Carre, Z., Delsol, R. and Eastwood, N. (2018) *The Colour of Injustice: 'Race', Drugs and Law Enforcement in England and Wales*, [online] Available from: www.release.org.uk/sites/default/files/pdf/publications/The%20Colour%20of%20Injustice.pdf

Spurrier, M. (2020) 'The Coronavirus Act is an attack on our liberties. MPs must seize this chance to scrap it', *The Guardian*, [online] 29 September, Available from: www.theguardian.com/commentisfree/2020/sep/29/coronavirus-act-liberties-powers-police-public-health-crisis

Thompson, V.E. (2021) 'Policing in Europe: disability justice and abolitionist intersectional care', *Race & Class*, 62(3): 61–76.

Walker, A. (2020) 'Manchester police refer taser shooting of man with child to IOPC', *The Guardian*, [online] 8 May, Available from: www.theguardian.com/uk-news/2020/may/08/manchester-police-taser-man-with-child-iopc-stretford

Whitehead, M. (2021) 'Poverty, health, and covid-19', *British Medical Journal*, 372: n376. doi: 10.1136/bmj.n376.

Y-Stop (nd) 'Should you record the police?', [online] Available from: https://y-stop.org/news/should-you-record-police#:~:text=You%20are%20allowed%20to%20film%20the%20police%20but%20it%20is,reach%20everywhere%20they%20need%20to

8

Crisis within a Crisis: Sex Workers, Emergency Response and Creative Service Provision

Rachel Fowler, Abbie Haines and Teela Sanders

Introduction

The context of being a sex worker in the United Kingdom (UK) brings about a complex interplay of quasi-criminalized laws which, while it is not illegal to sell or buy sex, makes it difficult to legitimately do sex work without criminal and/or social penalization. Laws criminalize sex workers by making it a crime for them to work together, through soliciting and kerbcrawling laws, and procuring laws which make it illegal for third parties (including other sex workers) to organize or assist in sex work. In addition, there is continually what has been called 'creeping abolitionism' (Scoular and Carline, 2014), where much of the governance of sex work falls under the 'deserving' and 'undeserving' binary – policies advocate exiting selling sex as a way of rehabilitation and moving away from deviant behaviour. These regulatory frameworks, which have focused on enforcement, antisocial behaviour and exclusionary tactics, have been called out consistently by research evidence and lived experience, but at the same time there has been no law reform away from a criminalized model. This framework of governance, treating sex work as a crime, is the bedrock of most sex workers' experiences, with high levels of violence reported across sex markets (street, indoor, online) (Campbell et al, 2019) and hate crime an everyday occurrence (Campbell and Sanders, 2021). This UK context is exacerbated by conditions of stigma, exclusion and marginalization, also documented extensively across the globe (Bjønness et al, 2021). It is this pre-pandemic background that the reader should be mindful of when considering the impact of COVID-19 and government responses.

Individuals, families and communities were affected by the COVID-19 government restrictions in many different ways, and this has been well documented across all types of media and reactive academic commentary. Sex workers and their communities of practitioners, peers and allies also have a specific story to document relating to how their lives were affected by the pandemic and how frontline workers responded to this monumental and abrupt change in lives, services and stability. There was an early call to arms, which doubled as a warning about the impact of reducing health services for sex workers (see Platt et al, 2020; Sanders, 2020; Singer et al, 2020). The International Committee on the Rights of Sex Workers in Europe (2021) produced an insightful report in April 2021 documenting how community-based peer sex worker organizations were at the forefront of provisions for sex workers. The importance of this level of practical and psychological support cannot be overstated, says the report, because:

> Marginalised and minority communities, such as people of colour, women, (undocumented) migrants, disabled and LGBT people have all faced deepening pre-existing inequalities during the COVID-19 crisis in Europe. The pandemic has significantly exacerbated these populations' social, economic, and political vulnerabilities and has exposed the ways in which excluded groups are forced to operate on the economic and social margins, in precarious circumstances, without state protection. (International Committee on the Rights of Sex Workers in Europe, 2021: 3)

While others have reflected on the socioeconomic effect and the health and safety effects of the pandemic on sex workers (Gichuna et al, 2020; Jozaghi and Bird, 2020; Fedorkó et al, 2021; Stuart and Grenfell, 2021), we focus on frontline service delivery perspectives on the direct needs of sex workers and how projects have responded to different needs in the context of a global crisis. We want to reflect on how the pandemic has shaped responses from the criminal justice system and other areas of welfare and safety support, for those who directly support individuals selling sex.

In this chapter, we examine both impact and response, covering the following topics:

- How sex workers were effected by government restrictions during the COVID-19 lockdowns and the impact this had on their lives. This covers the changes that took place in the sex industry, with brothel closures and policing of the streets.
- How the practitioners, especially those working with the criminal justice system, mobilized to navigate new ways of delivering services, adapting to different service user needs and a host of unexpected scenarios. We

reflect on the agility of services to recreate themselves, the excellent multiagency working that took place and the lessons learned from adapting in the crisis.

In order to do this, two authors, Abbie Haines and Rachel Fowler, who had a direct role in delivering and managing services for sex workers in different parts of the UK (Norwich and Merseyside, respectively) have come together in conversation with Teela Sanders to share reflections on this unique period of time.[1] Note that due to the nature of the organizations the two practitioners work for, much of the discussion here relates directly to female sex workers, although broader issues affecting the sex industry at large have influenced the lives of male and trans sex workers too.

We also share our reflections and experiences as members of a UK national practitioner forum in which best practice and approaches to support are shared. This forum has long-standing roots in the UK Network of Sex Work Projects (see The Guardian, 2014), set up in the late 1990s to bring together practitioners working in various sectors supporting sex workers. In 2012, the UK Network of Sex Work Projects set up the first ugly mugs national system in this country, which became the National Ugly Mugs (NUM) victim support charity. Reignited through the impact and dissemination work of the Beyond the Gaze project, which examined working conditions and practices in online sex work in the UK during 2015–18, the national practitioner forum brings together frontline workers from across the UK to discuss issues in their areas and the experiences of sex workers generally. One of the positive outcomes of the disruptions to working patterns brought on by government restrictions on mobility during COVID-19 has been the forum's move online, which meant it has been able to meet more regularly, enabling further support for practitioners and sharing of good practice.

But first a word on how the response was led, shining a spotlight on effective interventions from within the sex work community.

How were sex workers affected by the COVID-19 pandemic in the UK?

Disparities in effects on types of sex work and sex workers

There appeared to be three residing issues for sex workers across the world during the pandemic: first, the direct and immediate loss of income, pushing them to the economic margins of society, second, the paring back (or in some cases withdrawal) of health and welfare services for sex workers; and, third, the risk of increased surveillance from police as they enforced social distancing, with the ramping up of stigma towards sex workers as conduits for disease. Yet while the social distancing mantra was acceptable in order to keep everyone as safe as possible, the historical stigma attached to selling sex, and particularly women selling sex, continued as workers were treated as spreaders of disease – this time, coronavirus. Under the Contagious Diseases Act 1864, women 'prostitutes' were regulated, usually through lock hospitals, to prevent the spread of sexually transmitted diseases. There are concerns among the sex work community that COVID-19 could be the modern-day version, leading to further policing of those selling sex and COVID-19 restrictions becoming another mechanism of exclusion for those who do not have networks, resources, mainstream jobs or access to welfare systems. There were certainly groups who were doubly marginalized during the pandemic – migrant sex workers and those who do not have a wage from other income were particularly excluded. In a country where criminalization of sex work continues, the COVID-19 measures further hit vulnerable people who depend on an informal invisible economy which was temporarily shut down for several months. Niki Adams from the English Collective of Prostitutes (ECP) notes how COVID-19 has had major effects on sex workers because of their pre-existing position in society as a result of poverty, exclusion and racism:

'The virus comes on top of a crisis of poverty, especially among women. Most sex workers are mothers, mainly single mothers, who have been made poorer by austerity cuts. One and a half million people have been made deliberately destitute by government policies and four million children are living in poverty. That means that 100,000s of families in the UK rely on the income from sex work to survive.' (Quoted in International Committee on the Rights of Sex Workers in Europe, 2021: 6)

A survey of the demographics and needs of 222 sex workers who contacted the ECP during March–September 2020 reveals that their top three issues were emergency food, assistance with benefit claims and violence/stalking (ECP, 2020). Of those sex workers who made contact with the ECP during this time, 40 per cent were migrants. This subgroup experienced extensive barriers to accessing any support from government agencies:

Migrant women were particularly impacted by the pandemic. Many reported that lots of their friends had returned home before the lockdown, and that their usual support systems had broken down. In addition, many migrant women had 'no recourse to public funds' due to their immigration status, meaning that they could not apply for Universal Credit. Migrant women also struggled to access healthcare and other forms of state support, as the government refused to say publicly if migrants would be subject to deportation if they sought help. Other specific difficulties that migrant women faced included language barriers and a lack of access to a bank account and/or home address. (ECP, 2020: 2)

There is other evidence that as a direct result of financial hardship brought on by the closure of part-time jobs, people entered online sex work markets via adult entertainment platforms (Changing Lives, 2020). Speaking specifically about North East England, drawing on brief analysis of profiles on two adult platforms, Changing Lives (a support nongovernmental organization) makes a direct connection between women entering poverty and government closure of industries and 'stay at home' orders, and a usually indirect connection between women entering poverty and the rise in advertisements for the sale of sexual services. Other projects reported a change in who was working, particularly on the streets, as new people who were not previously known to projects were identified as selling sex.

When looking at the impact of the COVID-19 pandemic on sex work and sex workers, it is important to acknowledge the varied experiences of different types of worker to enable a nuanced understanding of how various lockdowns, government interventions and the overall pandemic impacted sex work and sex workers. Authors identified the distinct groups of female sex workers presenting to their service during the crisis period:

1. Older, more isolated women with specific and complex care needs, often returning to sex work after an absence – highly vulnerable, facing chronic health issues, digital exclusion and homelessness (may have been 'couch surfing')
2. Long-term homeless women with complex and long-term drug addiction – involved in street working and have been doing survival sex work for long periods
3. Younger women at transition age (18+) – vulnerable to several types of exploitation, including in 'COVID hotels',[2] and often did not abide by social distancing guidance due to mental health issues
4. Women in hostels doing sex work organized through their phones
5. New women joining online sex work because of financial problems

Authors confirmed that the increase in demand for their services was unprecedented. Abbie states that there was a 300 per cent increase in women accessing the service and that the level of multiple advantage among these women was high: on average, individuals faced over ten core issues. So they had a combination of needs relating to, for instance, mental health, drugs and alcohol, and housing as well as involvement with the criminal justice system. Needless to say, the projects saw intense and immediate changes to the sex industry, which directly affected their service delivery. In the following sections, we examine some specific issues that developed from immediate mobility and workplace limitations caused by the government restrictions, particularly during the first lockdown, from March to June 2020.

Brothel closures: immediate withdrawal of income

Collective working spaces and more formalized brothels, often tolerated by local authorities and police, were largely closed during the lockdown period. Police visited premises they were aware of to make sure they were closed. This meant that many of the women who the outreach workers contacted were not working. Their incomes had been withdrawn with immediate effect. The NUM documented, from a survey of 78 members in November 2020, that the loss of income was the most significant impact of the pandemic for sex workers (NUM et al, 2021: 21). The NUM et al (2021: 26) write: 'Sex workers have been forced into poverty by the Covid-19 pandemic, and through desperation to earn money, have engaged in risk-taking behaviours they would not ordinarily engage in.' Outreach workers like Rachel noted that when the women were not working in sex work, there were immediate challenges to their health, safety and well-being. Support work turned immediately to assisting with welfare benefit claims and supporting women in domestic violence situations, as they were forced to be home with their abuser. These links between domestic violence and the COVID-19 restrictions have been noted across the globe as an unintended consequence (Sharma and Borah, 2020).

Street working in a lockdown

The reflections from the authors who worked front line during the pandemic were that for those women engaged in street sex work, the experience of the pandemic was distinctive and characterized more by vulnerability and safeguarding risk in addition to increased risk of criminalization as well as decreased safety. Across outreach services, it has been noted that street work continued and at times increased, with women who had not worked in a long time returning to street-based sex work as well as women who were new to street-based sex work, due to financial pressures. This form of sex work has been historically more dangerous (Sanders, 2004), and it was at higher risk of criminality with the restrictions on mobility, given the new powers available to law enforcers, such as fines for breaking COVID-19 rules, on top of other forms of criminalization in relation to soliciting. Reaching out specifically to groups who were highly stigmatized and marginalized was crucial, as they faced increased destitution due to lack of income and other methods of income (begging, shoplifting) were taken away. Street-based sex work became increasingly risky both for women's health, as they were at increased risk of contracting COVID-19, and their safety, due to reduced demand in paying for sex – where supply outweighs demand in the sex industry, repercussions include competitiveness between sex workers, which can lead to tensions and aggression.

Services, however, did significantly adapt their modes of delivery to ensure they continued to reach out when so many other services had shut down. Delivery of services were adapted to walking services, as the previously used vans and cars involved too close contact. When lockdowns were eased, outreach returned to using vehicles, with additional safety measures including lateral flow tests, enhanced and updated risk assessments and social distancing used as much as possible. This was more like a 'window service', to maintain staff safety, rather than the direct contact which street outreach has normally been characterized by. The services delivered on the street were often the only ones available for all types of service user, as so many services had closed down during the lockdown, failed to reopen or had lost funding. One of the greatest concerns was that sexual health clinics (usually located in hospitals) were not open, so women were not getting access to free condoms. This meant that outreach services which did not usually have a harm reduction sexual health remit had to turn their hand to condom distribution. Yet it was a complex operation getting condoms to individuals who were not supposed to be on the streets – so boxes were left for people to access in churches, shops, doorways and known spots where women were known to wait for clients or drug suppliers. These on-the-ground solutions were initiated in order to get sexual health resources to women trying to earn money.

Digital poverty and communication

It is believed that there has been an increase in online modalities of sex work, as poverty, austerity and the pandemic pushed women in particular into sex work due to financial restraints. For instance, sex workers who were already set up on online adult entertainment platforms found it easier to protect their health and income by reducing in-person services and moving to image-, video- or phone-based interactions with clients. However working online requires particular skill sets and experience to earn sustainably and to protect one's safety (see Campbell et al, 2019). Here we have seen particular difficulties around digital exclusion, including lack of access to phones, laptops and/or internet, creating a barrier to working online. Ultimately, the existing digital divide based on class, education and resources was exacerbated among the sex work community during the crisis.

Also, specialist sex work support projects reported hidden concerns around sexual exploitation online. A review by Changing Lives of 900 online profiles found a strong link between new people engaging in online advertising to sell sex and COVID-19. They also flagged much younger women and girls advertising online, and linked this to child sexual exploitation. Further safeguarding concerns for adult women were also raised in relation to physical and sexual violence, and safety concerns exacerbated by a reduction in public services such as health and mental health support and safeguarding interventions (Changing Lives, 2020).

Digital resource poverty is a divider in the sex work community. Those who do not have access to technology, permanent Wi-Fi, and an address and bank account for a mobile phone contract, for instance, are prevented from using safer ways of selling sexual services. Regarding digital poverty and communication, outreach workers also recognized early on in the lockdown that street-based workers often did not have phones, so getting in contact with them was difficult. Funds were raised in many projects for cheap disposable phones to be distributed to vulnerable people in order to have that lifeline of contact.

Increased crime/risk and decreased reporting

According to the authors who worked on the front line, during the pandemic, reports of violence and crime among sex workers and those who are sexually exploited have never been higher. Disclosures of sexual violence and other crimes increased, and these were by domestic partners and men buying sex as well as people in the sex workers' own community on the streets or among the homeless community. Reporting crimes to the outreach workers was often where it stopped, with women reluctant to report to specialist services such as the NUM or the local police. Where projects had strong relationships with individual police officers who were working as either specialist points of contact or dedicated sex work liaison officers, there was more traction in reporting incidents to the police. The reflection on what was happening during the government restrictions was that people were reporting in crisis and really just needed support and intervention around mental health, housing and drug and alcohol, and this was less evident around sexual violence and assaults. In this regard, the outreach projects were vital lifelines providing this specialist support when many other services (particularly the NHS) were closed. Authors also noted the pattern that when lockdowns were imposed, reporting was centred on domestic abuse, but when lockdowns were eased and restrictions lifted, it was client violence that was being reported.

The changes to the sex industries during the COVID-19 restrictions, particularly in the first lockdown in Spring 2020, had the direct effect of making some spaces more dangerous for those who continued to work. In a survey by the NUM, respondents disclosed that they felt less in control of their work and were working for less money as clients had more bargaining power, and that changes to their working practices had made their work less safe (NUM et al, 2021: 21). Ongoing problems accessing welfare support in the form of Universal Credit exacerbated the reasons why sex workers needed to take greater risks than usual. The NUM also documented increased risks for those working online in relation to misuse of their content by others.

Access to the criminal justice system

Authors working on the front line noted that one of the most significant impacts of the government responses to COVID-19 was the extensive delays on cases being heard in court. The attrition rates of getting cases involving sex workers to court are significant, and the pandemic has made this much worse. With court times already long, the pandemic saw cases being postponed when they arrived in court, often adding months to the wait for a hearing. The emotional impact on sex workers, often individuals with pre-existing mental health conditions, has been extensive, jeopardizing cases and justice being reached. In cases which were in court immediately before the pandemic hit the UK in March 2020, significant delays had impacts on individuals' recovery journeys and desistance from harmful behaviours.

Another significant issue was raised among the sex worker client group. For many months, cases against them for minor crimes (begging, shoplifting, antisocial or aggressive behaviour) were not taken to court. Then, from the summer of 2021, with courts returning to regular procedures, it has not been unusual for them to have several court appearances in the same week for different cases – some as the victim and some as the perpetrator. The implications for support staff assisting individuals in these court appearances is extensive, with service users having significant needs around mental health and resilience in the criminal justice system.

For a small group of women, often at the transition ages of 18–25 years, prison was seen as one of the few safe spaces to go during the pandemic. For this group, there was a feeling that despite interventions, nothing could be done in the community to keep them safe. These women were often at very high risk of repeat domestic violence from multiple perpetrators and had long-term histories of exploitation and abuse. In these scenarios, being recalled to prison for breaches was common, and individuals felt this was a safe space during the pandemic as risks of victimhood in the community were so high.

These negative experiences, either as victim or perpetrator, are part of the reason many sex workers feel that the criminal justice system is out of reach for them. The reasons why sex workers do not contact the police are complex, but these are broadly around mistrust, stigma and not being taken seriously (Klambauer, 2018; Bowen et al, 2021; Campbell and Sanders, 2021). The NUM have regularly reported a decline in sex workers reporting to both their own scheme and to the police (Bowen et al, 2021). Bowen et al point out that the 'implications of sex workers not sharing information about dangerous individuals with police and choosing not to participate in court processes signal significant flaws in our legal system regarding safe and inequitable access and pose dangers for all of us' (2021: 885). The context of the pandemic, the halting of court procedures and the double-edged nature of the victim/perpetrator experience that sex workers sometimes have alienates them from the UK justice system.

Despite the failures of the criminal justice system discussed, many projects worked out ways to continue to provide the ISVA service to survivors of sexual violence. ISVAs continued to break down barriers for women experiencing multiple disadvantage when accessing sexual assault referral centres. They were able to keep supporting through reporting and providing emotional support to women whose court dates were greatly postponed due to closures and delays in the courts. Even when working from home, practitioners continued to provide emotional support that was a vital support for those experiencing sexual violence.

Who led the response?

Sex worker peer-led responses

Lam (2020) notes that, across the globe, sex worker peer-led organizations and the broader sex work community have led the response to the pandemic challenges for sex workers, in terms of provision and, importantly, for advocacy and resistance against repressive policing activities. Lam's evaluation of the types of resilience notes that these responses have been delivered by a group who are stigmatized, criminalized and disempowered even without the pandemic happening. In the UK, we have seen this agility, resilience and swift adaptation of services. The NUM were one of the pivotal charities that redesigned their service with immediate effect from March 2020 to respond to the needs of their sex worker members and to the lack of social protections afforded these workers. Sex work activist organization SWARM raised £251,000 from donations and a match fund gifted from adult platform VivaStreet, and managed this hardship fund with their partner, the NUM (see SWARM, 2020). These acts of mutual self-care and self-aid have been a mainstay characteristic of the sex work community, as noted in the analysis by Shimei (2022).

At the same time, the NUM wrote grant applications to community funds for vouchers and tapped into existing and new funds to support their membership, who were often left without no income at all. These emergency funds were lifesavers, literally, in the absence of direct funds for sex workers. The NUM also expanded the hours of their core case work service, offering crisis intervention for those who needed emotional support as well as practical support. Mental health support was a key priority, and the NUM adapted their crime prevention service by employing a therapist for online group therapy and offering webinars by 'experts by experience' to give advice to the community they serve (see NUM, 2020). This sums up the extreme efforts of frontline charities, like the NUM, and sex work support projects, which acted as emergency services during the lockdowns and those in-between times when life was not 'normal'. There were also some appropriate responses from adult entertainment websites, which reacted quickly to the fact that selling direct sexual services was effectively outlawed by the new COVID-19 restrictions. For example, early on in the pandemic, VivaStreet enabled free advertising for those setting up profiles on its site, while at the same time, to comply with government restrictions, they hid the face-to-face meeting adverts to protect identities. The closure of workplaces – particularly in the leisure and hospitality industry, affecting many workers – effectively promoted online indirect services such as webcamming and other content creation. During this time, we have also seen the rapid rise of subscription-based sites such as OnlyFans, which has opened up new opportunities for sexual content to be produced (and consumed) as labour (de Gallier, 2020).

Specialist sex work organizations and multiagency partnerships

During the pandemic, many mainstream health services were dramatically reduced or even closed for several months. Specialist support projects worked very hard and creatively to adapt their services to continue to assist sex workers, both face to face in their communities as well as through new ways of delivering remote services. For example, Manchester Action on Street Health continued its outreach service but also adapted to the harsh realities of lockdown for many of the service users. It set up a hardship fund, distributed essentials, such as food, clothing and condoms, gave out well-being packs to alleviate boredom and assisted people with lockdown compliance. Other organizations, such as Basis Yorkshire, made sure that COVID-19 compliance information was available in different languages for migrant service users and that they understood the rules. Deidre Bowen, Chief Executive Officer of POW Nottingham, one of the largest sex worker projects in the UK, notes:

> This has been a challenging time for POW but we have risen to that challenge, with the staff team demonstrating resilience, taking a person centred approach and being there for those who access our services. We have adapted to the changes the pandemic has imposed on us, with services running throughout and a continued drive to reach those often forgotten by society. (POW, 2020)

Flexibility in delivery seems to have been key for the specialist services that have continued to do outreach in the community, in-reach into workspaces and net-reach online. Reaching out to people through technology seems to have been a core shift and an important one to try and keep in contact with individuals when they are mobile and not visible in the usual ways. The crisis conditions have enhanced working relationships in local authorities, particularly with housing specialists and provision. These strengthened multiagency partnerships have centred safeguarding for vulnerable adults during the COVID-19 crisis with renewed relationships to continue effective work.

Improving practice through learning from a crisis

Those supporting sex workers across the markets have reflected on how they adapted their service in light of the government COVID-19 restrictions and the take-home lessons that should continue to inform their service in the post-pandemic era. First, services were ultra-flexible in both how they delivered services and what services they delivered. This was partly because of the shutdown of other vital services in the locality, and also out of creativity so that they could do all they were capable of. Adaptability of staff was key and enabled resources to be mobilized as quickly as possible. Some of the basic structural changes around outreach work enabled services to continue when most welfare support was stunted. Working outside normal hours and being flexible in adapting services was essential. Innovative ways of working with multi-needs service users was important, with staff thinking on their feet for much of the time as scenarios were presented. Second, key learning points centred on the importance of trauma-informed practice, working with individuals at their own pace and recognizing multiple and intersectional disadvantage. Gender- and trauma-informed accommodation was seen to be crucial to making women safe, and this was provided under crisis conditions to produce more stable results for women who had often been homeless for many years. These positive results were largely due to the removal of barriers to accessing housing that are often stumbling blocks to placing vulnerable women in accommodation. With the requirements of lockdowns and strict government rules around movement and social distancing, conditionality around housing was minimized. Keeping these processes, which enable housing options rather than reducing them for women, was seen as a very positive outcome to be continued.

Often the characteristics of existing services – such as flexibility, out-of-hours working, the importance of face-to-face and outreach engagement for the most excluded (including digitally excluded people) – were emphasized as best practice as these elements became essential in the pandemic response. Another factor that was very successful during the crisis was improved multiagency partnership working, as stronger relationships were built between statutory and third sector organizations, particularly around homelessness and housing provision. Fast-tracking individuals and removing criteria which had previously created barriers resulted in much-improved access to housing and drug treatments. These strengthened multiagency partnerships have led to COVID-19 prevention initiatives, such as Manchester Action on Street Health running vaccine programmes for sex workers.

Conclusion

Without doubt, specialist support projects and outreach workers experienced an increase in demand for their services during the pandemic, especially as so many other services were closed down. New referrals were sent from other organizations, and previous users who had not accessed services in a long time were returning. The support needs were greater and requests for support were more frequent level due to the circumstances. There was already a crisis in provision of health and support services for sex workers, with a decade of austerity extensively reducing specialist services, dedicated outreach and development of services to reach individuals switching to working online. COVID-19 restrictions made this situation worse and became another barrier to providing healthcare, drug intervention programmes and prevention services. Sex workers were faced with major disruption to services as drop-in facilities, outreach vans and street-based services all changed the way they worked to protect their own staff and abide by government guidelines while at the same time dealing with the changing needs of sex workers. Yet, in all of this, the dedicated practitioners had the well-being of sex workers at the fore of their mission, creatively changing their services and adapting their capabilities for service delivery. Projects provided support to access complex new and existing benefit systems, vouchers, food banks and basic supplies to protect people who often have very little in the way of a safety net.

Authors spoke about the legacy of COVID-19 and were pessimistic for the lives of many of their service users in the longer term. As frontline practitioners for many years, both authors specifically flagged the inability of the criminal justice system to cope with the backlog of cases and appropriately deal with cases where sex workers are victims of crimes. Mental health issues as a result of social isolation and increased trauma from violence and other abuses are often the priority need with the least amount of resources to address the issues. With caseloads increasingly high, staff burnout has increased, with experienced and knowledgeable practitioners leaving support work. The future of sex worker services looks increasingly under pressure, and with most projects funded through charities and philanthropy, their security is ever doubtful. Yet, at the same time, these services, alongside the sex work community peer support initiatives, have been a lifeline in a crisis.

Expanding funding to frontline organizations in the sex work community could address the ongoing and long-term implications of COVID-19 as well as the deepening inequalities and exclusion from the criminal justice system that many sex workers experience.

Notes

1. Abbie Haines is a team leader in a specialist women's outreach service in Norwich, East of England, and a specialist independent sexual violence advisor working mainly around sex work, sexual exploitation and women with multiple disadvantage. Rachel Fowler has worked in a support role with sex workers for over a decade and has been the specialist sex worker (Independent Sexual Violence Adviser – ISVA) in Merseyside for some time and is part-time service manager.
2. In order to move homeless people off the streets as an issue of public health safety and in line with the government mobility restrictions and the 'stay at home' message announced on 23 March by the Prime Minister, local authorities 'housed' homeless people in hotels that were effectively closed for usual business.

References

Bjønness, J., Nencel, L. and Skilbrei, M.L. (eds) (2021) *Reconfiguring Stigma in Studies of Sex for Sale*, Abingdon: Routledge.

Bowen, R., Hodsdon, R., Swindells, K. and Blake, C. (2021) 'Why report? Sex workers who use NUM opt out of sharing victimisation with police', *Sexuality Research and Social Policy*, 18: 885–96.

Campbell, R. and Sanders, T. (2021) *Sex Work and Hate Crime: Innovating Policy, Practice and Theory*, Cham: Palgrave Macmillan.

Campbell, R., Sanders, T., Scoular, J., Pitcher, J. and Cunningham, S. (2019) 'Risking safety and rights: online sex work, crimes and "blended safety repertoires"', *The British Journal of Sociology*, 70(4): 1539–60.

Changing Lives (2020) *NET REACH: Learning from online outreach with women selling sex during Covid-19*, [online] Available from: www.changing-lives.org.uk/wp-content/uploads/2020/12/Net-Reach-Report-FINAL.pdf

de Gallier, T. (2020) 'The hidden danger of selling nudes online', [online] 6 July, *BBC*, Available from: www.bbc.co.uk/bbcthree/article/5e7dad06-c48d-4509-b3e4-6a7a2783ce30

ECP (English Collective of Prostitutes) (2020) *Survey of Sex Workers' Access to Covid-19 Support in the UK*, [online] Available from: https://prostitutescollective.net/wp-content/uploads/2021/06/Covid-survey.pdf

Fedorkó, B., Stevenson, L. and Macioti, P.G. (2021) 'Sex workers on the frontline: an abridged version of the original ICRSE report: "The role of sex worker rights groups in providing support during the COVID-19 crisis in Europe"', *Global Public Health*, 17(10): 2258–67.

Gichuna, S., Hassan, R., Sanders, T., Campbell, R., Mutonyi, M. and Mwangi, P. (2020) 'Access to healthcare in a time of COVID-19: sex workers in crisis in Nairobi, Kenya', *Global Public Health*, 15(10): 1430–42.

International Committee on the Rights of Sex Workers in Europe (2021) *Sex Workers on the Frontline: The Role of Sex Worker Rights Groups in Providing Support during the COVID-19 Crisis in Europe*, [online] Available from: www.sexworkeurope.org/news/news-region/icrse-launches-its-new-report-sex-workers-frontline#overlay-context=news/news-region/icrse-launches-its-new-report-sex-workers-frontline

Jozaghi, E. and Bird, L. (2020) 'COVID-19 and sex workers: human rights, the struggle for safety and minimum income', *Canadian Journal of Public Health*, 111(3): 406–7.

Klambauer, E. (2018) 'Policing roulette: sex workers' perception of encounters with police officers in the indoor and outdoor sector in England', *Criminology & Criminal Justice*, 18(3): 255–72.

Lam, E. (2020) 'Pandemic sex workers' resilience: COVID-19 crisis met with rapid responses by sex worker communities', *International Social Work*, 63(6): 777–81.

NUM (National Ugly Mugs) (2020) *COVID-19 Emergency Response Project for UK Sex Workers*, [online] Available from: https://nationaluglymugs.org/wp-content/uploads/2021/04/COVID-19-REPORT-NUM.pdf

NUM, ECP and Umbrella Lane (2021) *Sex Workers Too: Summary of Evidence for VAWG 2022–2024 Consultation*, [online] Available from: https://nationaluglymugs.org/wp-content/uploads/2021/06/Sex-Workers-Too_NUM_ECP_UL_VAWG_Consultation_Submitted_19022021.pdf

Platt, L., Elmes, J., Stevenson, L., Holt, V., Rolles, S. and Stuart, R. (2020) 'Sex workers must not be forgotten in the COVID-19 response', *The Lancet*, 396(10243): 9–11.

POW (2020) 'A note from our CEO, Deidre Bowen', *Winter Newsletter*, [online] Available from: http://pow-advice.org.uk/wp-content/uploads/2020/11/POW-Newsletter-Winter-2020.pdf

Sanders, T. (2004) 'The risks of street prostitution: punters, police and protesters', *Urban Studies*, 41(9): 1703–17.

Sanders, T. (2020) 'Sex workers in the crisis of Covid', *British Journal of Community Justice*, [online] Available from: www.mmuperu.co.uk/bjcj/blog/sex-workers-in-the-crisis-of-covid

Scoular, J. and Carline, A. (2014) 'A critical account of a "creeping neo-abolitionism": regulating prostitution in England and Wales', *Criminology & Criminal Justice*, 14(5): 608–626.

Scoular, J. and O'Neill, M. (2007) 'Regulating prostitution: social inclusion, responsibilization and the politics of prostitution reform', *The British Journal of Criminology*, 47(5): 764–78.

Sharma, A. and Borah, S.B. (2020) 'Covid-19 and domestic violence: an indirect path to social and economic crisis', *Journal of Family Violence*. doi: 10.1007/s10896–020–00188–8.

Shimei, N. (2022) '"Though we are often invisible, we are always taking care of each other": mutual aid among sex workers', in T. Sanders, K. McGarry and P. Ryan (eds) *Sex Work, Labour and Relations*, Cham: Palgrave Macmillan, pp 291–314.

Singer, R., Crooks, N., Johnson, A.K., Lutnick, A. and Matthews, A. (2020) COVID-19 prevention and protecting sex workers: a call to action', *Archives of Sexual Behavior*, 49(8): 2739–41.

Stuart, R. and Grenfell, P. (2021) *Left Out in the Cold: The Extreme Unmet Health and Service Needs of Street Sex Workers in East London before and during the COVID-19 Pandemic*, [online] Available from: www.doctorsoftheworld.org.uk/wp-content/uploads/2021/05/Left-out-in-the-cold-full-report.pdf

SWARM (2020) *How We Ran a Mutual Aid Fund*, [online] Available from: https://static1.squarespace.com/static/58cea5cf197aea5216413671/t/5f3bfd8e95eb430ba8d5463b/1597767057163/SHFR_2020_Final.pdf

The Guardian (2014) 'Charity Award winner: the UK Network of Sex Work Projects – video', [online] 2 December, Available from: www.theguardian.com/voluntary-sector-network/video/2014/dec/02/uk-network-sex-work-projects-charity-awards-2014

9

COVID-19 and Drug Trends

Mark Monaghan and Ian Hamilton

Introduction

This chapter aims to begin the process of exploring the impact of COVID-19 on drug trends and markets in the United Kingdom (UK). It is too early to say what the full impact will be and what the legacy will be for alcohol and other drugs use. What we can assume, however, is that if national lockdowns and reduced opportunities for social drug and alcohol use have not impacted in any significant way on harmful consumption, then the trends witnessed over recent years will likely be continued and even magnified under the conditions of the pandemic. In this chapter, we start to piece together some of the key changes impacting on drug markets in the UK (with a particular focus on England) by triangulating data from a range of sources and interspersing this with some theoretical insights. We do this by considering emerging drug trends in relation to COVID-19, looking for points of continuity and change in the issues that preoccupied drug policy and practice over previous years. In doing so, we take a lead from the interim findings of the Release-sponsored survey, published in *Drugs in the time of COVID* (Aldrdige et al, 2021), but we seek to embellish the key findings from this report by drawing on a range of other sources and targeted surveys and other research. We also pursue separate lines of investigation where necessary.

Overall, we consider the impact of the pandemic on *supply*, but focusing more on changes in drug availability. We look at how drug distribution has been impacted by the responses to the pandemic (as well as specific responses to the drug issue). Moving on, we consider the impact of the pandemic on alcohol, noting some overlaps with the issues around other drugs. Finally, we explore the impact of the pandemic on drug harms. This is, at this stage, more speculative as the longer-term harms associated with the pandemic and drug use will only become apparent in time.

COVID-19 has altered life in ways that were once unimaginable. Over the course of the pandemic, there have been unprecedented restrictions placed on daily life, meaning that digital delivery has come to the fore of all kinds of activity, whether it be education and learning in schools, colleges and universities, the delivery of a range of public services or hospitality. In the drugs field, as the recent report by the government's Recovery Champion (Day, 2021) notes, professional services and peer-led communities made huge efforts to maintain the continuity of care, moving much face-to-face activity online:

> The pandemic has seen a huge increase in the use of digital technology, and especially videoconferencing platforms. For many this has been a vital lifeline, allowing them to connect to others to give and receive support. The Twelve-Step Fellowships (such as Alcoholics Anonymous, Narcotics Anonymous, Cocaine Anonymous) report a huge increase in online meetings, as well as an increase in newcomers to the Fellowship. It seems that many people found it easier to attend online meetings than attend in person. However, it remains to be seen whether this trend will continue, and many members of the Fellowships have told me how important it will be to return to face-to-face meetings as soon as it is safe to do so.

The impact of COVID-19 on recovery constitutes a particular challenge, and it is too early to say what that impact will be and what the legacy will be for alcohol and other drug use recovery. The adaption of services to provide online and virtual support meant that those without access to a computer or phone were disadvantaged, and those who are homeless or in temporary accommodation felt this most acutely (Kesten et al, 2021; Majeed et al, 2020). So, caution remains, and this chapter shows that the inequalities that existed within drug policy and interventions prior to the pandemic are likely to have become more entrenched throughout its duration. At their starkest, these inequalities show that ultimate harms – that is, deaths relating to drug use – tend to be disproportionately clustered among the most deprived neighbourhoods in England (Stevens, 2019).

Looking at the picture in Scotland, Walsh and colleagues (2021) comment in their discussion on 'deaths from "diseases of despair"' that drug- and alcohol-related deaths and suicide are clustered among the most vulnerable. Vulnerability here refers to the socioeconomically deprived, primarily from rampant de-industrialization in the late 1980s. Where drug deaths are concerned, this group are often labelled the 'Trainspotting generation', referring to long-time heroin users in their forties and fifties, thus contemporaries of the characters portrayed in Irvine Welsh's book and subsequent film. According to Dennis (2021), this group are often referred to as an 'ageing cohort' of heroin users who are overrepresented in the statistics, precisely because they are an ageing cohort of heroin users. In effect, the *Trainspotting* rhetoric serves to 'naturalize' these deaths. Dennis (2021) offers a devastating critique of the ageing cohort theory, showing how this serves to detract from the underlying causes of drug deaths, such as growing health inequalities (Hamilton, 2020a) magnified and exacerbated by austerity-driven cuts to essential services (Drummond, 2017) within a policy context that, over the previous decade, has moved away from services delivered on the principles of maintenance and harm reduction to those that have championed abstinence-based recovery (Monaghan, 2012; Duke, 2013; Dennis et al, 2020), while drug supply networks have, at the same time, multiplied and remain buoyant (Black, 2020).

National prevalence trends and other proxy measures

The scale of the illicit drug trade in the UK is titanic and has remained remarkably stable over time. In 2020, Dame Carol Black published the first part of her independent review of the size and shape of the drugs market in the UK, estimating it to be worth £9.4 billion per year. This is the trade itself. Indeed, when the costs and harms are factored in – those relating to health and crime, in particular – the cost to society is estimated to be in the region of £19 billion annually. For context, this is 20 times greater than the annual budget of England's fire service. The report also reveals that there were around 3 million drug users in 2020 (Black, 2020).

There are numerous sources of drugs data that can be used to analyze key trends and developments. In policy terms, the most commonly used figures are those from the Crime Survey for England and Wales (CSEW), although as the name suggests, this gives only partial coverage of the UK, as Scotland and Northern Ireland have their own versions. Previously known as the British Crime Survey (BCS), the CSEW is a face-to-face victimization survey. It currently asks approximately 43,000 respondents per annum about their experiences of a range of crimes in the 12 months prior to the interview taking place. The main aim of the CSEW is to provide robust trends for crime types and populations affected; the survey does not aim to provide an absolute count of crime and has notable exclusions. The CSEW excludes those crimes often termed 'victimless' (for example, possession of drugs), but since the mid-1990s, it has been providing data on drug use at the populations level.

The BSC/CSEW has been asking questions about drug use since 1992. Changes in methodology, from being paper based to computer aided, mean that comparisons and trends are more accurate from 1994 onwards (Ramsay and Percy, 1997). The CSEW is, then, a more useful indicator of long-term trends for the crime types and population it covers than police-recorded crime, because the former is unaffected by changes in levels of reporting to the police or police recording practices. This is not to say it is without criticism. According to the Office for National Statistics (ONS), the response rates for the CSEW were 70 per cent for the year ending March 2019 and 64 per cent for the year ending March 2020. This fall can be explained by the fact that in the year ending March 2020, fieldwork was suspended two weeks earlier than anticipated because of the coronavirus (COVID-19) pandemic. Commenting on the implications of crime survey response rates over time, Young (2004: 17) states that non-response rates can skew the findings of any survey:

> It goes without saying that such a large unknown population could easily skew every finding we victimologists present. At the most obvious level, it probably includes a disproportionate number of transients, of lower working class people hostile to officials with clipboards attempting to ask them about their lives, and of those who are most frightened to answer the door because of fear of crime. (Young, 2004: 169)

Where drugs are concerned, there is a further sampling issue. As the CSEW is a household survey, respondents from nontraditional households – for example, the homeless, students and prisoners, who are heavily represented in recent substance use – are likely to be missing. This also creates a gender bias in reporting, as young women are more likely to be in higher education than young men. The Higher Education Policy Institute recently reported that in 2018–19 the split of new entrants into higher education was 58 per cent young women compared to just 42 per cent young men (Cornell et al, 2020). By failing to sample students in higher education, we miss a key piece of intelligence on drug use and women.

There is, however, a lag in the data, with data releases providing an overview of the previous year. At the time of writing (July 2021), the latest data covers the year ending March 2020 and, therefore, offers no insight into changing patterns of consumption during the pandemic. Due to the COVID-19 pandemic, the decision was made to cancel collection of drug data as a subset of the CSEW in 2021. With this being the case, we restrict comment here on the longer-term trends of drug use as outlined by the CSEW and use other data sources to explore the changes during the pandemic.

The main finding from the 2020 release of the CSEW was that overall drug use continued to remain stable. Drug use was still most common in the 16–24 age group, but there were no notable rises or declines in this population nor indeed any other (Figure 9.1).

Data from the CSEW (ONS, 2020) shows that an estimated 1 in 11 adults aged 16 to 59 years were recent drug users – that is, those that had used

Figure 9.1: Percentage of adults aged 16 to 59 and 16 to 24 reporting use of any drug in the last year and last month, 1995 to 2020

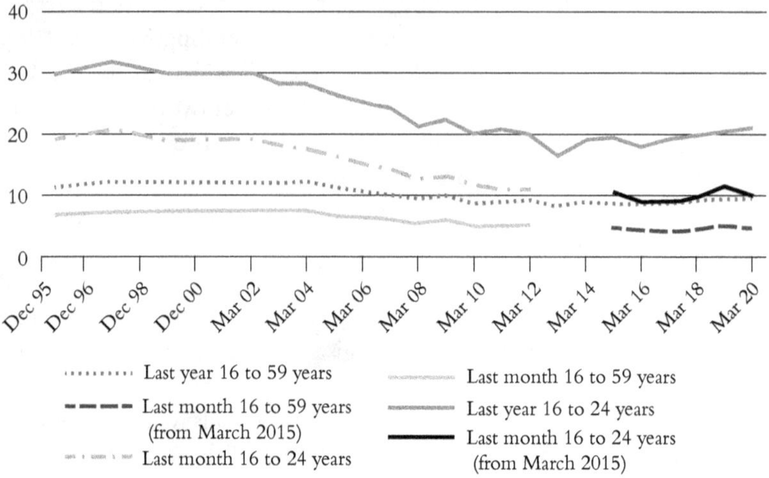

[Chart showing drug use percentages from Dec 95 to Mar 20, with legend items: Last year 16 to 59 years; Last month 16 to 59 years; Last month 16 to 59 years (from March 2015); Last year 16 to 24 years; Last month 16 to 24 years; Last month 16 to 24 years (from March 2015)]

Source: ONS Crime Survey for England and Wales

drugs in the previous year – which equates to approximately 3.2 million people or 9.4 per cent of the population in that age bracket. This was the same as in the previous year, though up by 0.8 per cent over the course of the previous decade. Where the younger age groups (16–24) are concerned, the number of recent drug users was approximately one in five. This means that approximately 1.3 million people aged 16–24 had used drugs at least once in the previous year, or around 20.3 per cent of this age group. This was down from a peak of just over 30 per cent in the early 1990s. Where 'frequent' drug use is concerned – people who had taken a drug more than once in the last year – CSEW data shows that 2.1 per cent of adults aged 16 to 59 years and 4.3 per cent of adults aged 16 to 24 years were in this category (Figure 9.2), which was similar to the estimates from 2019.

CSEW data also breaks down drug use by drug type. In 2020, it was estimated that 3.4 per cent of adults aged 16 to 59 years had taken a Class A drug (powder cocaine, crack cocaine, heroin, ecstasy, magic mushrooms, LSD, methadone and methamphetamine) in the last year. This equates to approximately 1.1 million people and was close to the previous year (3.7 per cent). Meanwhile, 7.4 per cent of adults aged 16 to 24 years had taken a Class A drug in the last year, which equates to approximately 467,000 people; again, this was not significantly different from the previous year. Although for the year ending March 2020, there was no change in last-year powder cocaine use among adults aged 16 to 59 years compared with the year ending March 2019, the proportion of frequent users fell from 14.4 per cent in year ending March 2019 to 8.7 per cent in year ending March 2020.

Figure 9.2: Percentage of adults aged 16 to 59 and 16 to 24 reporting use of any drug in the last year, by frequency of use, 2020

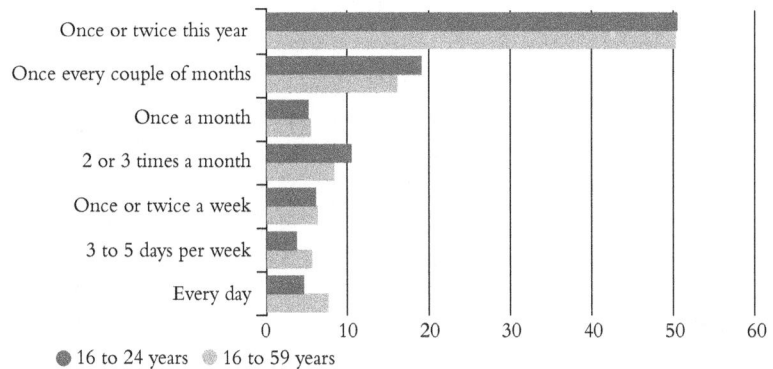

Source: ONS Crime Survey for England and Wales

Cannabis has for a long time been the nation's favourite 'illicit' drug, and it continues to be the most common drug used in the last year among adults aged 16 to 59 years and 16 to 24 years, taken by 7.8 per cent (approximately 2.6 million people) and 18.7 per cent (1.2 million), respectively. Longer-term downward trends in drug use, as shown in Figure 9.1, can be attributed to a declining popularity of cannabis among younger drug users, although this has levelled out in the past few years. This mirrors a decline in population levels of tobacco use. It is possible that some young people have avoided using cannabis as it is rolled with tobacco in a joint. ONS data on adult smoking habits in 2019 (ONS, 2020b) shows that the proportion of current smokers in the UK was 14.1 per cent, which equates to around 6.9 million people. This figure is a significant reduction in the proportion of current smokers since 2018, when 14.7 per cent smoked. It also prolongs the trend in falling smoking prevalence over the previous decade. Although not the scope of this chapter, it will be interesting to see whether COVID-19 has altered these trends.

Despite the decline in cannabis (and tobacco) use, there has been a parallel increase in those seeking help for problems related to cannabis (Hamilton et al, 2019). It is not clear whether this rising treatment demand is due to primary problems with cannabis or secondary issues with wider social problems, such as debt, housing and poverty. Interestingly, the use of some stimulants, such as amphetamine, have also been declining. In the year ending March 2020, amphetamine use in the last year among adults aged 16 to 59 years fell by 42 per cent (to 109,000 people) compared with the previous year, continuing the long-term decline since the year ending December 1995. Similarly, anabolic steroid use among 16- to 59-year-olds in the last year also fell compared with the previous year by approximately 100 per cent (from 62,000 to 31,000 people), following a period over the last decade where reported use was relatively flat.

The proportion of recent and frequent users is substantially higher for cannabis than any other drugs prohibited under the Misuse of Drugs Act 1971. Indeed, the rates for cocaine – the next most prevalent drug – are 2.6 per cent (around 873,000) among adults aged 16 to 59. The CSEW data shows no discernible change in recent cocaine use among those aged 16 to 59 and those aged 16 to 24 between 2019 and 2020. Longer term, however, the prevalence of powder cocaine use in 2020 was around four times greater than it was in the year ending December 1995 (at 0.6 per cent among those aged 16–59 and 1.4 per cent among those aged 16 to 24). Despite some fluctuation between 2009 and 2013, powder cocaine use is at a similar level as in the year ending March 2010. Where frequent use is concerned, there was a 28 per cent decrease from 1.1 per cent to 0.8 per cent (from around 361,000 to around 261,000 users) in adults aged 16–59. This was mainly driven by declining use among those aged 16–24, who accounted for 74 per cent of the decrease (around 74,000 people).

There is no breakdown in the 2020 CSEW data for opiate use, but it is estimated that the number of users is in the range of 300,000 per year (Black, 2020). The relative stability of drug indicators over the previous years affords us the platform to consider whether the emerging trends from the pandemic have disrupted the markets and, if so, in what ways; or if not, why not. The following sections consider these questions. Before we turn to this, the ONS (2020a) offers some pointers as to where to look in trying to ascertain how the pandemic may have affected drug markets and use. The first is to consider police data, though we are immediately reminded of its limitations. The ONS (2020a) states:

> Data recorded by the police showed that drug offences were 30% higher in April to June 2020 compared with April to June 2019. This was largely driven by rises in offences involving the possession of drugs, and reflected proactive police activity in pursuing crime during lockdown restrictions, rather than genuine changes in drug use.

In essence, police data reflects the nature of policing priorities more than changes in drug use and trends per se. But it was not just the police that changed strategy; as we show in this chapter, those at the top and bottom of the illicit drug market adapted too. Instead of frequently moving small quantities of drugs around the world, suppliers switched to larger but less frequent shipments of drugs. They adapted their delivery mechanisms also, including more use of private aircraft and the waterways, and contactless methods of payment (United Nations Office of Drugs and Crime –UNODC,

2021). Likewise, some street-level dealers adapted by wearing mail delivery or food delivery uniforms when moving drugs around, so that they were less conspicuous during the restrictions in movement imposed by COVID-19 regulations.

Drug availability

While data from the CSEW gives us an indication of recent and frequent use of drugs over time, more localized studies are required to give insights into the fluctuations of the markets in the context of COVID-19. One example is the Drugs in the Time of COVID study (Aldridge et al, 2021), sponsored by Release. The interim findings of the UK drug market response to lockdowns are presented in this report. This survey of 2,621 respondents provides real-time response to emerging trends in drug supply, using drug purchases as the measure. It breaks the analysis down chronologically, looking at four periods: before 23 March 2020, in 'anticipation' of the first national lockdown; between 23 March 2020 and 10 May, 'during' the first lockdown; from 11 May to 4 July, the 'easing' of the first lockdown; and 5 July to 17 September, the 'lifting' of the first lockdown.

The main focus of the survey are emerging trends in drug availability, quality and price, use of the darknet, supplier behaviour and harm(s) experienced. The survey shows fluctuations in drug availability at different points of the pandemic, based on whether respondents could find a seller who could provide their preferred drug or shopped around for their preferred drug and consequently went to a substitute substance.

In the sample, 56 per cent of respondents were aged 18–24 and a further 25 per cent were aged 25–34; 69 per cent identified as male; and 32 per cent were in full-time employment. This broadly aligns with the sociodemographic characteristics of people who use drugs as captured by the CSEW, which finds that prevalence of drug use is higher for men and (as shown in Figure 9.3) young adults.

In the Release survey, respondents were asked to reflect on their drug use before and during the pandemic: 43 per cent reported an increase in use and 36 per cent stated it had stayed the same, and 21 per cent said it had decreased. Of particular interest was the finding that reports of increased use were common across all drug types but more pronounced in cannabis. This mirrors findings from numerous studies (Barratt and Aldridge, 2020; UNODC, 2021). Indeed, Barratt and Aldridge (2020) suggest that early in the pandemic, some scarcity was apparent in supply chains for chemical substances, but this was not apparent in the cannabis markets as a consequence of shorter supply chains. Perhaps unsurprisingly, in the Release survey, the difference between increased and decreased use of drugs was smallest for drugs most associated with parties and going out, such as MDMA, cocaine

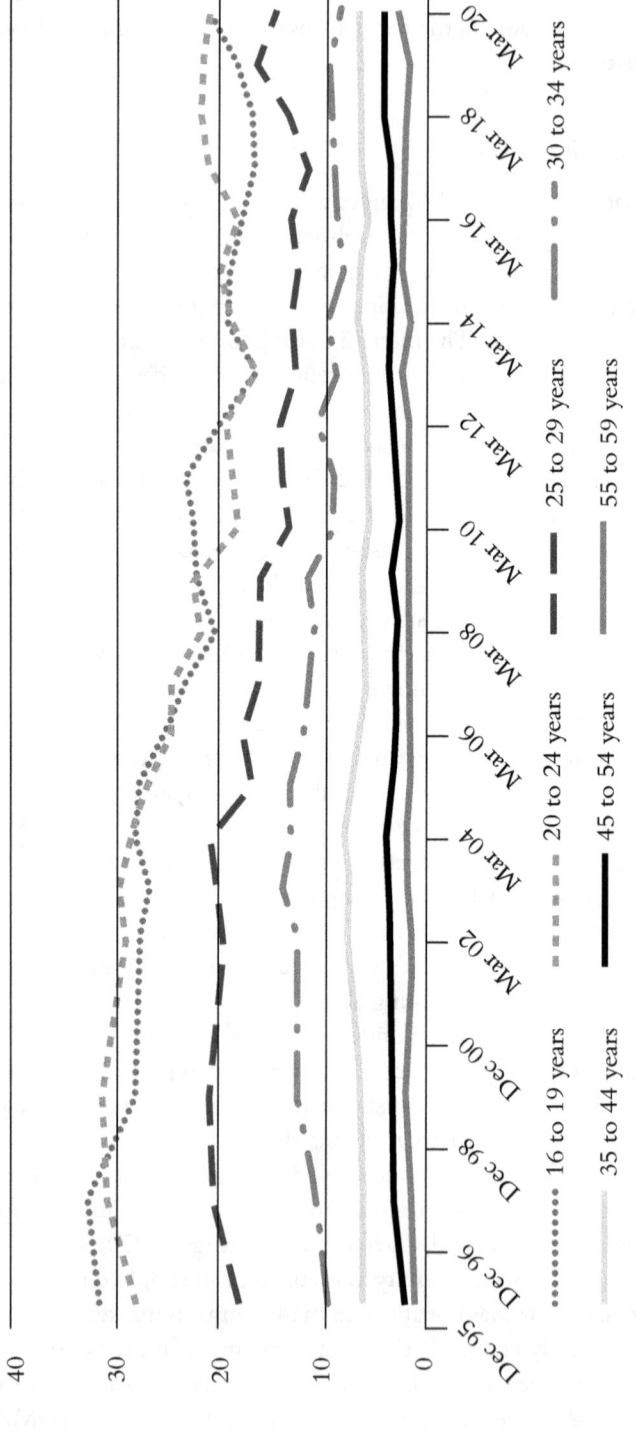

Figure 9.3: Percentage reporting use of any drug in the last year, by age group, 1995 to 2020

Source: ONS Crime Survey for England and Wales

and ecstasy. Further evidence comes from the Global Drugs Survey (nd), in which, for example, 21 per cent of cocaine users reported more frequent use, while 38 per cent reported less frequent use. In other words, while some respondents reported an increased use of these drugs almost the same amount of respondents reported decreased use too.

Consistent with longer-term trends, the Release survey found that cannabis was the most popular substance, with seven out of ten drug purchases relating to cannabis products. Interestingly, the report also notes that some drug users and suppliers may be switching over to cannabis due to restricted availability of other drugs. Herbal cannabis constitutes the bulk of the cannabis market with supplies of cannabis resin as low as 3 per cent of all transactions (Aldridge et al, 2021). In some ways, the increased use of cannabis during the pandemic shouldn't come as a surprise. The substance's psychoactive effects are well suited to solitary use as a depressant, particularly in comparison to stimulant drugs like cocaine or MDMA. COVID-19 restrictions also provided more opportunity for drug use, with the sharp reduction in commuting and significant increase in homeworking. All these factors have to be considered when looking at surveys reporting an increase in drug use by some groups. These practical facilitators of use are in addition to the perceived benefits of psychoactive drugs by some searching for ways to mitigate COVID-19-related stress and anxiety, and effectively self-medicating.

Although the subject of significant attention over recent years, synthetic cannabinoid receptor agonists (SCRAs), or spice, purchases were almost non-existent. This finding is consistent with other data that as SCRAs have become commonly associated with adverse health conditions and social harms, their use has declined in the general population, while this persists in vulnerable populations such as homeless people, prisoners and those recently released from prison (Grace et al, 2020; Gray et al, 2021) as well as those in prison (Duke, 2020). It is highly likely that this latter group are underrepresented in the Release survey sample. It is also likely that the supply of SCRAs has been disrupted by travel restrictions (Hamilton and Stevens, 2020), and they were noted in the *World Drugs Report* as being an issue (UNODC, 2021).

With the primary exception of those involved in home-growing cannabis, the use of drugs is contingent on being able to source a supplier. The consistency of the supply chain is an indicator of the buoyancy of the market. It could be assumed that travel restrictions, social distancing, lockdowns, quarantines and other measures introduced by governments across the world to combat the transmission of COVID-19 could, and perhaps should, have severely affected the flow of drugs from producer and transit countries into their destination markets. Indeed, a recent small-scale survey (n = 187) of addiction medical professionals perceptions across the world on disruptions to drug markets across the globe revealed a broad decrease in drug supply with a concomitant increase in price (Farhoudian et al, 2020). Where specific drugs were concerned, respondents perceived an increased use for alcohol (71.7 per cent of respondents), prescription opioids (70.9 per cent) and cannabis (63 per cent); decreased use was perceived for cocaine (67.5 per cent), amphetamines (59.7 per cent) and illicit opiates (58.2 per cent).

As the lockdowns lifted, there was emerging evidence that party drugs regained popularity in terms of demand, but it was demand that could not necessarily be matched by supply. Media reports in September 2021 have documented how emerging findings from drug testing services over the summer festival season in the UK showed increases in the consumption of fake ecstasy, where instead of buying MDMA, consumers have been sold substitute substances, including 4-CMC and 3-MMC. These are synthetic cathinones that can cause anxiety and paranoia, and they have higher potential for overdose as more intensive re-dosing takes place in search of the effect from the substance the user had intended to purchase (Tidy, 2021). A suggested explanation for the increasing prevalence of synthetic cathinones in the market is that suppliers are trying to cope with increased demand for party drugs post lockdown, magnified by a lull in production of MDMA as a response to decreased demand during lockdown (Tidy, 2021).

Drug distribution and enforcement responses

As we have already seen, noticeable trends are emerging from the contemporary literature on the availability of illicit drugs at different stages of the pandemic, and these can be mapped against longer-term trends predating the lockdowns. This section turns attention to the adaptability of the supply network as a consequence of measures introduced to address the spread of COVID-19 but also those specifically addressing drug distribution. Aldridge and colleagues (2021) suggest that supply issues became most acute in the period where the restrictions were lifted, which is likely to be a product of increased demand at that point in the pandemic from people who use drugs frequently. This mirrors what has happened in the wider economy, as ramping up industrial activity in the latter stages of the pandemic saw significant demand for energy, which created a fivefold increase in the price of energy to service these industries.

Earlier in the pandemic, the impact of increased restrictions around transportation did not seem to be having a significant impact on scarcity (Hamilton and Stevens, 2020), although scarcity has been reported elsewhere (Barrett and Aldridge, 2020). Instead, the social end of the supply change was where caution seemed to be applied, as sellers altered their behaviours and worked reduced hours to avoid detection – especially important in the context of increasing stop and search at the start of the pandemic, related to the more frequent use of Section 60 of the Criminal Justice and Public

Order Act 1994 whereby police can stop and search with no grounds for suspicion (Marsh, 2020). Furthermore, we might speculate that some of the decrease in accessibility to a regular supplier might stem from the reduced preponderance to engage in social supply chains by those who would otherwise have supplied drugs in this manner.

Pre pandemic, roughly half of all recreational drug users, according to Black (2020), obtained their drugs through social supply on the last occasion of use. Coomber and Moyle (2014) demonstrate how social supply is demarcated from more commercialized drug selling and takes place within friendship networks. It is often not for profit. Based on this, reduced opportunity for social use combined with a (perceived) sense of heightened surveillance during the pandemic could account for these findings. Although there have been disruptions, it is clear from the Release survey that the markets remain functional if not buoyant. It was noted by Aldridge and colleagues (2021) that changes to supply are likely down to the risk of apprehension in public spaces during lockdown restrictions, though research from Ayres and Ancrum (2020) shows that drug suppliers have adapted to the COVID-19 context and that mask wearing, in particular, has helped offset the threat of identification and apprehension.

Both Ayres and Ancrum (2020) and Aldridge and colleagues (2021) note that various COVID-19 precautions were taken by drug sellers during the pandemic. The broad trend here is that precautions were heightened during the lockdown period itself and seem to have dissipated over time, with the exception of mask wearing, which lasted for a while longer than other precautions. This is likely to be an artefact of the way mask wearing as a requirement came after the initial lockdown and it's lifting, despite its relatively late introduction into the armoury of interventions in the UK and a stalling of the implementation of the precautionary principle (Greenhalgh et al, 2020). Unlike Ayres and Ancrum's (2020) suppliers, the motivations of respondents in the Release survey for taking precautions seem to be focused on public health – reducing the handling of cash via online payments and using disinfectants and different packaging all seem to be aimed towards minimizing the spread of the virus. The timing is consistent with the emerging understandings of how the virus is transmitted, as there was emphasis on surface transmission as much as airborne transmission at that time (Greenhalgh et al, 2021).

With some barriers to 'business as usual' supply, there is emerging evidence from a survey of purchasing over the internet. The Black review (2020) shows how supply over the internet was a small but expanding part of the recreational drug market. This is consistent with advances in research in this area over time. Due to the often-clandestine nature of drug supply, often trends (such as those reported in this chapter) are, at best, estimates on the size and shape of the market. The Dark Net trade, however, provides opportunities for researchers and policy makers to look at an area of drug supply holistically, from vendor to consumer (Barrett and Aldridge, 2016). They provide a range of intelligence on drug trends, such as the needs and preferences of drug users (at least those who obtain drugs in this way).

In the context of the pandemic and notwithstanding the changes in supply, the majority of purchases still took place offline rather than on the dark web. It was perhaps too early to say that supply was moving online, as approximately 90 per cent of all purchases were not made this way. Furthermore, only 13 per cent of people surveyed who purchased drugs over the internet reported that this was the first time they had engaged in this form of supply. The authors suggest that COVID-19 may have generated interest in more digital forms of supply and that this shift may have been captured in the initial findings. This is distinct from purchases of illicit drugs that are facilitated and promoted via social media platforms such as Facebook and Snapchat. These sites provide details of those able to supply drugs, the cost and how they can be purchased, as opposed to the anonymous online market on the dark web.

County lines

Prior to the pandemic, changes to drug supply chains across the UK had been widely discussed in the context of 'county lines'. This term has been widely adopted, but there is some confusion as to its nature and extent. County lines rhetoric is frequently mentioned by the media, the police, senior politicians and ministers in their diagnoses of a range of interlinked social problems, centring on rising levels of violence, but these accounts are often in contrast to emerging research on the phenomenon. Much of the media commentary on county lines focuses on the role of the middle class, in terms of their victimization or their perpetration. The latter is often framed in terms of middle-class cocaine use fuelling exploitation within the drug supply system, as indicated by the following headlines:

- 'County lines drug gangs exploit middle-class children of busy working parents', *The Times* (Simpson, 2021)
- 'Middle class cocaine users fuelling county lines abuse' (West Midlands Police, 2021)
- 'Vile county-lines gangsters extort middle-class parents out of thousands by luring their kids into staged drugs robberies', *The Sun* (Aoraha, 2020)
- 'Police blast middle-class cocaine users for "fuelling child sex abuse" by supporting county lines drug gangs', *Mail Online* (Craven, 2019)

According to the Black review, the expansion of county lines is not linked to middle-class cocaine use, but is likely to have been driven by declining markets for heroin and crack cocaine in the major conurbations (National Crime Agency, 2017) and is also in recognition of 'the untapped markets in less established areas' often in England's satellite or coastal towns (Black, 2020: 45). There is, however, some emerging evidence of increase in the use of crack sometimes by entrenched opiate users, but not always leading to an escalation of violent activity stemming from the increased presence of organized crime groups in the supply chain. Data presented in the first Black report (2020) show that the proportion of drugs groups who supply crack increased from 25 per cent in 2015 to 36 per cent in 2019 and that this coincided with an upturn in drug-related homicide. Data from the ONS (2020a) on homicide in England and Wales up to March 2020 reveals that

> the proportion of homicides that have involved drug users or dealers, or have been related to drugs in any way, have increased over the last decade, from 39% in the year ending March 2010 to 48% in the year ending March 2020. In the last year, there were 337 homicides that were thought to involve drug users or dealers or were in some way drug-related, 26 more than the previous year (311).

In a series of critical articles on understandings of county lines as a driver of violence and the role of the middle class in this, Spicer (2019, 2021) argues county lines needs to be understood more by the extension of neoliberal rationality into drug supply chains. Spicer does not downplay that violence occurs in these situations, as county lines often entails the aggressive takeover of existing business and introducing economies of scale into new areas, accompanied by the development of a particular market brand. But the rational principles here mean that the levels of violence often attributed to drug markets are overstated on the grounds that violence is bad for business (Coomber, 2006). Much of this aggression is manifest in the exploitation of young county lines recruits, who are threatened with violence or with proxy threats to their families.

Moreover, we can see profit maximization at work in the kinds of dealing that takes place. It is widely known that the bulk of drugs are consumed by a relatively small number of high-end users. Data from the Home Office drug misuse statistics and Public Health England estimates of opiate and crack cocaine use, synthesized in the Black review (2020), show that powder cocaine and cannabis have a large number of infrequent users who tend to purchase small amounts. Conversely, there is a small number of frequent users of heroin and crack cocaine, who, to avoid the unpleasant and often harmful effects of withdrawal, will use on a near-daily basis. The report notes that as a consequence, each individual heroin/crack user represents a significant revenue source, as the 'annual spend of someone using both heroin and crack (~£19,000) is around 80% of the median wage in the UK (~£23,000 in 2016)' (Black, 2020: 62).

Emerging evidence on county line supply in relation to COVID-19 (University of Nottingham, 2021) shows that in response to changing allocations of resources, away from the night-time economy and into British Transport, the modus operandi of county lines activity changed. The rail network had been used in county lines to transport young people from urban hubs to satellite towns – frequently in exploitative ways. Under the conditions of the first lockdown, rail travel became less popular for county lines operators, for two main reasons. First, more surveillance of network meant a switch to road transport, but the use of drones and canal and waterways was also reported in one area of England. Second, there was a switch to using children in destination markets in supply rather than transporting them, often via exploitation and coercion, away from the urban centres. The use of local children in county lines also reduced the chance of 'cuckooed' homes being detected. Cuckooed homes are the residences of often-vulnerable populations in destination towns that are commandeered by county lines organizations as bases from which to distribute drugs in the new locality (Spicer et al, 2020).

Changing patterns of consumption and work under the conditions of lockdowns also facilitated the evolution of county lines activity. Brewster and colleagues (University of Nottingham, 2021) further note that actors frequently attempted to mask their activities, sometimes literally, by adopting disguises, and sometimes metaphorically. Often this would involve posing as (legitimate) delivery service drivers or workers in healthcare, construction or supermarkets. Similarly, when the rail network was used, young people in county lines were instructed to give legitimate reasons for travel, such as funerals of relatives or use of food banks (University of Nottingham, 2021).

Consistent with the data on availability, the data on supply and how this has been impacted by the pandemic is one of evolution as opposed to revolution. In many ways, both themes are indicators of the buoyancy and durability of drug markets that have remained intact despite the situational barriers presented by changes to daily life under COVID-19. In the next section, we seek to explore the impact of the pandemic on alcohol trends before turning to some thoughts on trends relating to drug harms.

Alcohol: still the nation's favourite drug

Although most of the focus of discussion around intoxicants in the context of the pandemic has focused on illicit drugs, there have been some notable patterns too in relation to alcohol consumption. The most obvious point is that a series of lockdowns has particularly impacted on the hospitality sector, with the prolonged and enforced closure of licensed and non-licensed premises. In some senses, this provides us with a neat natural experiment and enables us to ascertain whether there is a causal relationship between closure of premises and reduction of alcohol-related harm or whether a process of displacement occurs.

A key question is why start with a focus on harm rather than benefits. As Hamilton and Sumnall (2019) note, it is easy to forget the extent of alcohol toxicity. The alcohol industry curates a positive image of drinking and this frequently filters into policy documentation, which often subtly recognizes the prosocial aspects of drinking in a way that successive drug strategies have not (Monaghan and Yeomans, 2016). Indeed, although excessive drinking leads to social censure, it is clear that other forms of alcohol consumption are not only tolerated, but actually promoted due to their apparent economic benefits and prosociality.

Longer term, in the UK, alcohol consumption is, like tobacco, on a downward trend, decreasing by 18 per cent since 2004. This, however, masks a definitive increase in use among the heaviest drinkers (Holmes et al, 2019), which may partly explain the increase in alcohol-related deaths. The latest figures from the ONS (2021) reveal that a provisional total of 7,423 alcohol-specific deaths were registered in England and Wales in 2020. This a 16 per cent increase when compared with 2019 (6,209 deaths). The report goes on to note that 'equivalent to a provisional age-standardised rate of 13.0 deaths per 100,000 people, the alcohol-specific death rate in 2020 represents a statistically significant rise of 18.2% from the rate (11.0 deaths per 100,000) in 2019' (ONS, 2021).

The latest figures are a further reminder of the harms of alcohol and its toxicity. Perhaps reinforcing the power of the industry, the UK government made several changes to alcohol policy in response to the emerging COVID-19 pandemic. The government intervened early in the pandemic to ensure minimal disruption to supply of alcohol. They placed off-licences in the same category as pharmacies, deeming them to be 'essential' services (Hamilton, 2020b). The aim was to reduce the impact of closing pubs and restaurants. Consequently off-licence sales surged, offsetting the drop in sales of alcohol by pubs and restaurants. Alongside this, there is little or no alcohol prevention and education within schools and further education, and there would have been even less room for this under the conditions of school closures, home-schooling and online learning. Hamilton and Sumnall (2019) note that over time, general practitioners have been screening fewer new patients for high-risk heavy drinking and that 'since 2012, alcohol and drug treatment services have faced an average 30% cut in funding'. They state that '[a]ll of this has led to a costly burden on the NHS'.

In many ways, alcohol is the perfect drug for a pandemic. With government policy ensuring access and the drug's ability to immediately mitigate feelings of anxiety and stress, it is unsurprising that so many people turned to alcohol to soothe unwanted feelings and thoughts at this time. The pandemic amplified existing patterns of alcohol consumption. Multiple surveys measuring trends in drinking reported that those drinking elevated amounts prior to the pandemic increased their intake further during the pandemic (Hamilton, 2021). This contrasted with those who were abstinent or drinking low quantities of alcohol prior to the pandemic continuing to be abstinent or decreasing their already-low levels of consumption.

Although those who were drinking at hazardous levels added to their consumption, specialist support was in decline. So even if these individuals wanted support to address their excessive consumption, they would have found it challenging to access it. At a time when they were needed most, alcohol treatment services were especially difficult to access. Overall, it was telling that the only government intervention on alcohol was to ensure minimum disruption to supply. There was no attempt to provide public health messaging or interventions aimed at reducing the excessive consumption identified in these surveys, which effected hundreds of thousands of people. Further evidence of the harm caused by the rise in alcohol consumption for this subgroup of the population was apparent in the sharp rise in deaths attributable to alcohol reported early in 2021 (ONS, 2021). There was a 16.4 per cent rise in deaths between January and September 2020 over the same period in the previous year, continuing the rising trends in drug deaths, which don't appear to have been halted by the pandemic.

Drug harms

In England and Wales, drug-related poisonings are at the highest level since records began in 1993. According to figures published in August 2021 by the ONS, in 2020 there were 4,561 deaths related to drug poisoning in England and Wales, which equates to 79.5 deaths per million people. This was a rise of 3.8 per cent on the previous year. Men accounted for more than two thirds of the deaths, a trend consistent with previous years. Furthermore, two thirds of the registered poisoning deaths were related to drug misuse, with the highest rate among those aged between 45 and 49. ONS data also reveals how nearly half of all the drug deaths registered in 2020 involved use of an opiate, but there was also a 9.7 per cent increase in cocaine deaths, rising to 777, which is five times the number recorded in 2010.

Dennis (2021) notes that following the release of the 2014 annual report on drug-related deaths – which reported the record number at that time – a summit was convened by Public Health England and the Local Government Association to ascertain the reasons for the rising levels of drug-related deaths. A subsequent national enquiry found several risk factors, including a rise in heroin purity and potency, more people out of treatment who might otherwise be in the system, substantial regional differences linked to pre-existing inequalities and harmful increases in alcohol and polysubstance misuse. However, the risk factor that gained most commentary was being in the cohort of heroin users aged 40–49 – the Trainspotting generation.

As we noted at the outset, Dennis (2021) comments on the problems with the framing of this group, arguing that viewing rising levels of drug deaths as related to age can serve to depoliticize them and create the veneer that they are somehow naturally occurring and not deaths that have been brought forward:

> With this, the ageing cohort theory pushes the site of responsibility (and even blame) onto the individual – the irresponsible drug user who should really know better (especially at their age!). It is an all too easy link that neglects and flattens out different experiences that suggest age could function protectively. (Dennis, 2021: 1176)

The key question for this chapter is how these trends relate to the current pandemic. Again, it is perhaps too early to know for sure. However, the ONS note that the statistics are based on the year of death registration and that because of death registration delays, around half of these deaths will have occurred in the previous year (2019), and the majority will have occurred before the COVID-19 pandemic in the UK. Although that is the case, it is likely that the pandemic has had little impact on arresting the upward trend in drug-related poisoning. This is likely to have been exacerbated, although to what extent is hard to determine, by fake news and myths around drugs in the time of COVID-19. In particular unevidenced stories about the potency of fentanyl spread rapidly via social media early in the pandemic (Hamilton and Cavazos-Rhig, 2020). These stories suggested that mere skin contact with someone who had used fentanyl could trigger overdose. The consequences of such rumors were tragic, as some members of the public and health professionals were reluctant to intervene when witnessing an individual overdosing and in need of mouth-to-mouth resuscitation.

As with so many aspects of health, drug-related deaths have not been evenly spread across society. A consistent pattern of elevated rates has been experienced by those living in areas of highest social deprivation. This means that as an increasing number of people die due to drugs annually, it is the poorest communities that experience the greatest impact of these premature deaths. This is another factor that contributes to the disparity in life expectancy between areas of high and low social deprivation, with a gap in life expectancy of almost a decade between the wealthiest and the least wealthy areas in the UK. Paradoxically this is compounded by the deepest cuts to support services, such as specialist drug treatment being cut in communities with the highest rates of drug-related deaths.

As noted in the Black review (2020), from 2015, central funding for drug treatment services has declined. Conservative estimates suggest a 15 per cent reduction since 2015, although in some localities the figure is thought to be closer to 50 per cent. There is currently a higher proportion of long-term heroin users with failing health who are, therefore, at greater risk of poisoning from the increased availability of higher-purity heroin produced in Afghanistan. The isolation brought on by the pandemic with increased social distancing means a potentially higher chance that these rates will rise over the coming years. As mentioned earlier, poverty is also an issue. Deaths are clustered in areas of high deprivation, which serves to question the overarching emphasis on age, but as we have seen in trends on availability and distribution, there has been little disruption to business which might otherwise stall the upward trends of drug-related mortality.

Other policy developments, or indeed policy inertia, are likely to compound the harms. One concern identified early on was the interruption to the supply of opiate substitute medication for those in specialist drug treatment. Substitute drugs like methadone and buprenorphine are regulated as Class A drugs under the Misuse of Drugs Act 1971, and this restricts how and where they can be stored as well as who can prescribe and supply them. Many people in specialist drug treatment are subject to 'daily pick-up' regimes, where they attend a pharmacy on a daily basis to collect and consume their medication. So while members of the public were subject to lockdown restrictions that curtailed travel and contact with others, those in receipt of daily substitute medication were potentially being forced to do the opposite by continuing to access daily medication. There was some adaption by specialist drug services in terms of allowing some clients to move to weekly or fortnightly supplies of substitute prescriptions such as methadone or Subutex. It is not clear, so far, how well this worked or indeed if it will prompt a legacy shift in practice post COVID-19.

The Royal College of General Practitioners was one of many organizations, along with academics and health professionals, that lobbied the Home Office to loosen restrictions on this class of drugs so that timely supply and distribution could be maintained (Hamilton and Nutt, 2020). While the Home Secretary responded positively to the request, she made it clear that any changes would only be implemented on a case-by-case basis, not on the system as a whole. It was clear that while individual pharmacies could apply for the restrictions to be loosened, they were unlikely to have the time or will to engage in an overly bureaucratic process to achieve this. The blockage here can be contrasted with the more enabling approach taken to alcohol, but the iatrogenic nature of both responses is likely to be revealed over time.

Conclusion

This chapter is the start of a process of exploring the impact of COVID-19 on the drugs market. We have demonstrated that despite the wide-ranging changes to daily life during the pandemic, including far-reaching restrictions on the movement of goods, services and people, the illicit drug distribution chain remained intact and proved to be particularly dextrous. In the chapter, we sought to demonstrate that although national lockdowns reduced opportunities for social drug and alcohol use, this has not necessarily impacted on, and may even have magnified, the harmful consumption of specific intoxicants. Our analysis drew mainly from emerging findings and commentaries on the drug situation as the pandemic unfurled over time. We conclude that the illicit drugs and licit alcohol trade is in rude health despite the harm it visits on sections of the population. The pandemic has not altered this, and in spite of the extent of changes taking place at this time, there remains a stark line of continuity in drug and alcohol use.

References

Aldridge, J., Garius, L., Spicer, J., Harris, M., Moore, K. and Eastwood, N. (2021) *Drugs in the Time of COVID: The UK Drug Market Response to Lockdown Restrictions*, London: Release.

Aoraha, C. (2020) 'Vile county-lines gangsters extort middle-class parents out of thousands by luring their kids into staged drugs robberies', *The Sun*, [online] 12 November, Available from: www.thesun.co.uk/news/uknews/13179631/county-lines-gang-extort-middle-class-drug-robberies/

Ayres, T. and Ancrum, C. (2020) 'PPE and contactless delivery: drug dealers reveal how they are adapting to coronavirus', *The Conversation*, [online] 21 May, Available from: https://theconversation.com/ppe-and-contactless-delivery-drug-dealers-reveal-how-they-are-adapting-to-coronavirus-138952

Barratt, M.J. and Aldridge, J. (2016) 'Everything you always wanted to know about drug cryptomarkets* (*but were afraid to ask)', *International Journal of Drug Policy*, 35: 1–6.

Barratt, M.J. and Aldridge, J. (2020) 'No magic pocket: buying and selling on drug cryptomarkets in response to the COVID-19 pandemic and social restrictions', *International Journal of Drug Policy*, 83: 102894. doi: 10.1016/j.drugpo.2020.102894.

Black, C. (2020) *Review of Drugs – Evidence Relating to Drug Use, Supply and Effects, Including Current Trends and Future Risks*, [online] Available from: https://assets.publishing.service.gov.uk/government/uploads/system/uploads/attachment_data/file/882953/Review_of_Drugs_Evidence_Pack.pdf

Coomber, R. (2006) *Pusher Myths: Re-assessing the Drug Dealer*, London: Free Association.

Coomber, R. and Moyle, L. (2014) 'Beyond drug dealing: developing and extending the concept of "social supply" of illicit drugs to "minimally commercial supply"', *Drugs: Education, Prevention and Policy*, 21(2): 157–64.

Cornell, B., Hewitt, R. and Bekhradnia, B. (2020) *Mind the (Graduate Gender Pay) Gap*, HEPI Report 135, Oxford: Higher Education Policy Institute.

Craven, N. (2019) 'Police blast middle-class cocaine users for "fuelling child sex abuse" by supporting county lines drug gangs', *Mail Online*, [online] 9 November, Available from: www.dailymail.co.uk/news/article-7668783/Police-blast-middle-class-cocaine-users-fuelling-child-sex-abuse-county-lines-drug-gangs.html

Day, E. (2021) *UK Government Recovery Champion: Annual Report*, [online] Available from: https://assets.publishing.service.gov.uk/government/uploads/system/uploads/attachment_data/file/956729/Recovery_Champion_First_Annual_Report.pdf

Dennis, F. (2021) 'Drug fatalities and treatment fatalism: complicating the ageing cohort theory', *Sociology of Health & Illness*, 43(5): 1175–90.

Dennis, F., Rhodes, T. and Harris, M. (2020) 'More-than-harm reduction: engaging with alternative ontologies of "movement" in UK drug services', *International Journal of Drug Policy*, 82: 102771. doi: 10.1016/j.drugpo.2020.102771.

Drummond, C. (2017) 'Cuts to addiction services are a false economy', *BMJ*, 357: j2704. doi: 10.1136/bmj.j2704.

Duke, K. (2013) 'From crime to recovery: the reframing of British drugs policy?', *Journal of Drug Issues*, 43(1): 39–55.

Duke, K. (2020) 'Producing the "problem" of new psychoactive substances (NPS) in English prisons', *International Journal of Drug Policy*, 80: 102479. doi: 10.1016/j.drugpo.2019.05.022.

Farhoudian, A., Radfar, S.R., Ardabili, H.M., Rafei, P., Ebrahimy, M., and Zonoozi, A.K., et al (2020) 'A global survey on changes in the supply, price and use of illicit drugs and alcohol, and related complications during the 2020 COVID-19 pandemic', Preprint ahead of peer review, *medRxiv*. doi: 10.1101/2020.07.16.20155341.

Grace, S., Lloyd, C. and Perry, A. (2020) 'The spice trail: transitions in synthetic cannabis receptor agonists (SCRAs) use in English prisons and on release', *Drugs: Education, Prevention and Policy*, 27(4): 271–81.

Gray, P., Ralphs, R. and Williams, L. (2021) 'The use of synthetic cannabinoid receptor agonists (SCRAs) within the homeless population: motivations, harms and the implications for developing an appropriate response', *Addiction Research & Theory*, 29(1): 1–10.

Greenhalgh, T., Schmid, M.B., Czypionka, T., Bassler, D. and Gruer, L. (2020) 'Face masks for the public during the covid-19 crisis', *BMJ*, 369: m1435. doi: 10.1136/bmj.m1435.

Greenhalgh, T., Jimenez, J.L., Prather, K.A., Tufekci, Z., Fisman, D. and Schooley, R. (2021) 'Ten scientific reasons in support of airborne transmission of SARS-CoV-2', *The Lancet*, 397(10285): 1603–5.

Hamilton, I. (2020a) 'Drug related deaths are not spread equally in our communities', *thebmjopinion*, [online] 16 October, Available from: https://blogs.bmj.com/bmj/2020/10/16/ian-hamilton-drug-related-deaths-are-not-spread-equally-in-our communities/

Hamilton, I. (2020b) 'Is alcohol really essential during covid-19?', *thebmjopinion*, [online] 7 April, Available from: https://blogs.bmj.com/bmj/2020/04/07/ian-hamilton-is-alcohol-really-essential-during-covid-19/

Hamilton, I. (2021) 'Alcohol related deaths are on the rise, but we remain a nation in denial', *thebmjopinion*, [online] 11 February, Available from: https://blogs.bmj.com/bmj/2021/02/11/ian-hamilton-alcohol-related-deaths-are-on-the-rise-but-we-remain-a-nation-in-denial/

Hamilton, I. and Cavazos-Rehg, P. (2020) 'Misinformation about illicit drugs is spreading on social media – and the consequences could be dangerous', *The Conversation*, [online] 2 October, Available from: https://theconversation.com/misinformation-about-illicit-drugs-is-spreading-on-social-media-and-the-consequences-could-be-dangerous-146637

Hamilton, I. and Nutt, D. (2020) 'Coronavirus: why the law on morphine should be loosened', *The Conversation*, [online] 12 May, Available from: https://theconversation.com/coronavirus-why-the-law-on-morphine-should-be-loosened-138055

Hamilton, I. and Stevens, A. (2020) 'How coronavirus is changing the market for illicit drugs', *The Conversation*, [online] 26 March, Available from: https://theconversation.com/how-coronavirus-is-changing-the-market-for-illegal-drugs-134753

Hamilton, I and Sumnall, H. (2019) 'Alcohol deaths in the UK – the second highest since records began', *The Conversation*, [online] 3 December, Available from: https://theconversation.com/alcohol-deaths-in-the-uk-second-highest-since-records-began-127148

Hamilton, I., Monaghan, M. and Lloyd, C. (2019) 'Rising numbers of older and female cannabis users seeking treatment in England and Wales', *Drugs: Education, Prevention and Policy*, 26(2): 205–7.

Holmes, J., Ally, A.K., Meier, P.S. and Pryce, R. (2019) 'The collectivity of British alcohol consumption trends across different temporal processes: a quantile age–period–cohort analysis', *Addiction*, 114: 1970–80.

Kesten, J.M., Holland, A., Linton, M.J., Family, H., Scott, J., and Horwood, J., et al (2021) 'Living Under Coronavirus and Injecting Drugs in Bristol (LUCID-B): a qualitative study of experiences of COVID-19 among people who inject drugs', *International Journal of Drug Policy*, 103391. doi: 10.1016/j.drugpo. 2021.103391.

Majeed, A., Maile, E. and Coronini-Cronberg, S. (2020) 'Covid-19 is magnifying the digital divide', *thebmjopinion*, [online] 1 September, Available from: https://blogs.bmj.com/bmj/2020/09/01/covid-19-is-magnifying-the-digital-divide/

Marsh, S. (2020) 'Met police increased use of section 60 stop and search during lockdown', *The Guardian*, [online] 27 July, Available from: www.theguardian.com/uk-news/2020/jul/27/met-police-increased-use-of-section-60-stop-and-search-during-lockdown

Monaghan, M. (2012) 'The recent evolution of UK drug strategies: from maintenance to behaviour change?', *People, Place & Policy Online*, 6(1): 29–40.

Monaghan, M. and Yeomans, H. (2016) 'Mixing drink and drugs: "underclass" politics, the recovery agenda and the partial convergence of English alcohol and drugs policy', *International Journal of Drug Policy*, 37: 122–8.

National Crime Agency (2017) *County Lines Violence, Exploitation & Drug Supply 2017*, [online] Available from: www.nationalcrimeagency.gov.uk/who-we-are/publications/234-county-lines-violen-ce-exploitation-drug-supply-2017/file

ONS (Office for National Statistics) (2020a) 'Homicide in England and Wales: Year Ending 2020', [online] Available from: www.ons.gov.uk/peoplepopulationandcommunity/crimeandjustice/articles/homicideinenglandandwales/yearendingmarch2020

ONS (2020b) 'Adult smoking habits in the UK: 2019', Office for National Statistics, [online] Available from: https://www.ons.gov.uk/peoplepopulationandcommunity/healthandsocialcare/healthandlifeexpectancies/bulletins/adultsmokinghabitsingreatbritain/2019#:~:text=In%20the%20UK%2C%20in%202019,2018%20to%2014.1%25%20in%202019

ONS (2021) 'Quarterly alcohol-specific deaths in England and Wales: 2001 to 2019 registrations and Quarter 1 (Jan to Mar) to Quarter 4 (Oct to Dec) 2020 provisional registrations', Available from: www.ons.gov.uk/peoplepopulationandcommunity/birthsdeathsandmarriages/deaths/bulletins/quarterlyalcoholspecificdeathsinenglandandwales/2001to2019registrationsandquarter1jantomartoquarter4octtodec2020provisionalregistrations#alcohol-specific-deaths-in-england-and-wales

Ramsay, M. and Percy, A. (1997) 'A national household survey of drug misuse in Britain: a decade of development', *Addiction*, 98(2): 931–937.

Simpson, J. (2021) 'County lines drug gangs exploit middle-class children of busy working parents', *The Times*, [online] 2 March, Available from: www.thetimes.co.uk/article/county-lines-drug-gangs-exploit-middle-class-children-of-busy-working-parents-g56rqd9kd

Spicer, J. (2019) '"That's their brand, their business": how police officers are interpreting county lines', *Policing and Society*, 29(8): 873–86.

Spicer, J. (2021) 'Between gang talk and prohibition: the transfer of blame for county lines', *International Journal of Drug Policy*, 87: 102667. doi.org/10.1016/j.drugpo.2020.102667

Spicer, J., Moyle, L. and Coomber, R. (2020) 'The variable and evolving nature of "cuckooing" as a form of criminal exploitation in street level drug markets', *Trends in Organized Crime*, 23(4): 301–23.

Stevens, A. (2019) '"Being human" and the "moral sidestep" in drug policy: explaining government inaction on opioid-related deaths in the UK', *Addictive Behaviors*, 90: 444–50.

Tidy, R. (2021) 'here's why there's so much fake MDMA in the UK right now', *Vice*, [online] 2 September, Available from: www.vice.com/en/article/xgx3ja/heres-why-theres-so-much-fake-mdma-in-the-uk-right-now

University of Nottingham (2021) *Policing County Lines, Impact of Covid-19*, Interim Research Briefing, [online] Available from: www.nottingham.ac.uk/research/beacons-of-excellence/rights-lab/resources/reports-and-briefings/2021/february/briefing-policing-county-lines-during-covid-19.pdf

UNODC (United Nations Office of Drugs and Crime) (2021) 'World Drug Report 2021', [online] Available from: www.unodc.org/unodc/en/data-and-analysis/wdr2021.html

Walsh, D., McCartney, G., Minton, J., Parkinson, J., Shipton, D. and Whyte, B. (2021) 'Deaths from "diseases of despair" in Britain: comparing suicide, alcohol-related and drug-related mortality for birth cohorts in Scotland, England and Wales, and selected cities', *Journal of Epidemiology & Community Health*, 75(12): 1195–1202.

West Midlands Police (2021) 'Middle class cocaine users fuelling county lines abuse', [online] 3 February, Available from: www.west-midlands.police.uk/news/middle-class-cocaine-users-fuelling-county-lines-abuse

Young, J. (2004) 'Voodoo criminology and the numbers game', in J. Ferrell, K. Hayward, W. Morrison and M. Presdee (eds) *Cultural Criminology Unleashed*, London: GlassHouse Press, pp 13–28.

10

Professional Qualification in Probation and COVID-19

Andrew Fowler, Laura Martin, Aileen Watson and Tom Brown

Introduction

This chapter explores the ways in which students have experienced the Professional Qualification in Probation (PQiP) during the COVID-19 pandemic. It includes comments drawn from focus groups with students in a range of cohorts at various stages of the qualification when the pandemic occurred. The findings lead to reflections on the implications for probation education moving forward. The impact of the COVID-19 pandemic on probation has been documented by the House of Commons Justice Committee (2020) in their report *Coronavirus (COVID-19): The impact on probation systems*, which details the move to the exceptional delivery model that changed the way probation services were delivered. Unfortunately, there was no mention of PQiP students within the Justice Committee's report. We are interested in learning more about the students who transitioned from the workplace to working from home, and those students who started the qualification when already working from home. Given that the report states that staff '[m]orale and wellbeing are being affected' (House of Commons Justice Select Committee, 2020) by the current circumstances, there is further support for research that explores the 'wellness' of probation trainees.

The aspiring probation officers were entering the service at a time of tumultuous change. During this period, the Justice Select Committee (2020) reported that probation practice adapted by using Skype, phone and messaging services for supervision, while people assessed as high risk received doorstep visits. Further to this, sentence requirements could not be completed where they involved unpaid work or offending behaviour programme interventions. In addition, an already-stretched workforce, with high caseloads and not enough staff, suffered the absence of 2,000 staff per day due to COVID-19. Moreover, Phillips (2020) flags a request from HM Prison & Probation Service (HMPPS) for the frequency of contact with people on probation at this time to be doubled. With 224,174 individuals on probation in the community in March 2021 (GOV.UK Justice Data, 2021), this was also a difficult time for people on probation and in prison experiencing supervision, exacerbating the 'pains' of supervision (McNeill 2019, 2020). This has all come at a time when probation services in England and Wales are undergoing significant reforms following the failure of Transforming Rehabilitation. To enter a new organization, start a new role and complete a degree at this time would have been challenging. To have done all this and become competent probation practitioners, developing skills in supervision, risk assessment, report writing, enforcement procedures and multiagency work, is commendable. This chapter captures the experiences of people on the PQiP during the pandemic and a period when the government sought to correct their own unsuccessful strategy to reform probation services.

Transforming rehabilitation, the reunification of probation and probation training

Transforming Rehabilitation was the purported 'strategy for reform' and the government's initial White Paper detailing wholesale changes to probation services (Ministry of Justice, 2013). This background is important because, as Carr (2020) emphasizes, probation officer education also represents broader questions about penal philosophies, the purpose of probation and the wider criminal justice system. This observation is pertinent at the time of the implementation of the Transforming Rehabilitation agenda in 2015/16. The split of probation provision between 21 private/third sector community rehabilitation companies (low- and medium-risk individuals) and the public sector National Probation Service (high-risk individuals) left probation organizations short of staff (Smyth and Watson, 2018), and this had an impact on training new probation officers. The qualification has changed over time to reflect the changing demands of both the probation role and the staffing demands of the service. In terms of content, there has been more emphasis on risk and working with high-risk individuals; and the structure of the programme has changed to decrease the amount of time taken to complete the qualification. In 2021, Transforming Rehabilitation came to an end, and the current PQIP learners will begin their careers in a reunified Probation Service. There are few who will mourn the end of Transforming Rehabilitation, but there will be challenges ahead as the service seeks to rebuild and forge a coherent identity while trying, like the rest of society, to emerge from the shadow of the pandemic.

The PQIP programme is the third version of probation officer training since the move away from social work in 1994. As this chapter shows, this shift from social work training reflected a political desire to mould the identity of probation as a criminal justice, rather than a social work, agency with an emphasis on accountability and 'regularisation of practice' (Raynor and Vanstone, 2016). A brief summary of the development of probation training is given in the next section, starting from the 1990s.

Probation training

The development of the probation qualification is reviewed in chronological order from the 1990s to the time of writing. In the 1990s, Home Secretary Michael Howard ended the affiliation between probation training and social work through the Certificate in Qualification of Social Work (CQSW) or Diploma in Social Work (DipSW). This was replaced by the Diploma in Probation Studies (DipPS) in 1998 (Nellis, 2001), which Dominey (2010: 154) argues brought in a 'work-based distance learning model'. This involved students being given time to access university education rather than being 'lent' to the probation service on placement. This approach reflects shifts in the approach to training in other helping professions – for example, nursing and social work. The DipPS also introduced a work-based competency assessment, in the form of National Vocational Qualifications (NVQs), which is coterminous with the academic work and involves assessment by a work-based NVQ assessor. The work-based distance learning model polarized opinion. For instance, Treadwell (2007: 504) calls for 'pedagogical logic' to justify 'distance delivery' and underlines the lack of engagement with students on DipPS courses delivered at a distance, while Dominey (2010) offers some rationale that distance and online learning can increase accessibility and maintain levels of contact experienced in face-to-face learning.

In 2010, the DipPS became the Probation Qualification Framework (PQF). The PQF retained the vocational qualification from the DipPS and could be completed as a three-year degree or over 15 months for those with an existing and relevant degree. Skinner and Goldhill (2013), citing Treadwell's (2006: 1) earlier concern about an 'enforcement-driven mentality', argued that the curriculum became tailored to the priorities of the National Offender Management Service to protect the public and reduce reoffending. The argument for the PQF was to introduce a flexible route to qualification and increase staffing levels, making it easier for existing probation service officers to gain access to a qualification. In contrast to previous iterations of the qualification, the PQF involved a 'blended learning' approach including online content with some face-to-face teaching. Davies (2009) explains that the value of blended learning for probation students, who are often situated over a broad geographical area, lies in students being able to access learning at any time in any place. On completion of the qualification, Cracknell (2016: 216) reflects that the training on the PQF was overly focused on 'learning processes and prioritising public protection'. However, Watson and Smyth's research into student experience on the PQF found values that endure in the probation habitus, emphasized the importance of interaction with peers for learning and found a 'general high degree of satisfaction' (2018: 70).

Currently, to become a qualified probation officer, a person must complete the PQiP. The PQiP replaced the PQF in 2016 and is a vocational qualification that can take 15 or 21 months to complete, depending on the individual's level of academic experience. It is a rolling programme with three intakes each year. At the time the research was completed, there were three academic institutions delivering the training broadly in the North, the Midlands and the South. Pre COVID-19, the PQiP adopted a blended learning approach involving face-to-face workshops, online delivery and student-led learning, the majority of which was self-paced and asynchronous. Canton and Dominey (2018) argue that compared to the DipSW, the PQiP asks aspiring probation officers to complete more study in their own time, at their own expense and with less support from tutors at the university. Due to the pandemic, with health and safety precautions including the need for social distancing and restrictions on travel, the delivery of learning moved entirely online from March 2020.

In addition, the context for delivering supervision to people on probation adapted to make use of videoconferencing and online technology to facilitate remote contact. While some have argued in support of blended learning (Madoc-Jones and Buchanan, 2003; Stout and Dominey, 2006), none imagined or advocated for a purely online delivery of the probation qualification. Madoc-Jones et al (2003) also argue that face-to-face teaching is important for motivation, dialogic learning and support. In Davies and Durrance's (2009) research, trainee probation officers reported that they wanted physical contact, which they found really supportive. Davies and Durrance (2009) speculate that this is due to the warmth and/or immediacy of that support. Consistently, the commentary on probation education acknowledges the lack of research into probation officer education (Treadwell, 2006, 2007; Dominey, 2010; Watson and Smyth, 2018). To the authors' knowledge, this is the first piece of empirical research with probation students completing the PQiP considering wellness and self-care.

An area that has received more attention over the last decade in the context of criminal justice practice is the theme of emotional literacy and emotional labour in probation practice (Knight, 2014; Fowler et al, 2017). Interestingly, in the recent Strengthening Probation, Building Confidence

(HM Prison & Probation Service, 2019) consultation, 340 respondents answered the following question:

> Q10: Which skills, training or competencies do you think are essential for responsible officers authorised to deliver probation services, and how do you think these differ depending on the types of offender's staff are working with?

Over a third of respondents classed life experience and interpersonal skills as the main attributes a probation officer should have. These respondents listed relevant skills such as empathy, motivational skills, compassion and emotional intelligence. This highlights the importance of emotional literacy (Knight, 2014) and emotional skills for effective practice (Fowler et al, 2017) in probation work.

There was also a belief that aspiring probation officers should complete a degree or formal qualification. Around a fifth of respondents stated that a degree or other form of formal qualification is essential for the responsible officer role. This highlights some degree of challenge for an educational programme for aspiring probation workers to support learners to be both emotionally and academically competent. With emotion work, there are also implications for self-care, as Lee (2017) argues that self-care practices and trauma-informed training are critical to reducing the risk of vicarious trauma from the impact of clients' trauma stories.

Method

This chapter draws on five focus groups undertaken with students on the PQiP. The decision to conduct focus groups allowed for the sharing of stories, recognizing the value of listening to individual accounts as well as the capacity for these stories to help others shape and share their own experiences (Digard, 2014). The participants were drawn from PQiP cohorts at Sheffield Hallam University and employed by the Probation Services in the North of England. All had either completed or were completing the qualification at the time of their participation in the focus groups. This allowed for a diverse range of individuals contributing to the research, in terms of the stage of their involvement with the PQiP as well as the range of academic routes taken.

The 16 participants were recruited using convenience sampling based on announcements at module sites as well as direct email. Eighty-eight per cent of the participants were women, reflecting the gender imbalance of professional probation training as well as the wider probation service (Annison, 2013). The disproportionate impact of the pandemic on women is explored later with reference to the experiences of the research participants (McNeill, 2020). The focus groups were semi-structured, using an interview guide to encourage participants to talk about the quality of their learning experiences on the PQiP and their wellness (Hettler, 1976). The focus groups lasted approximately 60 minutes and were facilitated by senior lecturers working on the PQiP. Case and Haines (2014: 59) highlight that connectedness within the research team can facilitate a deeper level of engagement and a 'nuanced understanding of the realities of everyday lives and practice contexts'. However, it is also important to recognize that power differentials between researchers and participants may have influenced the extent to which those involved in the focus groups felt able to be candid (Lumsden and Winter, 2014). The findings suggest that the participants were able to speak frankly about their experiences, both in terms of the personal impact of the pandemic as well as how far the content and delivery of the PQiP met their expectations and needs.

The research was approved by Sheffield Hallam University's Research Ethics Committee. Participants' names have been anonymized for this chapter, with pseudonyms used. The research aim was to explore the cumulative effect of being online on student wellness, the quality of the learning experience and the implications for ongoing delivery of the PQiP.

Professional Qualification in Probation during the pandemic

As we have heard, the PQiP was not designed to be delivered purely online. However, from March 2020, probation teaching moved to online delivery, as did aspects of people's personal and work lives.

"It all felt the same for a period of time": spillage and spillover

'I think doing the qualification online as well as then having to work for a good three months 100 per cent online, and my social life moving 100 per cent online, I found it really hard. Not having, with the qualification, as much discussion.' (Tammy)

'I've got two young kids, both in primary school, and when COVID started, one was in nursery, one was in primary, but they were off, as with most people, even though we're both key workers. To begin with, I think it was like a lot of other parents, we decided, to begin with, to keep them off. So, yes, that was difficult and I think being able to sort of manage the time and differentiate the time between, you know, work work, uni work, it all felt the same for a period of time and it was hard to differentiate you know, working day, university day. They all kind of felt the same and that made it difficult to be disciplined, I suppose, on study days, because you're there on the same desk.' (Rick)

The cumulative strain expressed by Tammy and Rick provided layers of difficulty with no differentiation between study, work and home life or family time. For Tammy, most of the study activity was spent online. Rick expresses the inherent issues related to having children at home when working and studying.

Both participants experienced sameness in their days. This is also captured in a blog post by McNeill (2020) in which he refers to 'blurred lines' during COVID-19 for probation workers. He also notes that domestic responsibilities fall to a predominantly female workforce, who may experience gendered burdens of caring at home. The activities of working, studying, parenting and socializing all spilled into the same location and time-space, which made it hard to 'differentiate' or manage the work/life boundary. The concept of 'spillover' (Kalliath and Kalliath, 2015; Westaby et al, 2016) has been previously considered in probation work.

Spillover theory suggests that 'despite the physical and temporal boundaries that exist between work and family, behaviours and emotions from one domain spill over to the other. Spillover can occur from work-to-family contributing to Work-Family-Conflict and from family-to-work contributing to Family-Work-Conflict' (Staines, 1980, in Kalliath and Kalliath, 2015: 244). Westaby et al (2016) found considerable levels of spillover between work and family lives for probation officers, and examples of this boundary being managed. However, for our participants, during the pandemic, the physical and temporal boundaries collapsed into the same place and time-space. Mandy makes this collapse of boundaries clear, as she found herself in a domestic space that was also used for work, which led to reading further about high-risk work during a recreational period in their day. For these participants, the boundary became indistinct:

'I was away in halls, you were at uni, the uni library, there was still that separation of like work and home, you know, than rarely, obviously only for like essays would like your work ever come home, whereas obviously now, the information for like my learning and for your, you know, your PQiP workbooks is now at home as well, you know. And if, like me, you haven't got your office, like an office or a spare room for an office, like, you just, you are in your living room and it's just like, or in your kitchen, and it's just weird that you are in the [same] place as, you know, where you'll be trying to relax and like an hour's time, you know. And at that point, instead, you are reading about how to work with high risk.' (Mandy)

The pandemic made visible the challenges for students on the PQiP, some of which cannot necessarily be attributed to the consequences of COVID-19. The PQiP is a demanding and academically rigorous course which requires commitment, dedication and careful time management. Saskia made clear the spillage from work-based commitments into study time and the inherent challenge to 'ring-fence' time for study.

> 'it's very hard to, to ring-fence that time specifically for uni work, which I'm sure will be something everybody says, regardless of a pandemic or what, because it's, it is a lot of work.' (Saskia)

Nadia and Sam highlighted the compromises in domestic life and the need to have support from partners to meet the requirements of the course:

> 'I need to do some work, I got things due in, like on a Sunday, and that means obviously my other half has to look after our daughter and keep her entertained for that, for that day, by himself.' (Nadia)

> '[It's] understanding family members as well. Because you need that support, you know.' (Sam)

However, for one participant, the pandemic felt like the ideal time to complete the PQiP as there was "nothing else to do":

> 'I just thought well with COVID, so, right, what would I be doing, there's nothing else to do. So, if anything, we're kind of lucky to be doing it [PQiP] at this time, because it didn't feel like, you know, everybody else was out having a fantastic life.' (Janine)

"You sometimes feel like you are sort of cast adrift, don't you?"
Probation habitus?

The PQiP involves students studying at one of three academic institutions, which deliver to the North, Midlands and South cohorts in England and Wales. Within these cohorts, students come from disparate rural and urban locations. Due to COVID-19 safety measures, the face-to-face sessions that are part of the blended delivery model could no longer be facilitated. As a consequence, delivery of the PQiP came to be completely online. This was also the case for the work within probation services, which moved to remote delivery. Tammy explains that she went from travelling to "multiple" training sessions at work and meeting new people to using Microsoft Teams videoconferencing for communication online after the pandemic happened:

'I went from going to Sheffield CRC [community rehabilitation company] office multiple times a week for training because we'd got our own Sodexo induction as well. All my training with the NPS [National Probation Service] was in York, so I went from getting the train every week and going there to then completely online. And especially when it's PQiP and you're meeting new people and then suddenly you're on Teams, where at the beginning everyone's getting used to it and no one wants to speak. That bit was harder for me than the uni side ... being online, if that makes sense.' (Tammy)

While Tammy felt the pressure of trying to build relationships online in work, Nadia missed the face-to-face contact and Sam expresses resignation about the impact of the pandemic, that being online cannot 'substitute' what is gained from face-to-face contact with colleagues and peers:

'You are all in the same boat and you sometimes feel like you are sort of cast adrift, don't you? ... Missing a bit of the face-to-face thing. I think especially because you're kind of remote from your colleagues and people who are on the PQiP as well, so it's not like you're sat together and can, all that's online as well, when you're talking about the work.' (Nadia)

'But there is no substitute, that's the word I was looking for, for face to face. But that, that's something, that's the pandemic, it's just the way of the world now, isn't [it], we've all got to get used to it.' (Sam)

Through the lens of 'secondary habitus', Grant (2016) explains the role of structured activities, including university education. Grant speculates that aspiring probation officers arrive with welfare-oriented ways of thinking that transcend the punitive penal context in which they arrive (see also Deering, 2010). Martin (2020) further emphasizes the durability of probation values when reflecting on an exercise conducted during the university induction for new PQiP students, where they were asked to respond to the question 'Why probation?' Their responses were collated in a word cloud and frequently recurring words from over 100 participants included: 'support', 'assist', 'empower' and 'empathise' (Martin, 2020). Martin (2020: 33) suggests that 'it is hard to reconcile such comments with ambivalence about the value of relationships or an overt focus on assessment and risk management'. It is noted that the culture in probation has a doxa found in 'linguistic, social and psychological practices' (Grant, 2016: 762) which somehow mediates the prevailing policy context of control. This recognition of the importance of practice culture in probation settings raises questions about how doxa was experienced during the pandemic by new entrants to the probation service who were not co-located in an office with qualified probation officers. While there are established members of staff (such as practice tutor assessors – PTAs) who undoubtedly influence the approaches, attitudes and culture of those working towards probation qualifications, opportunities to access such support were reduced due to the imposition of remote working. Both Matthews (2009) and Cracknell (2016) reflect on their own experiences of probation training and highlight the dissonance between the ideals and values that might lead people into probation training and the realities of practice, which are characterized more by bureaucratic endeavours than relational encounters with people on probation. In emphasizing the role of the workplace in supporting individuals to forge their professional identity and make sense of practice, Trede et al (2012) highlight the potential for this dissonance to be exacerbated as trainees are not exposed to opportunities to observe and participate in the dialogical and social encounters envisaged by Grant (2016). The focus groups made visible the importance and value placed on such peer support as well as considerations in its absence.

"I've never actually made a, made a friend": communities of coping

The need, desire and benefits of peer support were made clear by participants in the focus groups. While Megan and Astrid expressed their need and desire to have more face-to-face contact with their peers on the PQiP, Nadia experienced some benefit from a group formed early on using the social media messaging service WhatsApp:

> 'You know, I think the support is there, but, but like, like it's been mentioned, it's, it is just the face to face with our peers. Because even, even when I was at uni before, you know, it wasn't so much the, the face to face of the lecture that I found important, but that, that peer support, I guess.' (Megan)

> 'I will have benefited from more if it was in person as well, just being able to discuss things with other, with other PQiPs really, rather than sort of sitting at home by myself doing the materials.' (Astrid)

> 'I mean, I only really have contact with a few, because we were kind of put together at the start, because we were all on the 21-month route. None of which I've met sort of face to face. But there's ongoing kind of conversation around this one particular person who's very organized, who everyone knows put in their conversation when's the next assignment due, or we check ... she's got a list of things, she's really organized. That's been quite useful, so we do kind of use that. Not as much now as what it was at the start, but otherwise interaction

with others has just been through kind of whatever training has been put on, whilst in work.' (Nadia)

Many people expressed that work-based training was the main place they met peers. However, some people felt isolated and lonely:

'I've not got to know anyone from university ... because we don't actually physically go in to uni, and we don't have, like, chatrooms like this to chat to other people that are on the course ... I've never actually made a, made a friend.' (Sam)

The participants expressed some regret that they did not get a chance to experience the camaraderie of the PQiP in the same way that previous cohorts did. Mandy and Sally expressed the feeling that it is important to have positive relationships on a learning programme that is, in Mandy's words, "so intense and so challenging":

'you are probably in the range to get the train down together, you know, because I know from talking to colleagues in the office ... they were like NQOs [newly qualified officers] when I first came in the team. But I know from, like, listening to them about how ... I guess for them, I think how much easier it was for them to build good relationships.' (Sally)

'It's a bit like, bit like my training from the prison service, where when you're training, you kind of make friends. Because it's so intense and so challenging. I guess people have similar, although it's like obviously for a longer period of time, but like it's like still, you know, you know, a lot to do for it, that them relationships would probably be harder for us to build in a way.' (Mandy)

This sentiment relates to an earlier yearning for support which could be described as 'communities of coping'. This was a feature of findings from research on experiences of criminology PhD students (Waters et al, 2020), which recognized the tendency for people to cope 'communally and socially' (Korczynski, 2003: 58). By sharing feelings and experiences with others, the PhD students recognized their emotional experiences were not unique and felt better able to cope with the isolation of academic study.

While there were invariably challenges studying online, some students found this mode of learning suited them:

'Because I don't really know how things worked beforehand, because we've always had it online, but I know like a couple of people in the office have said oh yes, waiting for your train to Sheffield, and getting back late at night, and although it seems quite fun, I think like this job's quite stressful enough, so the thought of like starting and finishing your day and being at home and the second you finish, as long as you're strict with yourself, you're done, rather than then, because I live like … probably from door to door, if I was to come to Sheffield, it would probably take like three and a half hours, like one way, do you know what I mean? So for me, it's probably been a lot better.' (Amy)

'I have to admit, I found going online, finding all the information I need through the library and everything, that's been fine, you know. There's been more than enough information there.' (Sam)

'I really enjoyed the blended learning approach. I think there were really difficult times because of COVID, but the positives to grow from that is having done the courses and the formal input sessions online, it's basically saved four days sitting on a train to Sheffield and back.' (Janine)

The overriding feeling was that the journey to university was an additional stress and in some ways the pandemic resulted in a more convenient approach to learning. There is much to reflect on from hearing these accounts of participation on the PQiP during COVID-19.

Lessons learned

There are many lessons to be learned from the pandemic for students, staff and the future of probation training. It is also important to recognize that while the focus of this chapter is the experience of aspiring probation officers during the pandemic, the findings from the focus groups provide insight into the wider strengths and opportunities for development in the PQiP. As we have seen, the pandemic brought to the fore the tacit aspects of the probation qualification experience that were prohibited during lockdown restrictions. The PQiP candidates were no longer based in the office, and this stifled development of informal networks of support among peers. This section considers three aspects of the programme: digital learning; wellness and self-care strategies employed by students; and academic support offered by the teaching teams.

"It's good just to be able to go on it anytime": digital learning

The impact of removal of in-person taught sessions on the academic component of the PQiP was lessened due to the fact that the blended learning nature of the course was already heavily weighted towards asynchronous, independent learning. As previously discussed, a number of participants reinforced the benefits of a flexible approach to study and the consistent availability of a range of learning resources, noting, for example, the positives of screencast versus in-person lectures:

> 'the lectures are recorded, so like you can go back to them in future, whereas if it was face to face, although you might have the PowerPoint, you don't, it's not a recorded thing.' (Astrid)

> 'Whenever you're logging on to do stuff, having everything there is really useful. Because you weren't just relying 100 per cent on your notes and your own research search pulling stuff up. You always had the backbone of what you were going to do.' (Janine)

This positive reinforcement of our 'business as usual' approach to the variety of materials and self-paced learning aligns with the intentions of HMPPS to maintain a blended approach to learning within the PQiP during the pandemic (Carr, 2020). Martin (2020) highlights the importance of active engagement in the process of learning to bring about a sense of 'rootedness' (Ashton and Stone, 2018: xviii) in the academic foundations of probation practice. It was clear also from the participants that they placed value on the opportunity to learn collectively and that this had not translated well into the online environment. For example, Nadia alluded to working in isolation and the lack of opportunity to develop relationships and reflect on practice collectively, and Astrid also highlighted that the relational aspects of learning were not manifest within the programme.

As a blended learning course, the PQiP already faced challenges in relation to opportunities for students to come together and discuss key theories and models, and debate their application to practice, and these challenges were further exacerbated by the pandemic. Treadwell's (2006) reflection on his own experiences as a probation trainee highlights concerns around limited in-person engagement and a belief that the pedagogical decision to transition to a predominantly online delivery model was insufficiently articulated. However, while responses from focus group participants generally noted the positives of having access to online materials and the flexibility of engaging at a time and space that suited them, alongside this was a recognition that knowledge is socially constructed and that they would benefit from hearing the perspectives of others as well as having opportunities to subject their own beliefs to reflective scrutiny (Mathieson, 2015). From a pragmatic point of view, the focus groups reinforced the need for inclusion of in-person teaching on the programme but also suggested that staff should think more creatively about how students might engage in meaningful dialogue with their peers within an online environment. Burnett (2011) frames this as the need to take account of the professional, academic and interpersonal contexts our students operate within and the impact of these on their ability to engage with the PQiP. Articulating a response to this would help address Treadwell's (2006) concerns over a lack of pedagogical justification for the use of blended teaching in professional probation education (Biggs and Tang, 2007). As previously discussed, the merging of these three contexts for the duration of the pandemic raised questions around not only opportunities for meaningful education but also how students have managed their wellness.

Linked to the consideration of spillover (Westaby et al, 2016), it was clear that the pandemic had a significant impact on the wellness of many of our PQiP learners. However, as the earlier discussion around the encroachment of the academic programme into evenings and weekends indicates, these negative impacts were not confined solely to the period of lockdown.

"I am very, very reluctant to do any work-based stuff on those days, I kind of shut myself away and it's 'do not disturb'": wellness and self-care

Students employed a variety of strategies to safeguard themselves. One example is Janine's decision to utilize separate laptops for work and study to limit distractions from the workplace on study days. Rick was also very clear about protecting his study days from workplace intrusions. This suggests a wider issue around the protection employers are affording students in terms of ring-fencing their study days, as well as the challenges for individuals of prioritizing their academic work over the demands of caseloads. This is explored later in relation to the need to facilitate creation of supportive networks. A pertinent example of the inconsistency of workplace support came from Lana, who spoke of the lack of recognition of the integrative nature of the programme:

> 'If I expressed, like, I was worried about a particular essay, it was very much oh well you have to do that yourself, it is home learning, it is not undergrad, it's not this, it's not that, you should just know to go and look stuff. I made a little bit of a frustration at not having any face-to-face learning and my manager just said, well it's not face-to-face learning anyway, regardless of COVID, you should just be doing this yourself.' (Lana)

Earlier, both Mandy and Astrid highlighted that they have allocated time at the weekend to undertake academic work. The cumulative impact of living, working and studying in the same environment was a factor for Sally, Astrid and Mandy, with Astrid commenting on her lack of productivity after "an intense day at work doing work-related stuff, to then close one laptop and open another to do the academic side".

The National Wellness Institute (2021) defines wellness as an 'an active process through which people become aware of, and make choices toward, a more successful existence'. A successful existence involves paying attention to six dimensions: occupational, physical, emotional, spiritual, intellectual and social. Through the application of this concept, it is apparent that through the need to balance the competing priorities of work, study and home life, the PQiP brings with it the possibility of disruption around the occupational and intellectual dimensions. In addition, the opportunity for transformation within these domains is potentially limited because, as Mezirow (1997: 7) highlights, 'we transform our frames of reference through critical reflection on the assumptions on which our interpretations, beliefs, and habits of mind or points of view are based'. This depth of critical reflection rightly takes time, and we need to ensure this is available within the programme and encourage learners, where possible, to move beyond surface engagement with the academic programme (McGregor, cited in Biggs and Tang, 2007). In this sense, surface engagement is linked to the achievement of performance rather than learning-related goals and is associated with instrumental or strategic approaches to studying (Yorke, 2006). While this approach may lead to positive assessment outcomes, it does not necessarily provide for the transformative experience envisaged by Mezirow (1997). The notion that surface engagement is a self-care strategy as opposed to indicative of a lack of motivation is discussed later.

We can also see the pandemic as restricting opportunities for enhancement of the social and physical domains, as people were required to remain in their homes primarily and social interaction was minimized. As such, it was recognized that students' spiritual and emotional wellness would be affected and that there was a need for an enhanced student support offer from the teaching team. The benefits of this offer were to provide not only additional opportunities for lecturer–student interaction but also online spaces for students to learn from each other. While these were mainly assessment-focused sessions, they offered reassurance that others were experiencing similar challenges and sought to reduce feelings of being excluded from collaborative encounters:

> 'I've struggled with working from home to be, to be fair ... just sat at home, like, I've found it harder for me ... I was stuck in a flat, I had no, didn't even have a garden, you know what I mean, so I'm stuck.' (Mandy)

> 'I didn't have, in my office, anybody else doing the qualification either. So it was just radio silence, other than input from the lecturers. Yes, it was a bit lonely.' (Janine)

"I've found the communication better than I expected, really": academic support

When completing the PQiP, each learner is allocated an academic tutor who offers pastoral support throughout the 15- or 21-month course. On each module, there is also tutor support to help the students understand content and complete assessments. A common theme across the focus groups was praise for additional academic support and, in particular, the swiftness of staff responses to requests for help. The availability of staff was in itself a feature of the pandemic. With teaching teams being home based themselves and also seeking to navigate the diminishing boundaries between work and home life meant that they were more frequently online outside of traditional working hours. Also they had increased access to PQiP students due to the move to homeworking and the rise in use of videoconferencing:

> 'It was all a bit new and everything, but everyone was quick and prompt and responded. And then beyond, I think it was only a couple of occasions, I asked sort of an academic-related question and it was fairly quick back. So that side of it was absolutely spot on.' (Rick)

> 'There's always somebody there and I think that's impressed upon you, via email, you know, wherever, it just pops up, don't forget we're there. So, you know, it's not like, you [are] probably cast less adrift by university than you are by work.' (Sam)

> 'I found that the course tutors have been really available.' (Sally)

For those that felt isolated, academic tutor support was invaluable and at times served to mitigate feelings of loneliness. Sam and Saskia also appreciated the structure offered by the scheduled drop-ins and the availability of additional guidance to support the completion of module assessments:

> 'Again, I think it's because it was quite a lonely experience so having [academic tutor] just going how are you finding it, oh yes that's – and she's quite chatty. It was just good, I found that really good.' (Tammy)

> 'I mean, even just dropping a email to the tutor on the module and they just point you, you know, in the right direction.' (Sam)

Therefore, while positive and reassuring that the focus group participants found staff to be both accessible and helpful, it will be important moving forward to look at how levels of engagement and support can be maintained as university and probation working environments start to resemble pre-pandemic operations. For example, when learners return to their office spaces, the time and space to 'drop in' to support sessions might be restricted, as communal offices and the increased demands of in-person contact are likely to limit flexibility. As pandemic restrictions ease, the porous or indistinct boundaries between work, study and home (McNeill, 2020) are likely to become more tangible, as flexible approaches to studying might not continue to be appropriate or achievable.

Moving forward: approaches to learning

"It's made a massive difference": creating support networks

The PQiP programme, like professional education programmes in social work, nursing and midwifery, integrates academic and practice learning in a network of different organizations and individuals involved in supporting learners. Our participants were positive about the support offered by academic colleagues but were conscious of the need to have equivalent support in the workplace:

> I've got quite a good relationship with, like, my PTA and my manager, where I can go and say, like, I'm … too much is being expected of me at this stage. So, trying to work within the guidelines and what's been advised for us at each stage. And I'll, if I feel like I've got time, then I'll offer to take on like an extra case or I'll, I'll offer to do like a CMS [case management system] task to help out probation officers and things like that. But I'm trying to be really strict in terms of not taking on more work than I need to at this stage, really.' (Astrid)

While Astrid told us about the need for clear guidelines and an outline of expectations at each stage, Sally spoke of the need to be assertive to avoid feeling overwhelmed:

> 'My caseload was very, up to like 31, 32, and it was, I was struggling so much and then … but I was assertive, kind of, for me, and mentioned it to my PTA. And it's gone right down now, it's made a massive difference.' (Sally)

The good practice by Astrid's PTA and manager should be the experience of all PQiP learners so that those who feel less confident or unable to assert their needs are not put in a position of taking on more than they can cope with.

As we have heard, the experience of working from home has been particularly difficult for PQiP learners, who are trying to gain experience and build the skills they need to work effectively as probation officers. The reliance on technology to communicate with other practitioners was experienced quite negatively by Astrid, who welcomed the return to office working and the chance to interact with other practitioners:

> 'Like, since COVID, with literally, well we've started going in the office more recently, but completely reliant really on, like, emails and using Teams, and it's quite easy for people to just ignore your questions, or I've had it that people assume someone else will get back to you. So, I think, hopefully, with going back into the office more, that people can sort of put a face to name and you are not just someone who keeps pestering them on emails, and they might be more willing to help, really.' (Astrid)

This is not to say that technology cannot facilitate positive social interaction and ongoing learning, but careful consideration is required around how communication tools can be used to promote professional development (Allen et al, 2020). The pandemic necessarily led to the ad hoc adoption of communication tools and a multitude of ways to contact people. Going forward, organizations need to evaluate how they use these tools to engage individuals effectively in ongoing professional development rather than leaving them feeling ignored or, conversely, overwhelmed with messages to be responded to. This is particularly important for individuals such as our participants, who are new to their role and embarking on a process of professional socialization (Grant, 2016). The working environment can have a significant impact on the practice and identity of new workers, whether this is office based or virtual. As highlighted earlier, ongoing support in the workplace will be vital for learners trying to navigate the transition to a post-pandemic working environment.

"It is quite hard for them to adjust": building communities of practice

In recent years, probation officer training has taken a blended learning approach with a mix of face-to-face and online learning. The feedback that we have received consistently from learners is that they would prefer more face-to-face time with tutors and a more 'traditional' university experience. This perhaps reflects the way many of our learners have experienced academic learning in the past and what feels the most comfortable and familiar for them. Questions about the pedagogical underpinning for this were addressed earlier in this chapter, but in addition to this aspect, the face-to-face element of the programme has felt important in helping to foster learning through a sense of building a community of practice. Wenger's (1998) concept of community of practice focuses on learning through participation and social interaction. A community of practice is described as a 'social process of negotiating competence in a domain over time' (Farnsworth et al, 2016: 143).

This concept sits well with the PQiP programme, as learners develop their knowledge and skills through participation to move from being peripheral to full members of the probation community. The concern throughout the pandemic was that the moves to online study and homeworking would leave learners stuck at the peripheral levels with few opportunities to develop their learning through interaction with others, resulting potentially in an uncertain sense of their own professional identity.

The challenges of the pandemic have emphasized the need for us to be focused on inclusivity and to understand the differences in the way our learners experience the programme. While a face-to-face teaching session had been welcomed by many, for others the travel and planning required had caused considerable levels of stress and anxiety, which impacted on their levels of engagement. The move to more online learning alleviated some of these concerns and enabled a more relaxed approach to the teaching sessions. Higher education institutions responded to the pandemic with what could be termed 'emergency remote teaching' (Bozkurt and Sharma, 2020), which meant a sharp pivot from normal practice for many lecturers and students. A transition from this emergency situation to a more considered and pedagogically informed approach to online learning may have significant benefits for many students. Online learning requires specific skills and capabilities among lecturers and students, and while these can be learned, there needs to be support in the workplace to enable this to happen effectively (Egan and Crotty, 2020; Gasevic, 2020).

However, we do need to work towards demystifying the world of online learning and acknowledge the difficulty that some of our learners will have with this experience. Many of our learners have been out of formal education for an extended period, and the experience of trying to navigate the world of online learning (in addition to learning their probation role) can be overwhelming. The social cues that help us to navigate a face-to-face learning experience may be absent in the online environment, and it may take learners some time to interpret the virtual learning environment and engage in a way that is meaningful (Lofstom and Negvi, 2007). There is a need to ensure that more time is allocated to induction processes and that there can be flexibility in what is provided to account for different learning needs and preferences:

> 'When I was at Hallam ... we had, like, a session of how to use Library Gateway and get sort of the best out of it, and I found that I was often giving tips to sort of fellow PQiPs of, like, how you search for articles and, you know, you can reference on there, and people didn't have a clue. So I think, sort of, maybe giving a session around how to use Blackboard and Library Gateway in the future might be quite helpful for people who have not got any experience of it before. Especially

people who haven't either been to uni for sort of 10 to 15 years. It is quite hard for them to adjust to it, I think.' (Lana)

"I was burning myself out a bit": instrumental learning as self-care

A prominent theme from our research has been the potential for our learners to become overwhelmed by the programme and the compacted nature of the learning. This has been exacerbated by the pandemic when the boundaries between home, work and study have become blurred. Our participants highlighted that this led to a shift towards a more strategic or instrumental approach to learning, mainly as a means of managing their own well-being:

> 'I was burning myself out a bit, and I thought I can't go through the process. And I thought, no, I'm going to have my assignment in mind and just really steer my learning towards the topics that I'm doing rather than trying to, you know, absorb everything, because it was just a bit of an information overload.' (Janine)

> 'I have spoken to, like, tutors and stuff about it. They tended to be, you know, pragmatic and realistic about that it's not, it's not like we're doing a straightforward undergraduate or a postgraduate degree. It's, there needs to be that degree of … and like you say, if I did everything, I'd burn out, I wouldn't have time to do it.' (Rick)

> 'It's like you're definitely focusing on the content that's most relevant to what you're focus is for the assignments. And I suppose there's always that hope that you get the opportunity to go back and look through a bit more, but in reality I'm not sure how realistic that is.' (Nadia)

As academics, we are attuned to encouraging a more holistic or deeper level of learning. This is felt acutely on a programme such as the PQiP, where we are trying to motivate learners to critically reflect on their role and practice and to engage them with the theory and knowledge that will underpin their decision making about complex issues and individuals. However, we must be mindful that learners may, as a means of self-care, approach their learning strategically. The role for academics is to acknowledge this more peripheral approach to learning and help learners find their way to become a more engaged and central part of a community of practice without burdening them with additional tasks.

Our participants highlighted the need for us to provide accessible and easy-to-manage learning materials where there was the possibility for "scaling up" or taking their learning further. Sam identified that while learners could just work towards achieving a pass mark, it was clear how they could develop from there with the additional reading and activities provided:

> 'You can do as much as you want, really, because there's the, the option to read enough to pass your module or there's the option to read a little bit more ... I suppose that is the beauty of the online thing, because you are pointed towards it.' (Sam)

This demonstrates that learners such as Sam are constructing their own version of knowledge rather than being dependent on what is taught to them. Our role is to develop effective mechanisms for students to scaffold their learning (Biggs and Tang, 2007).

Online lectures were popular, but again there is a need to make these accessible and for academics to have an understanding of optimum length and content for learner engagement:

> 'I would say in terms of the lectures, you know, I felt, I felt fine watching like a 20-minute lecture, but anything longer than that was ... I would say, too much.' (Saskia)

> 'One of them was quite long and, like, you could zone out. Yeah, 20, 25 minutes is enough, but I know one of them, was the rehabilitation one, can't remember, but it was, it went on for nearly an hour and it was a little bit, I didn't really take a lot of notice towards the end.' (Sam)

There is an argument here for simplification and standardization of key learning materials with opportunities provided for those learners who want to go beyond this and expand their learning. We need a more empathic approach that is understanding of the pressures faced by many of our learners. There has been a tendency in the past to focus on 'what they need to know' rather than the process of learning and how that is experienced by our students. The challenge going forward for professional training is to find ways to use the online environment to create new and valued opportunities for interaction and engagement that can help learners feel that they are participating fully in a community of practice which will help them to develop their sense of professional identity and confidence (Allen et al, 2020).

Conclusion

Returning to Carr (2020), probation officer education also represents broader questions about penal philosophies, the purpose of probation and the wider criminal justice system. Probation education operates within the current penal thinking, policy context and direction of the criminal justice system. As we have seen from the literature, probation students' values, attitudes and motivations for working in probation can transcend the worrying punitive direction within criminal justice and ideas about the purposes of probation services; this is despite concern that probation training is enforcement orientated, centred around public protection or processes. It would be interesting to learn more about 'if' and 'how' these values, attitudes and traditions were maintained during the PQiP without the same professional socialization experienced by previous cohorts. It is important to draw attention to this group, who were largely forgotten at a policy level during the pandemic, albeit during an exceptionally disruptive period globally. This research offers some insight into the PQiP student experience during the pandemic, the lessons learned and nature of probation learning going forward.

What emerged in this research is that counter to Canton and Dominey's (2018) pre-pandemic concern that the PQiP would result in less support from tutors, during the pandemic student support really came to the fore for our participants. However, the spillage of work into home life dissolved boundaries between domestic spaces, academic study and probation work. For some aspiring probation officers there was peer support and for others it was a lonely time. Regardless, the value of academic support was a recurring theme among our participants. In addition, the pandemic made visible the emotional demands and consequences of probation training, which stresses the importance of communities of practice and communities of coping for participants. The are some important considerations for the academic institutions providing probation education, including the role of the university in facilitating communities of practice and how this can be done online, and ensuring there is equal access to all learning opportunities. A legacy of the pandemic will undoubtedly be some lasting changes in the delivery of probation education.

Furthermore, the transition to remote working during the pandemic could result in the maintenance of some practices that have proved to be effective for probation work, which in turn has implications for probation education. For instance, the pendulum could swing towards agile working (McDermott, 2016). This would mean increased attention in higher education to the technologies, skills and approaches that make remote working effective. It is imperative that part of this dialogue considers:

- the emotional consequences of remote working for PQiP students;
- the spillage of probation work into domestic spaces;
- the strategies used by students to manage study/work/life boundaries; and
- the emotional consequences of the work, which need to be acknowledged more at an organizational level and within higher education.

Given the demands of the PQiP programme, students require understanding and empathy from their senior probation officers, their partners and family members, and the university. This is needed to protect study days and time to read and complete essays, enable access to learning opportunities in a meaningful way and help students cope with the emotional consequences of the work. The use of instrumental learning as a tool for self-care during the pandemic reveals the size of the challenge and how aspiring probation officers coped while completing the qualification at this time. It also highlights some strengths of the academic programme and the relationships that sustained participants through their experiences of the PQiP during COVID-19.

References

Allen, L.M, Hay, M., Armstrong, E. and Palermo, C. (2020) 'Applying a social theory of learning to explain the possible impacts of continuing professional development (CPD) programs', *Medical Teacher*, 42(10): 1140–7.

Annison, J. (2013) 'Change and the Probation Service in England and Wales: a gendered lens', *European Journal of Probation*, 5(1): 44–64.

Ashton, S. and Stone, R. (2018) *An A-Z of Creative Teaching in Higher Education*, London: Sage.

Biggs, J.B. and Tang, C.S. (2007) *Teaching for Quality Learning at University: What the Student Does*, Maidenhead: Open University Press.

Bozkurt, A. and Sharma, R. (2020) 'Emergency remote teaching in a time of global crisis due to CoronaVirus pandemic', *Asian Journal of Distance Education*, 15(1): i–vi.

Burnett, C. (2011) 'Medium for empowerment or a "centre for everything": students' experience of control in virtual learning environments within a university context', *Education and Information Technologies*, 16(3): 245–58.

Canton, R. and Dominey, J. (2018) *Probation* (2nd edn), London: Routledge.

Carr, N. (2020) *Recruitment, Training and Professional Development of Probation Staff*, Academic Insights 2020/02, [online] Available from: www.justiceinspectorates.gov.uk/hmiprobation/wp-content/uploads/sites/5/2020/02/Academic-Insights-Carr-Final.pdf

Case, S. and Haines, K. (2014) 'Reflective friend research: the relational aspects of social scientific research', in K. Lumsden and A. Winter (eds) *Reflexivity in Criminological Research Experiences with the Powerful and the Powerless*, Houndmills: Palgrave Macmillan, pp 58–74.

Cracknell, M. (2016) 'Reflections on undertaking the probation qualifying framework scheme during the transforming rehabilitation changes', *Probation Journal*, 63(2): 211–18.

Davies, K. and Durrance, P. (2009) 'Probation training: the experience of learners and teachers', *Social Work Education*, 28(2): 204–21.

Deering, J. (2010) 'Attitudes and beliefs of trainee probation officers: a "new breed"?' *Probation Journal*, 57(1): 9–26.

Digard, L. (2014) 'Encoding risk: probation work and sex offenders' narrative identities', *Punishment & Society*, 16(4): 428–47.

Dominey, J. (2010) 'Work-based distance learning for probation practice: doing the job properly', *Napo*, 57(2): 153–62.

Egan, K. and Crotty, Y. (2020) 'Sustaining and prolonged pivot: appraising challenges facing higher education stakeholders in switching to online learning', *International Journal for Transformative Research*, 7(1): 1–9.

Farnsworth, V., Kleanthous, I. and Wenger-Trayner, E. (2016) 'Communities of practice as a social theory of learning: a conversation with Etienne Wenger', *British Journal of Educational Studies*, 64(2): 139–60.

Fowler, A., Phillips, J. and Westaby, C. (2017) 'Understanding emotions as effective practice in English probation: the performance of emotional labour in building relationships' in P. Ugwudike, P. Raynor and J. Annison (eds) *Evidence-based Skills in Criminal Justice: International Research on Supporting Rehabilitation and Desistance*, Bristol: Policy Press, pp 243–62.

Gasevic, D. (2020) 'COVID-19: the steep learning curve for online education', *Lens: Pioneering Research Stories*, [online] Available from: https://lens.monash.edu/@educatio n/2020/04/26/1380195?slug=covid-19-the-steep-learningcurve-for-online-education

GOV.UK Justice Data (2021) 'Probation data', [online] Available from: https://data.justice.gov.uk/probation

Grant, S. (2016) 'Constructing the durable penal agent: tracing the development of habitus within English probation officers and Scottish criminal justice social workers', *The British Journal Of Criminology*, 56(4): 750–68.

HMPPS (HM Prison & Probation Service) (2019) *Strengthening Probation, Improving Confidence*, [online] Available from: https://assets.publishing.serv ice.gov.uk/government/uploads/system/uploads/attachment_data/file/802175/strengthening-probation-consultation-response.PDF

House of Commons Justice Committee (2020) *Coronavirus (COVID-19): The Impact on Probation Systems*, Third Report of Session 2019–21, HC 461, [online] Available from: https://committees.parliament.uk/publications/1944/documents/18919/default/

House of Commons Justice Select Committee (2020) 'How has coronavirus impacted the justice system?' [online] 5 August, Available from: https://houseofcommons.shorthandstories.com/justice-coronavirus-impact-on-probation-prisons-courts-legal-professions/index.html

Kalliath, P. and Kalliath, T. (2015) 'Work-family conflict and its impact on job satisfaction of social workers', *The British Journal of Social Work*, 45(1): 241–59.

Knight, C. (2014) *Emotional Literacy in Criminal Justice Professional Practice with Offenders*, Houndmills: Palgrave Macmillan.

Korczynski, M. (2003) 'Communities of coping: collective emotional labour in service work', *Organization*, 10(1): 55–79.

Lee, R. (2017) 'The impact of engaging with clients' trauma stories: personal and organizational strategies to manage probation practitioners' risk of developing vicarious traumatization', *Probation Journal*, 64(4): 372–87.

Lofstrum, E. and Negvi, A. (2007) 'From strategic planning to meaningful learning: diverse perspectives on the development of web-based teaching and learning in higher education', *British Journal of Educational Technology*, 38(2): 312–24.

Lumsden, K. and Winter, A. (2014) *Reflexivity in Criminological Research Experiences with the Powerful and the Powerless*, Houndmills: Palgrave Macmillan, pp 58–74.

Madoc-Jones, I. and Buchanan, J. (2003) 'Welsh language, identity and probation practice: the context for change', *Probation Journal*, 50(3): 225–38.

Martin, L. (2020) 'Hanging on in there: the enduring value base of probation practitioners', *Probation Quarterly*, 14: 32–5.

Mathieson, S. (2015) 'Student learning', in H. Fry, S. Ketteridge and S. Marshall (eds) *A Handbook for Teaching and Learning in Higher Education* (4th edn), Abingdon: Routledge, pp 63–79.

Matthews, J. (2009) '"People first: probation officer perspectives on probation work" – a practitioner's response', *Probation Journal*, 56(1): 61–7.

McDermott, S.-A. (2016) 'Probation without boundaries? "Agile working" in the community rehabilitation company "transformed" landscape', *Probation Journal*, 63(2): 193–201.

McNeill, F. (2019) 'Mass supervision, misrecognition and the "Malopticon"', *Punishment & Society*, 21(2): 207–30.

McNeill, F. (2020) 'Penal supervision in a pandemic', *Scottish Centre for Crime & Justice Research*, [online] 4 May, Available from: https://sccjrblog.wordpress.com/2020/05/04/penal-supervision-in-a-pandemic/

Mezirow, J. (1997) 'Transformative learning: theory to practice', *New Directions for Adult and Continuing Education*, 74: 5–12.

Ministry of Justice (2013) *Transforming Rehabilitation: A Strategy for Reform*, Cm 8619, [online], Available from: https://consult.justice.gov.uk/digital-communications/transforming-rehabilitation/results/transforming-rehabilitation-response.pdf

National Wellness Institute (2021) 'The six dimensions of wellness', [online] Available from: https://nationalwellness.org/resources/six-dimensions-of-wellness/

Nellis, M. (2001) 'The Diploma in Probation Studies in the Midland region: celebration and critique after the first two years', *The Howard Journal of Criminal Justice*, 40(4): 377–401.

Phillips, J. (2020) 'Delivering probation during the Covid-19 pandemic', *The Sheffield Institute for Policy Studies*, [online] 30 April, Available from: https://sheffieldinstituteforpolicystudies.com/2020/04/30/delivering-probation-duringthe-covid-19-pandemic/

Raynor, P. and Vanstone, M. (2016) 'Moving away from social work and halfway back again: new research on skills in probation', *The British Journal of Social Work*, 46(4): 1131–47.

Skinner, C. and Goldhill, R. (2013) 'Changes in probation training in England and Wales: the Probation Qualification Framework (PQF) three years on', *European Journal of Probation*, 5(3): 41–55.

Smyth, G. and Watson, A. (2018) 'Training for a transformed service', *Probation Journal*, 65(1): 61–76.

Staines, G. (1980) 'Spillover versus compensation: a review of the literature between work and nonwork', *Human Relations*, 33(2): 119–29.

Stout, B. and Dominey, J. (2006) 'Counterblast: in defence of distance learning', *The Howard Journal of Criminal Justice*, 45(5): 537–40.

Treadwell, J (2006) 'Some personal reflections on probation training', *The Howard Journal of Criminal Justice*, 45(1): 1–13.

Treadwell, J. and Mantle, G. (2007) 'Probation education, why the hush? A reply to Stout and Dominey's December 2006 Counterblast', *The Howard Journal of Criminal Justice*, 46(5): 500–11.

Trede, F., Macklin, R. and Bridges, D. (2012) 'Professional identity development: a review of the higher education literature', *Studies in Higher Education*, 37(3): 365–84.

Waters, J., Westaby, C., Fowler, A. and Phillips, J. (2020) 'The emotional labour of doctoral criminological researchers', *Methodological Innovations*, 13(2). doi: 10.1177/205979912092.

Wenger, E. (1998) *Communities of Practice: Learning, Meaning and Identity*, New York: Cambridge University Press.

Westaby, C., Phillips, J. and Fowler, A. (2016) 'Spillover and work–family conflict in probation practice: managing the boundary between work and home life', *European Journal of Probation*, 8(3): 113–27.

Yorke, M. (2006) *Student Engagement: Deep, Surface or Strategic*, Keynote address to the 9th Pacific Rim Conference on the First Year in Higher Education, Griffith University, Australia.

PART III

The View from the Inside

So far in this collection, we have seen contributions from academics, practitioners and those with lived experience in the community. Such chapters have provided a vital understanding of the practicalities of delivering and experiencing criminal justice during the pandemic. When designing this collection, however, it became apparent that another, often-overlooked set of voices was missing – that of those serving prison sentences. It is this gap that Part III seeks to address through the unedited presentation of artistic expression from the residents of two prisons: HMP Parc (in Wales) and HMP Manchester (in England).

There is a growing body of literature demonstrating the positive impact arts-based initiatives can have within the prison environment (Anderson et al, 2011). Such initiatives have been shown to improve relationships between residents and prison staff (Menning, 2010), improve participants self-esteem and self-confidence (Cox and Gelsthorpe, 2012) and help participants 'imagine different possible futures, different social networks, different identities and different lifestyles' (Anderson et al, 2011: 40). There is also a growing body of evidence demonstrating the impact of involvement in arts-based initiatives on successful desistance and rehabilitation efforts, with art classes being identified as a 'catalyst for change' in some cases (Bilby et al, 2013: 20; see also Maruna, 2001). Finally, it has been shown that art allows residents to 'spend time doing something which is absorbing, engaging and ultimately enjoyable' (Bilby et al, 2013: 21) but also takes them 'out of the prison zone' (Bilby et al, 2013: 18). Within the context of strict lockdown measures across the prison estate as a consequence of the exceptional regime management plan, with residents spending up to 23 hours a day in their cells, arts-based interventions could be seen to be a way to escape the monotony of prison life in lockdown (Callaghan, 2020).

The pieces presented in Chapters 11 and 12 are the result of two separate initiatives run by HMP Parc and HMP Manchester during the first and second lockdowns in England and Wales (March 2020 to January 2021), with introductions from the practitioners implementing each initiative. They reflect not only the thoughts and feelings of the residents, but also a snapshot in time of the experience of incarceration during this period. With research data, there is often a concern that the accounts provided are 'fragmented, lifted out of context, trimmed to support particular criminological theories or policy initiatives in ways that make nonsense of taking offender perspectives seriously' (Weaver and Weaver, 2013: 260). Here, the work from these initiatives is presented its entirety, unedited and without comment from the authors. It is hoped that this presents a more authentic account of how the pandemic has been experienced by people in prison.

References

Anderson, K., Colvin, S., McNeill, F., Nellis, M., Overy,K., Sparks, R. and Tett, L. (2011) *Inspiring Change: Final Project Report of the Evaluation Team. Grant report for Creative Scotland*, Glasgow: Scottish Centre for Crime & Justice Research, University of Glasgow.

Bilby, C., Caulfield, L. and Ridley, L. (2013) *Re-imagining Futures: Exploring Arts Interventions and the Process of Desistance*, London: Arts Alliance.

Callaghan, T. (2021) *CAPPTIVE – Covid-19 Action Prisons Project: Tracking Innovation, Valuing Experience. How Prisons Are Responding to Covid-19*, London: Prison Reform Trust.

Cox, A. and Gelsthorpe, L. (2012) 'Creative encounters: whatever happened to the arts in prisons?' in L.K. Cheliotis (ed) *The Arts of Imprisonment*, Farnham: Ashgate, pp 257–76.

Maruna, S. (2001) *Making Good: How Ex-convicts Reform and Rebuild Their Lives*, Washington, D.C.: American Psychological Association.

Menning, N. (2010) 'Singing with conviction: New Zealand prisons and Maori populations', *International Journal of Community Music*, 3(1): 111–20.

Weaver, A. and Weaver, B. (2013), 'Autobiography, empirical research and critical theory in desistance: a view from the inside out', *Probation Journal*, 60(3): 259–277.

11

The Box Project at HMP Parc

Introduction by Phil Forder

Introduction

Art has always been one of the most popular subjects taught in prison, with many finding a sense of meaning and achievement previously not thought possible. I believe art has this ability because it is from the heart and bypasses many of the obstacles that traditional schooling can inculcate. However, education departments, especially when facing cuts, often marginalize the arts in favour of more mainstream subjects, thinking them to be less useful in the job market and more expensive to deliver. As those who have taught art know, this is short-sighted as many prisoners find paths to inner fulfilment and expression that not only offer much-needed therapy but also bring about life-changing self-perceptions.

Nowhere has this been more clearly illustrated than in the Box Project at HMP Parc, which began as a result of COVID-19 in March 2020 with all our prisoners in lockdown. For those enrolled in the art classes, individual packs of brushes, watercolours, pencils, erasers, sketchbooks, sharpeners and 'ideas books' were assembled to distribute to the students so they could carry on their work, albeit in isolation. An insignificant problem to be overcome was to find a container of sorts to put this equipment in. There was nothing that we already had that was suitable, everything being either too large or too flimsy. Eventually it was decided that we would have to buy something in. This was already becoming an expensive project, but the prison, very wisely, decided to buy 100 robust white cardboard boxes to deliver the kits in (see Figure 11.1).

Little did we know at the time how important this decision was to become. The boxes were wonderfully pristine and, like a brand-new exercise book in the hands of a child, were an open invitation to paint, decorate or write on. The Box Project was born and the results that came back were better than anyone expected.

Figure 11.1: A box of art supplies

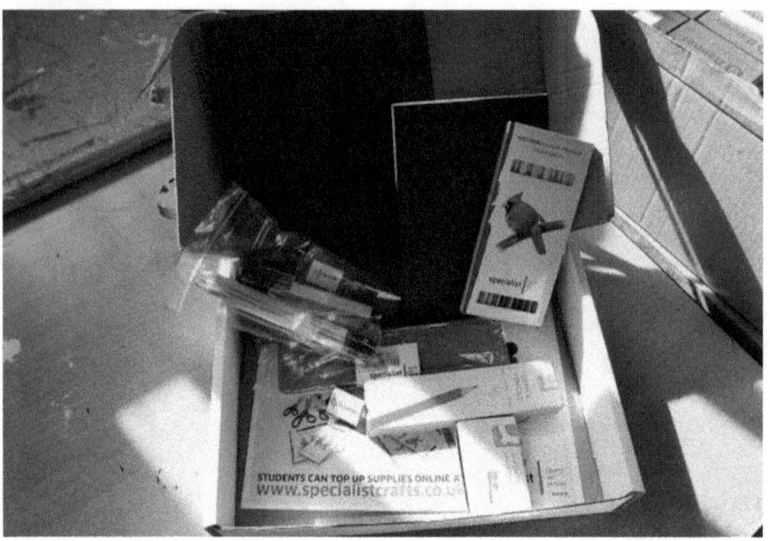

Due to the prolonged isolation, the efficacy of the project soon became clear, with requests coming in from those not involved in the art classes to also be included. As a result, another 100 sets in another 100 boxes were bought and subsequently delivered.

It would be impossible in a chapter such as this to include a lengthy appraisal of the results from each box, though each is worthy in its own right. But the results speak for themselves, offering a profound insight into the personal lives of men coping with very difficult circumstances heaped on an already difficult situation. They clearly show concern for loved ones, praise for the NHS, pressure of stress caused by isolation, recognition of Black Lives Matter, missed opportunities and dreams, hobbies and interests and also copious amounts of 'prison humour', which was unexpected under the circumstances. But then again, isn't humour just another way of coping?

We have all heard the expression 'necessity is the mother of invention' and nowhere is this clearer than in prison, where access to resources is heavily restricted and any opportunity will be utilized creatively. (One of the best paintings I have ever seen was completed using prison coffee when the paint had run out.) There is one entry, entitled 'My breakfast', that clearly illustrates this resourcefulness where literally a breakfast pack has been used in such a way that would hold its own in any conceptual art show.

So to sum up, I would like to thank the men for sharing with us some of their deepest feelings and thoughts through these amazing pieces of art. It takes courage to be so honest about our feelings, especially in a place not known for sensitivity, and the onus is clearly on the viewer to respect these personal insights. To try and psychoanalyze them would, in many ways, be a betrayal of confidence. Funnily enough, the first box to be returned was 'The apple of a prisoner's eye', which included a slice of apple stuck onto the box. After a while, the apple turned brown and then went rotten, which caused the man, on seeing it, to reflect: "You know what! That's exactly what happens in life, things start of looking great and then inevitably they turn horrible. Maybe I should do things differently next time and avoid using fruit."

Figure 11.2: Box 1, outside

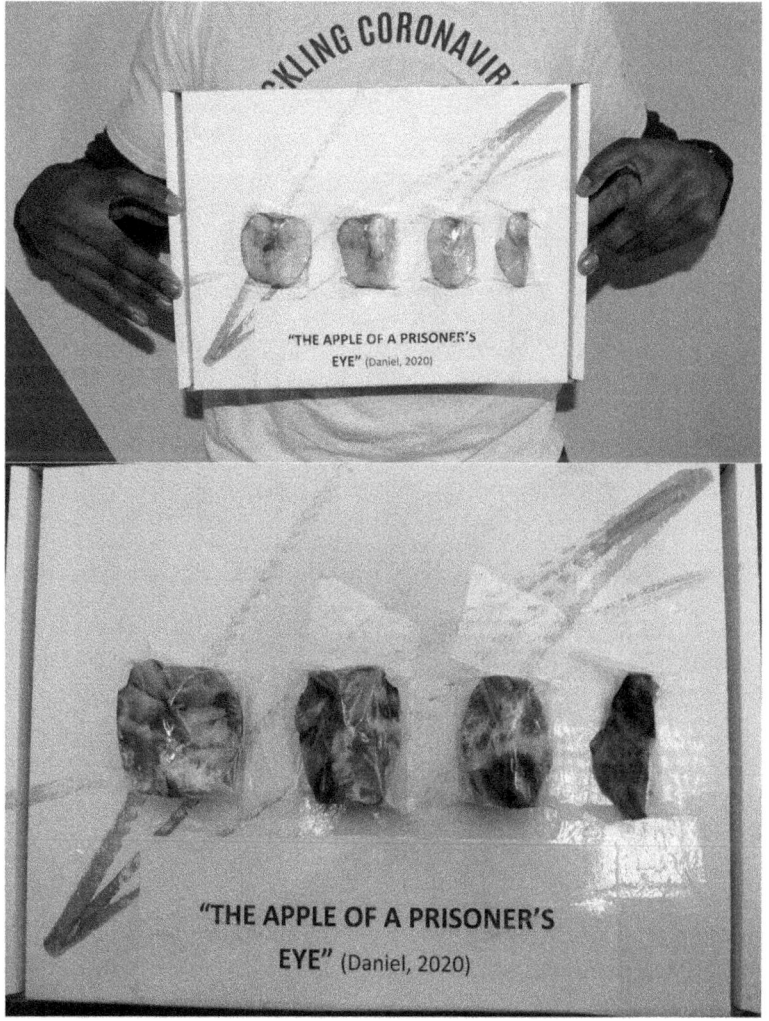

Figure 11.3: Box 2, outside and inside

Figure 11.4: Box 3, outside

Figure 11.5: Box 4, outside

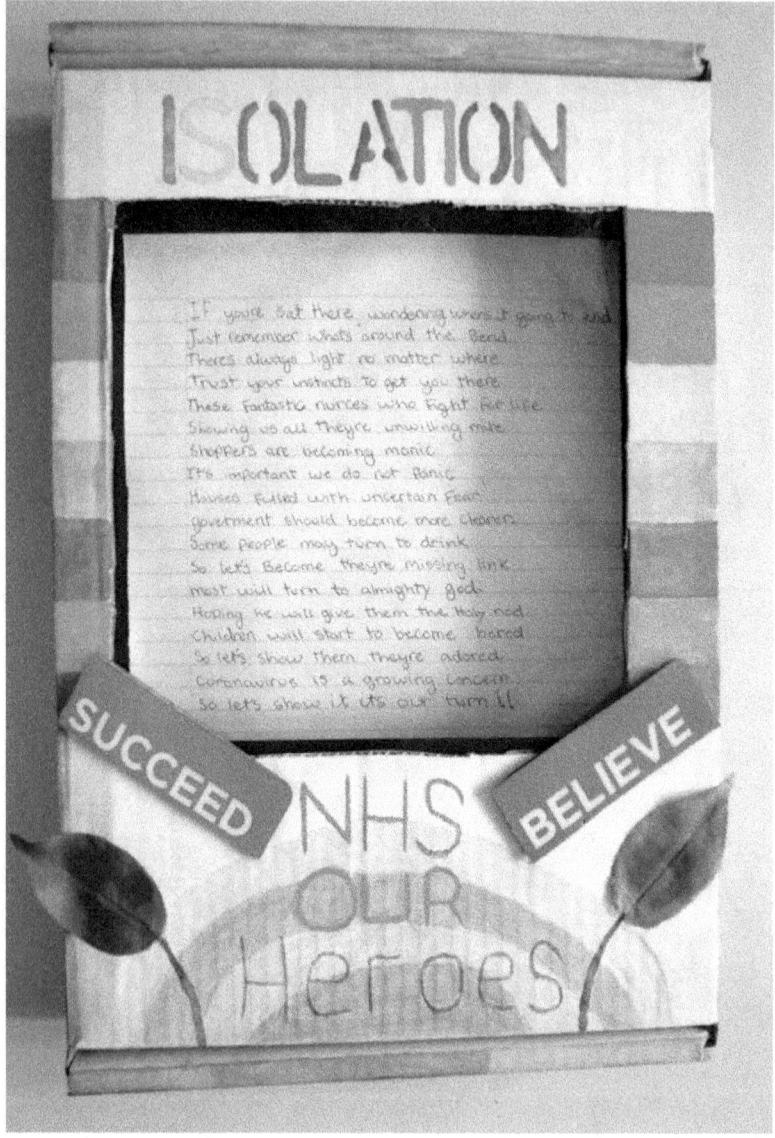

Figure 11.6: Box 5, outside

Figure 11.7: Box 6, outside

Figure 11.8a: Box 7, inside

Figure 11.8b: Box 7, outside

Figure 11.9: Box 8, outside

Figure 11.10: Box 9, outside

Figure 11.11: Box 10, outside

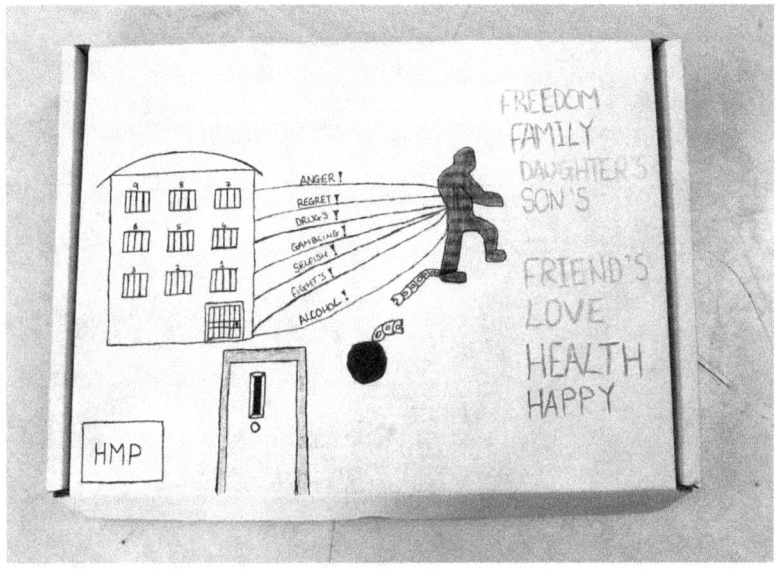

Figure 11.12: Box 11, outside

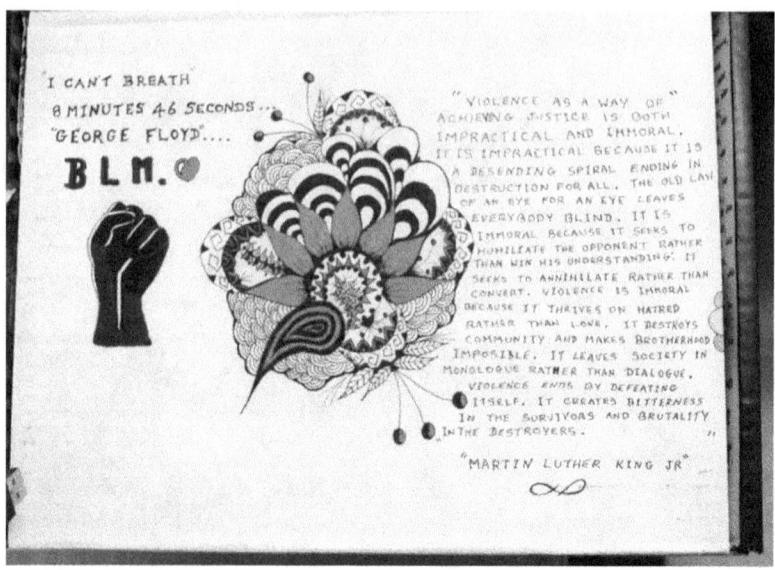

Figure 11.13: Box 12, inside lid

Figure 11.14a: Box 13, letter

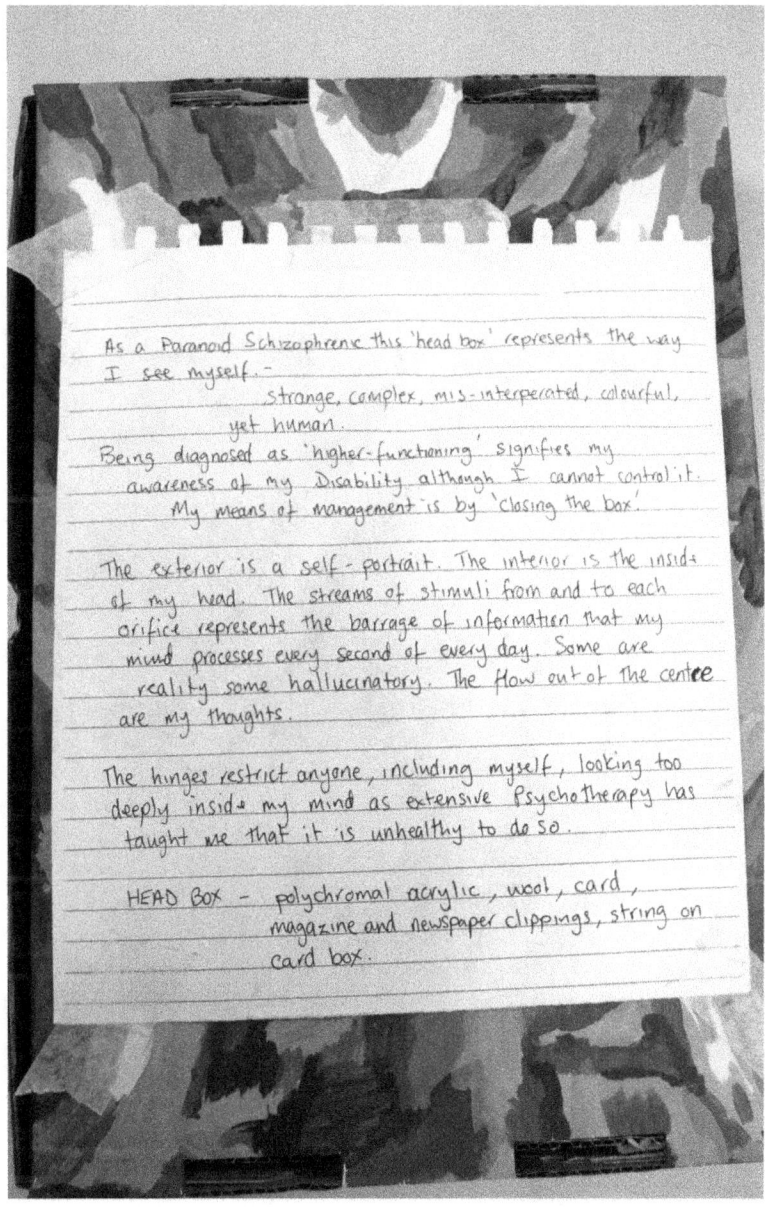

Figure 11.14b: Box 13, outside

Figure 11.14c: Box 13, inside

Figure 11.15a: Box 14, outside

Figure 11.15b: Box 14, inside

Figure 11.15c: Box 14, inside lid

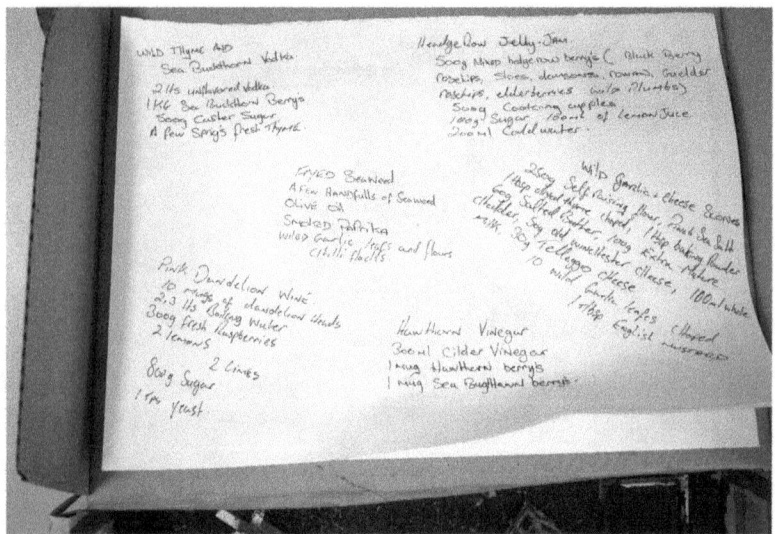

Figure 11.16: Box 15, outside

Figure 11.17a: Box 16, outside

Figure 11.17b: Box 16, letter

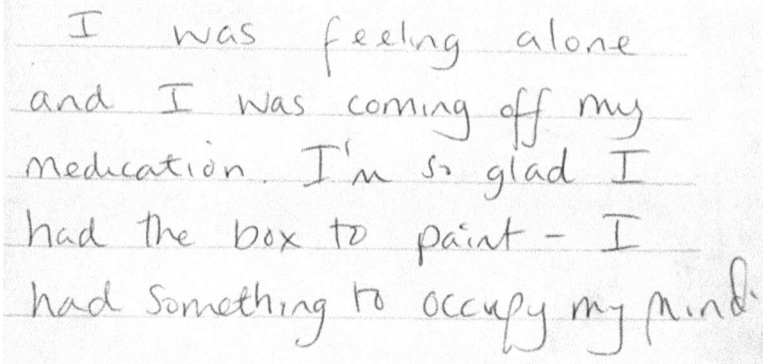

I was feeling alone and I was coming off my medication. I'm so glad I had the box to paint – I had something to occupy my mind.

Figure 11.18a: Box 17, outside

Figure 11.18b: Box 17, letter

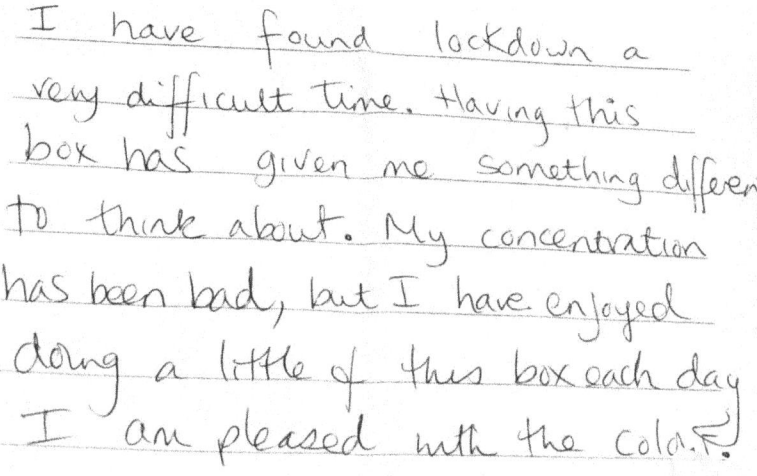

Figure 11.19a: Box 18, outside

Figure 11.19b: Box 18, inside

Figure 11.19c: Box 18, inside lid

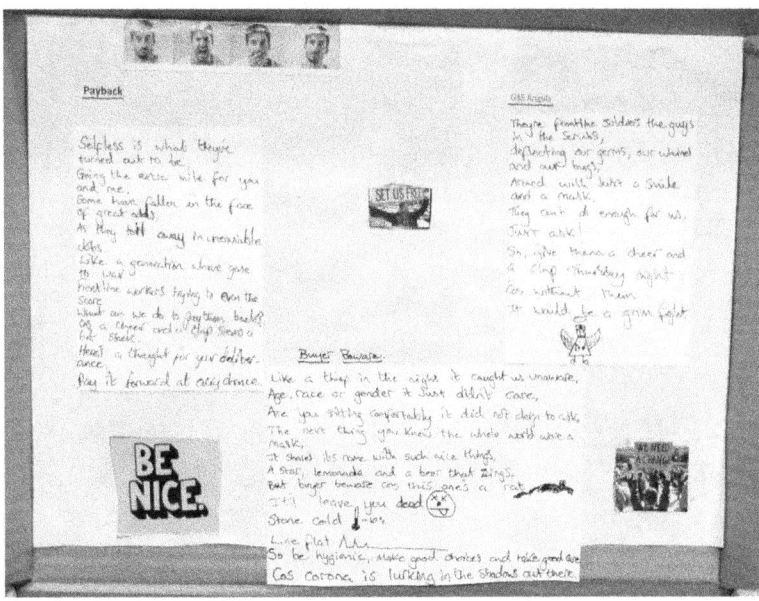

Figure 11.19d: Box 18, manual

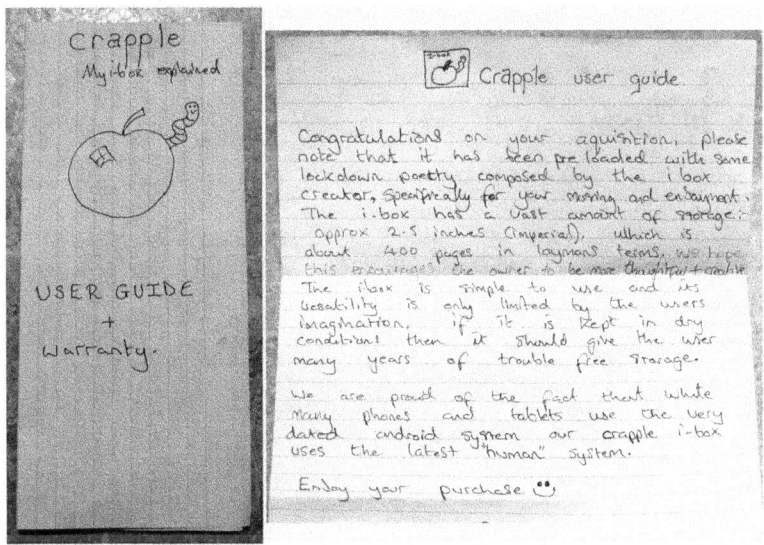

Figure 11.20: Box 19, outside

Figure 11.21a: Box 20, inside lid

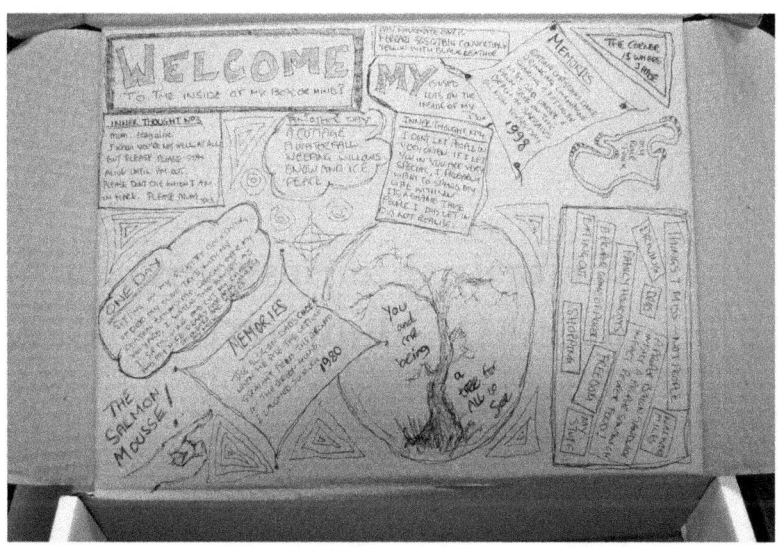

Figure 11.21b: Box 20, inside

12

Write Inside Sessions at HMP Manchester

Introduction by Maureen Carnighan

Introduction

At the end of March, it was looking increasingly like there would be a lockdown at HMP Manchester, and at the time we were expecting this to last a few weeks. I decided to organize a competition for the men which might keep them occupied for some of this time. I contacted Jonathan Aitkin and explained that I was going to ask them to write a letter to their 13-year-old selves. Jonathan Aitken is a former Cabinet Minister who was given an 18-month prison sentence in 1999 for perjury. Now a reverend and in his eighties, Jonathan currently works as a chaplain in Pentonville jail. He kindly agreed to judge and offered me a cash prize of £50 for the winner, from his prison charity. I organized a leaflet to explain, which I was hoping would be distributed around the wings.

Three weeks turned into three months, and then it became apparent that the Education Department would be closed indefinitely. I had to change the competition into something more in-depth and long term. I thought that writing might help provide 'medicine for the mind' during the lockdown. I produced a creative writing pack and contacted another three published authors, two with Manchester connections, David Nolan and Joseph Knox, and also Erwin James, an author who had served a life sentence and is currently editing *Inside Time*, the prisoners' newspaper.

All three writers, without hesitation, offered to be judges. I asked the men to write about their experiences of life in the prison during the pandemic, or about something that was very important to them or, in fact, anything they wanted to write about.

The work they produced was extremely varied. I did receive some letters from men who wrote to their younger selves, the original competition idea, and these were brutally honest and poignant. Some are featured in a booklet. One piece came in on the back of an envelope, and the writer explained he had never written 'a story' before. Others wrote about their heroes. There were many moving autobiographical accounts, book reviews and a great deal of poetry. Several wrote very accurate descriptions of their experiences during the early pandemic. Some of the material made me laugh out loud, but more of it I found to be extremely moving and revealing. More importantly, I felt that so much of the writing showed the men in a positive light, concerned about others, their families and the outside world at a weird and problematic time. I felt they came across as human beings who had made mistakes which they regretted, not the usual impression given of prisoners as monsters who deserve everything that comes their way.

I passed on the work to the four judges and, without asking them, all the authors wrote feedback for the writers. For me, this was the best part of the project. To provide this for them enabled me to see self-esteem grow before my eyes. Sometimes I read it out to them on the phones which had been hurriedly fitted in cells to enable contact. Again, hearing the change in their voices when they heard the comments written by 'proper authors' was a complete joy.

It was difficult for the judges to come up with just one winner, so a shortlist was drawn up and the cash prize, very generously, became £100 split between several of the writers. The commitment given by the authors on this project was incredible.

It seemed a shame to leave it there, so I asked the head of Learning and Skills at HMP Manchester if it would possible to produce a booklet containing the men's work and get it published in the prison print workshop. She spoke to the governor, and he agreed. They both read all the pieces of work I wanted included and, surprisingly, approved nearly all of them.

In late May, we finally got the finished product. It was an A5 full-colour booklet, 128 pages long, complete with drawings, photographs and illustrations.

Having talked about it with the men involved, we decided that it would be great if we could raise some donations from the booklet for the Prisoners' Education Trust (PET). This charity provides funding for prisoners to take distance-learning courses and some Open University Access courses which would not usually be available to them. I work with the PET on a daily basis and know what a difference they make to individuals' futures.

I thought the easiest way to distribute the booklets would be by using a JustGiving page. I would then be able to send out the booklets to those who made donations. The prison initially rejected this idea. They were concerned about 'public perceptions'. After some persuasion, they agreed, and in a few months we had raised over £1,200. This might seem like a very small amount, but it meant a great deal to the writers. Opportunities to support others are infrequent in a prison environment. Clearly, a charity like the PET will always struggle to compete against other charities, prisoners very much seen as undeserving of anything.

Manchester Central Reference Library generously bought several copies of the booklet and gave exhibition space for extracts and drawings from July to October in 2021, which also helped promote it, and this year the brand new Manchester Poetry Museum at Manchester Metropolitan University has asked us to provide material they can use in a display. This exhibition of the men's work is due to start in September 2022 and the director of Manchester Poetry Museum is keen to use students from Manchester Metropolitan University in a poetry project with the prison. Erwin James and David Nolan both offered to come to the prison to do writing workshops, but because of COVID-19 restrictions and officer staffing shortages, this hasn't happened, but hopefully will do at some future point.

I feel very lucky to have been given the chance to organize this project. I really enjoyed reading their work, getting to know the individual writers and hearing their ideas. From a very selfish point of view, it helped me feel useful at a time when I wasn't allowed in the prison full time and often wasn't able to get on the wings. During a 30-year career as a teacher in schools, this project has given me more job satisfaction than anything else I have ever done. To work with authors who have been so generous with their time, to be able to give the contributors a copy of their work which has been published and to see the confidence-boosting effect of this has been a total pleasure. For the writers to know that their work has been exhibited in the Central Reference Library and their descriptions of their COVID-19 experiences at HMP Manchester will be in the archive section has contributed to their self-belief as writers. As the distance-learning coordinator at HMP Manchester, I have also been able to identify individuals who I believe can further develop their skills as writers through courses which the PET can hopefully fund.

We got several great reviews for the book, including this one from Jimmy McGovern, writer of the prison drama *Time* and prison visitor for several decades: 'It's not easy to get ANYTHING done in a prison. To get something of this quality done is simply miraculous. It's a tremendous achievement.'

Two years have now passed since I decided to run a competition for the prisoners at the start of the first lockdown. Many of the men whose work was in the booklet have continued to write. One is doing a degree in creative writing through the Open University, two are doing other distance-learning creative writing courses and another is doing a foundation course in journalism. With encouragement, one of the first writers and illustrators to give me his work has taken to entering his poetry into competitions, where he frequently wins prizes. I regularly read their work and see their talent and confidence growing. Several have moved on to other prisons, where I hope they are continuing to write and to study. One contributor, who was transferred out, was kind enough to write and send me the sequel to the first part of his story, which finished on a real 'cliffhanger'. Readers of the booklets have asked me about the character of Finagnon, and I have been able to give them the second instalment. When I am on the wings visiting distance learners, I am often given poetry and other writing, which is usually impressive work. I just wish I was in a position to do another collection.

Most of the prisoners I work with are tenacious people who have their own plans for rehabilitation despite serving life sentences with many years left to serve. They don't take drugs. They want to use the meagre opportunities for higher education in our prison to get qualifications, and do it despite the many obstacles in place which prevent this from happening. They have jobs as cleaners, care orderlies or in the prison kitchens. They are probably not typical of the general prison population. They work extremely hard in order to get good grades despite not being able to contact tutors directly if they don't understand something. They do not have any access to the internet facilities available to students on the outside. They could and should be a much bigger group than they are. The extra problems that COVID-19 created in terms of being unable to hand in assessments or contact me with any issues made this even more difficult. Even delivering course material created enormous problems during lockdowns. Their determination to succeed at studying has been relentless, and I am greatly impressed by them.

The COVID-19 experience was for many prisoners a very frightening time. As one prisoner told me at the very start of the pandemic: "Everyone hates us, we're all going to die and nobody will care." As the pandemic went on, there was a real sense from many of the prisoners that they were 'in it together' with the people on the outside. I think this came across in their writing.

I have always felt that one of the strengths of this collection of writing is that it gives a positive insight into prisoners at a very strange time, when they became even more vulnerable – still remaining so. Their work describes their regret and the misery that is daily life when you are denied basic freedoms. This is often misunderstood because if you have never been imprisoned, isolated and made totally vulnerable, you can't properly understand what this means, especially for those who incarcerated for many years.

When people know I work in a prison, they often tell me that it can't be that bad, because most prisoners have televisions; in other words, it's 'a cushy number'. Maybe, now we have all had experience of several lockdowns, it is easier to imagine that watching TV loses its appeal pretty quickly. Life without access to friends and family, without the freedom to access the places we want to be, isn't the easy experience that the media often presents.

To end on a positive, every now and again someone asks if the booklet is still available, and I am able to get them a copy knowing that another donation will go to the PET and this will help a prisoner somewhere get on a course. The collection of writing in this chapter is only a fraction of what came from the overall project, representing the considerable creativity that exists inside the prison walls.

Painted rainbows

I know it's easy to see the negative impact of Covid-19,
But over the past few months this is what I've seen.

I saw courageous NHS staff risking their lives selflessly,
Day after day, humbly saving the helpless relentlessly.

I saw our people clap for carers every single Thursday,
I saw all colours, creeds and classes shown they're equally worthy.

I saw people give love and compassion in abundance without the power of touch,
I saw our communities coming together, giving so much.

I believe these testing times have also been a lesson,
To love one another, see life as a blessing.

And slowly, but surely, as time passes and all the pain goes,
We'll see the beauty and significance in our children's rainbows.

BG

COVID-19 diary by Lee F

March 2020 will be engraved in our minds forever for lots of people, mums, dads children, grandparents, along with close friends.

On 16th March, at HMP Manchester, Strangeways, I finished work, collected my meal and went behind my door to chill out and watch the news – in particular, 'Breaking News'. On almost every channel I went through were the news reporters and journalists feeding the nation about the new public health crisis – Covid 19, a highly infectious virus.

Italy was the hotspot destination that we were seeing, all their hospitals overwhelmed with the mystery virus that nobody knew very much about, let alone the doctors and nurses. This was the talk of the workplace amongst the lads during the week on our break-times. Everyone was expecting the prison to go into lockdown, in line with the outside world.

My work is on the Industrial Cleaning course, as an orderly, training lads on the various aspects of cleaning and on different electrical equipment like buffing machines which a lot of lads in jail will be familiar with as a lot of cons have done the course to enable them to become cleaners on the wings. I am also Bio-Hazard trained to clean any kind of body fluids, blood, spit urine and faeces.

This was a great job at one point as we got five pounds for a minor clean and 10 for a major clean and was a way of earning some extra money.

Friday 19th March.

An officer came to the BICS office to speak to my boss and the lads. He asked me if I would be a 'Covid Cleaner' so I asked what it entailed and he gave me a brief rundown. The Governor requested Covid Cleaners to set up on all wings 7 days a week. I said 'no'. I wasn't willing to leave my job as I had worked there for three and a half years. I had that loyalty to my instructor and boss. That's when my boss said 'No! Go for it. When it's done your job will be here for you.' So I said 'I'II do it!' And the money was good, £25 a week, to this day, 8th October. Seven months down the line, I'm still a Covid Cleaner, continuously spraying and wiping doors, gates and locks.

Tuesday 23rd March.

I got up as usual. 7am – Kettle on, washed, brushed my teeth, made my bed, made my morning coffee and switched on ITV. Piers Morgan was on about Covid. 8am is unlock time but we weren't unlocked. I thought either it's a staff meeting or maybe an incident within the jail that has delayed things. 8.30am – I muted my TV and you could hear a pin drop on the Wing. So I carried on watching morning news and every channel was on the Covid outbreak.

It was a world-wide pandemic. Airplanes grounded, pubs ordered to shut, restaurants, cafes and nonessential shops all to close. The world has officially gone CRAZY with this virus! 9.20am someone shouted out of their door, 'Everyone, check your phone credit.' So I pressed 118 for my balance and there was £5 on top of the sixteen pounds I had. I knew then Strangeways was officially on total lockdown.

Officers went door to door letting us all know, 'We're on lockdown lads and we are doing control un-locks for medication.' I thought, that's why my boss told me to accept the Covid job. Maybe he knew we were going into lockdown but couldn't say. I will make a point of asking him when I see him!

As a cleaning orderly, I usually give advice to people, Cons and staff, and I must admit, I do have a bit of OCD, my attention to detail does stand out, I'm told. 10.00am, my door opened with Mr S, the Cleaning officer, who asked me to go to the 1s landing so he could do a briefing with all the cleaners and Covid cleaners. He asked us to clean all the doors, locks, handles, flaps, the kiosk machines, etc. then issued all Covid cleaners with buckets, clothes and gloves and we were on our way.

The days passed, with Boris and Co. doing their daily appearances on the TV, newspapers telling us how so many people were dying. I wouldn't be human if it didn't stress me out a bit!!? When that door shut, I thought, this is real and serious shit.

For 27 years I've been coming to jail and I've seen a few changes in that time. From slop out to having a sink and toilet in the cell. From the Strangeways riots in the early 90s, three to four sharing a cell, to a single cell. But the big one, for those who can remember was from having a Robert's Rambler radio with big square PP9 battery, to the whole of the prison system having a TV in our cells for the first time (all down to the Strangeways Riots).

In those years, I've done many, many lockdowns, where the Northern Search Team would come into a jail and go through all the wings, workshops, etc. but they would usually last 3 days maximum. This is the first time there has been a lockdown like this and we are now 7 months into it! Wow! No visits, no gym, only urgent health care appointments, no dentists, no work, twenty-three and a half hours bang-up unless you are a servery worker or cleaner. I honestly feel for all those lads and girls who I think are 'suffering in silence behind that door.'

They say that mental health cases in the community are going through the roof. They have a bit more freedom and can still do some of what they want though. In jail you get a 5-minute shower and half an hour's exercise and that is your daily routine. I see lads who are struggling more and more, lads that don't have family and friends for support and have no money to buy essentials. The prison gives you £2.50 plus £2.50 Covid pay. £5 a week, an absolute joke. The jail should pay lads a living wage to get by without getting into debt. A lot of lads are sitting behind their doors with nothing and I think that is wrong. No regime, no work, no visits is bad enough for some but all that with no finances, it is an even bigger worry.

You've got to give them credit for how they've conducted themselves through this pandemic. Prison is hard enough to cope with without all this. Now staff are going off sick and isolating, it is having a knock-on effect.

Visits and purple visits are now running. Each wing has their set days and times and there are strict rules to follow. Purple visits have been a good thing too. Now we're are in the second wave of the virus. Winter is coming and Christmas. This is a tough time for everyone outside and inside the prison.

Strangeways has had low confirmed cases of Covid and that has been down to all the Covid cleaning on the wings and the testing by Southampton University's research team, where lads could volunteer to be tested over a nine-week period. There are cases amongst the officers and even a governor was sent home. Strangeways does take this virus seriously and everyone's health seriously from what I know and see, and this gives me a bit of reassurance. Life still goes on behind these walls and gates and cameras. So, everyone must stay strong and remain focused.

Strange times – Strangeways – Covid

> I'm catching a tan between the bars, hah, hah,
> My head is spinning with emotional scars,
> Imagination drifts off, I'm on planet mars,
> I can hear the engines from the passing cars,
> No longer in a cloud and smoking spice,
> I got a little help from the drugs team, DARS,
> The coronavirus has took this world by storm,
> A deadly pandemic has just been born,
> So many families stricken and torn,
> The devil is blowing his triumphant horn,
> Will mankind ever see a new dawn?
> May family lay together upon our bright green lawn.
> These really are some weird, strange times,
> I'm never lost for words, but I'm struggling with rhymes,
> I should be at home, why did I commit such pointless crimes?
> My pain is echoing throughout these lines,
> Without my children, nothing binds,
> Crazy dreams with so many signs.
> I'm spitting real life issues in all my grimes.
> The NHS staff are overrun, this beautiful world has just lost its fun.
> My Dad has got cancer, I'm thinking of you, your son.
> So worried about my sister and mum,
> I will not cry, the tears won't come.
> I need to be strong and stop acting so dumb.
> Inmates are going crazy in their cells.
> Now we're experiencing two nightmare hells,
> Shout for help, I'm hearing bells,
> The officer's footsteps and so many yells.
> God only knows when I'll see my kids again,
> Just keep calm and have a little count to ten.
> But I want to explode and scream 'When? When? When?'
> Even the strongest crack and we're all grown men.
> Hearing my family when I pick up the phone,
> My daughter cries, 'Daddy you're all alone',

I can't sound upset, I can't break my tone.
Learning courage is something that's shown.
I need to be a king upon my throne.
'Don't go outside', instead I moan.
I'm missing so much and my children have grown.
There is definitely no place like my loving home.
Watching the news just fills me with dread,
I close my eyes and lay on my bed.
So many people are already dead,
I flick the channels and watch a movie instead,
But the fear is there and I start seeing red,
My stomach does some somersaults, whilst I'm being fed,
So many images flashing inside my head,
Panic kicks in and turns me wild,
I'm feeling afraid, like a lost, lonely child,
I need some fresh air, something mild,
Punching numbers already dialled.
When will the doctors ever find a cure?
The streets will be quiet until they are sure,
Something positive, something pure.
How much longer? How much more?
How long am I spending behind this door?
This evil virus is killing the rich and the poor.
The sick need to fight,
This world will unite,
Together as one, the future is bright,
This isn't the end of our human light,
I pray to God in bed at night,
Look into the stars and never lose sight,
I can see the tops of some trees,
Gently blowing in the springtime breeze,
A 106-year-old woman has just fought off the disease,
Now that's the spirit, yes, yes, please,
I salute, I'm on my knees,
Praying for Great Britain and all the people over the seas.

GG

Actually, we're here – PR

When growing up, I had read almost constantly from when I first learnt how. Whilst I had my own bookcase, which was overflowing with all sorts of genres and authors – Lewis, Kipling, Cooper, Blyton, Garner; above all others, I loved the stories about (and from) the Middle Ages. *The Canterbury*

Tales, the sagas of Beowulf, King Arthur and Robin Hood always kept me enthralled, but my mother insisted that I also spent time outside. (Apparently, going around the world in eighty days with Phileas Fogg didn't count.) So what was a six-year old boy to do but recreate and re-enact the battles from days of yore?

I was Launcelot, dueling Gawain before racing to protect Arthur from Mordred. I was outwitting the dastardly Sheriff of Nottingham, all for the love of Maid Marian. Dragons, knights, brigands and rogues all then defeated by a squeaky voiced chevalier.

Once lockdown had begun and my beloved and my beloved family felt a million miles away, memories of these freedoms and follies, those idle hours of decades gone by, they are all I have left.

Over six months down the line, I've been in quarantine, isolation (and exile). I cannot yet see my fiancée, and its longer still since from when I last saw my family. Days with no routine are the norm and no routine is, for me, like having my body vigorously rubbed with a cheese grater.

At first I was in a different prison but one Monday the door opened and the call came. Thirty minutes to pack up and ship out. So the last bastion of normality – the friendships there are now taken too. There's just me left. We're not in Kansas anymore.

HMP Manchester, Strangeways of old. It's got a hell of a reputation. Blood pressure, diastolic and systolic, is through the roof. Pulse is beating out a samba rhythm. In quarantine, surrounded by the vulnerables and gen. pop. and the incessant shouting, the mating call of the lesser-spotted idiot. Officers who are overstretched, understaffed and less than two weeks into the job in some cases. They're doing everything they can and they really are helpful as possible but they have no time. You hear all the raging and anger over the least things and you wonder if someone's bought a one-way ticket to 'Stabby Town'. The longest fourteen days of my life are over – it's time for the residential wings.

Isolation is pervasive. I feel, for twenty-two hours a day, that I'm drowning in fresh air. Alone, whether you like it or not. No visits, no consistency, garbled communication but the staff shortages mean everything is hit and miss. If you're lucky, you work but if you're forgotten, you're high and dry.

We're told to 'Chill out' by the officers but when you're caged like a beast for days on end, you simply *cannot* relax. Stress levels are higher than Everest and the wing is crackling as if it's charged with static. You hear people turn on themselves. Funding cuts mean no counselling service. Our very essence is being routed, it's a massacre of humanity. Can we see the light at the end of the tunnel? Not really, unless it's some pimply Herbert with a flamethrower.

Someone infinitely wiser than I am said, 'No man is an island.' We're on islands now but they are going the way of Atlantis, floundering and sinking. Life is presently akin to being rescued by the Lusitania when you were aboard the Titanic. The forgotten, we are the forgotten. We're calling out to you, through vocal cords unused to asking for help, but we don't know if there's anyone there who will hear our silent screams. Even if there were, we're the lowest priority. If we're heard, who will care? Who would come? No man is an island, sure, but for whom the bell tolls (sorry, that's an awful pun) is we here. We're here. We're still human. Remember us, before you become us.

COVID-19 in the 'big house' – MM

I was sentenced to six years at Liverpool Crown Courts in 2019. I had only just lost my dad with COPD. Arriving at every prisoner's five-star abode, which is situated on Hornby Road, it was no different from any other previous time, other than this one was in March 2020. I was located on the five's landing, cell 7, Wing A.

It all started with the 'lunatics lantern', as my late father would call it. I saw the news about this devastating infection that was sweeping through the world and killing people on a huge level, every day, more and more. I remember thinking if my dad was still alive, he would be witnessing this terrible infection. In a way, I was glad he died when he did, with me and him in the community. At his age, 72, and with his complications, asthma, COPD this infection would no doubt have killed him. I believe this.

As I watched the news on the TV my thoughts drifted off to the bulletins of the disasters of 9/11 and Princess Diana, then back to the present. Watching the news, I felt disbelief. Is this out of a film? Is this the end of the world? It was written that man will destroy and this is man-made?

I was working the Liverpool prison in the laundry as a keyworker providing clean materials for other prisons in the country when I heard that people who were infected overseas are now being flown to the UK to John Lennon Airport, then police escorted them to Arrow Park Hospital in the Wirral. I couldn't believe it! My God, are these people in government real? Can't they see its going to be even worse?

Then, that's when I get sick with flu-like symptoms. At first, I was scared to say anything to anyone and after some thought I went to the medication hatch on the wing and saw an M.O. to tell her. She immediately said, 'Go and isolate Mark,' which I did.

After I told an officer I was self-isolating, he came back to my cell and placed on my door a big sticker stating, 'This prisoner is isolating – 7 days – Caution'. I was throwing up in my toilet and my head was banging, coughing and phlegm up my nose which was also running. It was like the flu, but the worst flu I'd ever had. Shivering in my bed, thoughts ran through my head. What if I don't wake up? The thought of dying in prison was so scary. The more I watched the news and the death toll rising, the more I was getting depressed, frightened, worried and upset. I just wouldn't watch the news anymore. Also, the fact that this was all new to our world. People just didn't understand it and that frightens us humans.

A prison officer opened my observation panel. With a mask, visor, gloves and PPE on, he said, 'Stand at the back of the cell, Mark.' This was for my food to be placed inside my cell. I felt embarrassed and upset. I felt like a leper and this made me more frightened, to see the way my fellow humans were behaving towards me.

By the third day of my isolation, I realized that I couldn't taste my food and I couldn't smell anything. (Disappointing for the palate, even though prison food isn't very nice.) Then I was visited by Health Care staff who gave me an examination, antibiotics and off he went. I took them straight away to get them into my system.

I thought of my mum, dad and brother, who had all passed away. How must they have felt before they died? I had to expect, if it was my time, to take it like a man and not be that scared. At least I'd be with my loved ones. This was so upsetting at the time but I woke up the next day and then the next day. After the sixth day of isolating I slowly started to feel better. No more coughing, I just felt so, so weak, weak as a kitten, no energy whatsoever.

Finally, on the seventh day my door was unlocked like everyone else's. Then all the lads were asking, and the prison officers also, 'You OK mate?'

It's a lucky escape that I had. I lived through this time. Who knows why I'm still here? You can ask yourself is it because I've got faith? A strong body? Medication I was given? Or was it because my family were watching over me, sending me out spiritual healing? Whatever saved my life, I'm here to tell the story of the Big House during Lockdown Covid-19.

13

Conclusion: The Lessons – Recovery and Pandemic Preparedness

Christopher Kay and Stephen Case

Understanding and responding to pandemics in criminal justice: the need for a holistic approach

In the introduction to this collection, we introduced the notion that it is important to understand the impact of COVID-19 on the criminal justice system in England and Wales holistically. We argued that to understand the ways in which the pandemic changed the facilitation and experience of crime and justice, we needed to see not just the ways it effected the functioning of individual agencies but also the interconnections between these agencies, and that this is where real learning around recovery and future pandemic preparedness can be obtained. We believe that the contents of this collection make a strong argument for this approach.

Throughout the chapters, reference has been made to the interrelated impacts of criminal justice agencies on the operation and experience of crime and justice during the pandemic. Multiple chapters referenced the closure and increased backlog of cases going through the criminal courts as causing considerable concerns further down the line. Chapter 4 showed that the closure of courts during the first lockdowns not only created a backlog of cases, but also made it difficult for some of the key objectives of probation work to be undertaken. While this was a concern on a practical level, particularly in relation to the long-term impact of probation supervision, the chapter also argued that it could potentially pose a threat to the legitimacy of the service. Should a client breach their community order, the closure of courts meant that returning a case to court would simply not be possible, reducing practitioners' abilities to enforce sentences. Legitimacy was also raised in Chapter 3 in relation to portal justice.

Chapter 5 again raised concerns about the impact of court closures and case backlogs on the prison system. The chapter recognized that the increasing backlog of cases meant fewer people were being given prison sentences and that this, combined with the natural outflow of residents at the end of their sentences, allowed for a reduction in the prison population. This raises a number of concerns. First, the situation with the court system meant that individuals on remand were spending much longer in custody than was previously the case. This would be, at best, troubling during non-pandemic times, but the situation across the prison estate with the Exceptional Regime Management Plan (ERMP) and later COVID-19 regulations also meant that residents were spending considerably longer in cells with little in the way of purposeful activity to occupy them (as noted in Chapter 5 and addressed in Chapters 11 and 12). This subsequently led to increasing concerns regarding the mental health and well-being of residents during this time. The time taken to get a case to court was referred to in Chapter 8 as 'one of the most significant impacts of the government responses to COVID-19', causing a considerable emotional impact on sex workers and often compounding pre-existing mental health conditions among this group.

Second, the increased length of remand periods disproportionately affected residents from minority ethnic communities, who were more likely to be remanded to custody awaiting trial. The impact of imprisonment during the pandemic was also discussed in Chapter 4, recognizing that the situation in the prison system may have shaped practitioner decision making around recall and enforcement. Chapter 6 examined the impact of court, custodial and community COVID-19 policies on justice-involved children and identified many of the same issues in the youth justice system that have affected adult criminal justice provisions. The chapter argued that COVID-19-related policies in criminal justice were not only a risk to the development of a Child First approach to youth justice but also prevented children from accessing their rights.

It was also noted in multiple chapters that frontline workers found themselves taking on more responsibilities owing to the fact that support services they would usually call on were closed. Chapter 3 noted that the changing relationship with partner agencies represented a fundamental shift in police operations. The chapter argued that the police service had cultivated external relationships to ensure that issues such as domestic violence, drug dependency, mental health and homelessness could receive the appropriate support, but the initial lockdown periods saw the majority of these services close their doors (at least physically), therefore changing this dynamic. As noted in Chapter 2, 'police officers needed to manufacture ways of handling complex cases without the same levels of support'. Chapter 8 also highlighted concerns that frontline workers were adapting their roles as a result of a considerable number of outreach services closing due to the pandemic and then failing to reopen or simply losing funding. This created a range of safeguarding issues which frontline workers and charity organizations needed to work around.

Alongside the more direct connections among criminal justice agencies discussed in this collection, multiple core themes emerged surrounding notions such as the function and implementation of COVID-19 regulations, the facilitation of justice during lockdown periods, the pre-existing state of criminal justice and the calls for innovation during this period. Each of these, we argue, further our call for a more holistic understanding of crime and justice during COVID-19, especially if we are to recover from this and prepare for any future pandemics.

Exacerbating pre-existing issues: resilience and preparedness

One of the core themes that emerged throughout the collection is that while COVID-19 created some new issues (in relation to the development of a testing infrastructure and the rapid need for agile working), it mostly exacerbated issues that had existed long before the start of the pandemic. Every agency within the criminal justice system has seen years of budget cuts, reduced resources and periods of considerable transformation. By 2018, police numbers had dropped to their lowest since the 1980s. Such was the concern that in 2021, the Conservative government pledged to recruit an additional 20,000 police officers by 2023 (Criminal Justice Joint Inspection, 2021). At the time of writing, roughly 9,000 additional police officers have been recruited. But even if the target is reached, numbers will still be lower than the total police workforce in 2010. A similar theme was evident in relation to the court system (Chapter 3). The 2018 annual report by the Lord Chief Justice identified significant issues with regards to recruitment and staff morale. The report left a damning indictment of the condition of court buildings in England and Wales, stating that 'the public should not be expected to visit dilapidated buildings and neither is it reasonable to expect staff or judges to work in conditions which would not be tolerated elsewhere' (Lord Chief Justice, 2018: 5). It also noted that 'the backlog of urgent maintenance needed to ensure that all our buildings are in a decent condition will only be reduced by the injection of substantial funds' (Lord Chief Justice, 2018: 5). The probation service was facing re-nationalization after emerging from a prolonged and tumultuous period under the Transforming Rehabilitation agenda, which, since its introduction in 2013, had caused significant damage in terms of increased numbers of serious further offences, reduced staffing levels and threats to the legitimacy of the service (see Chapter 4). The prison service was equally experiencing budget cuts and a dilapidating prison estate. As discussed in Chapter 5, the prison estate was considerably overcrowded and unsanitary, having been in a state of increasing disrepair before the introduction of COVID-19, with an annual attrition of 500 prison cells per year due to the level of disrepair and an estimated £900 million maintenance backlog across the estate.

As a result, the criminal justice system lacked the resilience to be able to deal with the pandemic as effectively as it perhaps could have. Davies et al (2020) examined the resilience of a range of public services before the start of the pandemic and included three agencies in the criminal justice system: the police, the court system and the prison service. Their report identifies concerns across all three agencies in relation to preparedness but, perhaps more important, the resilience needed to undertake the implementation of COVID-19 policies. It also noted that there were considerable concerns about the performance of these agencies and that buildings and equipment were worse 'on the eve of the crisis than ... in 2010' (Davies et al, 2020: 11).

This context was, perhaps unsurprisingly, identified as a significant issue by each of the chapters in this collection. As such, when thinking about the recovery of the criminal justice system post COVID-19, we must also think about not just restoring the system to where it was before the pandemic but also *increasing* the levels of resilience across the system as a whole. Such an approach makes sense in relation to future pandemic preparedness as well as the effective day-to-day running of the system. The first lesson to be taken from this collection, then, is:

1. Considerable investment needs to be placed in the criminal justice system in England and Wales in relation to staffing, buildings, equipment and infrastructure if we are to be better placed to deal with pandemics in the future.

The importance of frontline workers

Almost every chapter in the collection recognized the importance, speed and innovation of frontline workers in implementing COVID-19 policies and supporting service users through this process. Chapter 2 identified how, when faced with new COVID-19 regulations, the challenges of policing during lockdown and reduced support from external partners, frontline police needed to quickly find new ways to approach police work. Chapter 4 asserted that frontline probation staff continued to support people on probation, alongside their colleagues and local communities, almost in spite of the pandemic and the related regulations which had made probation work difficult. Chapter 5 highlighted the importance of prison staff not only in implementing regime management policies to reduce transmission of the virus, but also in communicating these changes quickly and effectively to residents, thereby reducing stress and seemingly gaining support for the measures (for a while at least). Chapter 6 recognized the speed and innovative action that occurred within YOTs to ensure that there remained an element of contact between young people and their workers, recognizing the importance of such contact in maintaining engagement. Chapter 8 praised the rapid efforts of charitable organizations, such as National Ugly Mugs, and sex work support projects which 'acted as emergency services during the lockdowns and those in-between times when life was not "normal"' (Chapter 8). Chapter 10 found that while the shift to remote working affected the amount of in-person contact that could be offered in the training of probation officers, the teaching team on the PQiP programme made student support a priority during this time, providing additional opportunities for student–lecturer interaction as well as online spaces for students to learn from each other. Finally, the work presented in 'The view from the Inside' reflects the key role that frontline workers had in supporting residents during the implementation of COVID-19 regulations (also discussed in Chapter 5).

While it is absolutely right to praise the work of frontline staff who were responsible for implementing COVID-19 policy during this time, the chapters also raised concerns in this regard. The spillover of work and study into family life was recognized in multiple chapters in the collection. The views of frontline police in Chapter 2 highlighted the emotional impact of doing the job during the pandemic and how this carried over into family life, affecting people who hadn't necessarily "signed up for emergency work", This chapter evidenced tensions both in relation to officers potentially bringing the virus home with them and in their having to manage the public's stress head on, with the perception they were "the only visible service out there". For frontline staff who were now required to work from home, further well-being concerns began to arise. For instance, it was noted in Chapter 4, that the move to working from home for probation workers meant there was less space to detach from the 'emotional dirty work' (Ward and McMurray, 2020). Participants in the chapter noted that there was no safe space to switch off as home had now become the office, and this blurred line also resulted in longer working hours and needing to work flexibly around family commitments, all of which added to household tensions.

Other concerns were raised in relation to frontline workers throughout the collection. It was suggested that frontline workers were, at times, left to deal with issues on the ground with limited guidance from above, ironing out the creases in COVID-19 policy and practice while it was being implemented. Further well-being concerns were raised for frontline workers whose roles were essentially expanded due to the reduced availability of external support services. As noted in Chapter 8, for example, 'support work turned immediately to assisting with welfare benefit claims and supporting women in domestic violence situations, as they were forced to be home with their abuser'.

Aside from these specific tensions identified in the chapters in this collection, it should also be remembered that the pandemic hit a service with limited levels of resilience. Frontline workers were responding to the pandemic within the context of increased workloads and considerable staff shortages due to underfunding, but also sickness and precautionary isolation periods. It is also important to recognize that a pandemic represents an extended and ongoing emergency. At the time of writing, the world is well into the second year of living with COVID-19. The concerns raised in this collection have not only been considerable, but are also long term. As such, attention must be paid to how these can be managed, both now and in any future pandemics.

There are multiple lessons that can be taken from this discussion, both in relation to recovery from the COVID-19 pandemic and general pandemic preparedness moving forward. This collection has also demonstrated the following:

2. Frontline workers need greater access to both organizational support and peer support and communities of coping, particularly during periods of online or remote working.
3. There needs to be a greater level of investment in both staff support services and recruitment in order to boost the resilience of services, both now and moving forward.

The implementation of digital technology: virtual justice?

The use of technology in an attempt to reduce the impact of the pandemic on both frontline workers and service users was evident throughout the collection. Whereas some agencies had already been implementing technological developments in their services, such as the improvements in digital infrastructure around case management and virtual hearings (Chapter 3), others required a little more development, such as with the use of virtual visits for people in prison (Chapter 5). In others, technology allowed for remote supervision, ensuring that probation workers were still able to deliver some form of community supervision, particularly when a range of other community order requirements and enforcement measures (unpaid work, breach hearings and so on) could not be completed (Chapter 4). Technology was also utilized to develop good practice in youth justice. Chapter 6 noted that digital media was utilized not only to facilitate virtual contact between young offenders and their family members and support workers, but also to promote engagement through activities like online quizzes and lessons delivered via online videos.

While the shift to remote and online ways of working certainly has its advantages and has been shown to be effective in a range of settings, the chapters in this collection have also noted a degree of caution when considering whether remote working and digital technologies have a permanent place in a post-COVID-19 world, and the precautions that should be taken if they do.

First, a range of procedural concerns have been raised in several chapters in this collection. It was noted in Chapter 3 that there were often practical difficulties in facilitating virtual court hearings. On a purely practical level, sometimes the technology simply does not work, thereby restricting engagement. When it is working, however, there are other concerns that need to be taken into account. Virtual hearings have been shown to reduce interactions between court participants, to change the level of communication between defendants and legal advocates, and to preclude court users from understanding processes and outcomes. Chapter 3 also highlighted, in a similar way to that discussed earlier, that the use of technology in this way has the potential to blur boundaries; only in this case, as McKay (2022) argues, the boundaries being blurred may be those between prison and court, which runs the risk of court work being shaped by the contextual environment of the defendant.

Similar concerns around virtual court hearings were expressed in Chapter 6, with specific reference to virtual hearings with children. In this chapter, it was argued that such hearings run the risk of eroding the rights of children, under the UNCRC (United Nations, 1989), to fully participate in court proceedings, since this implies a good level of understanding throughout the process which may not be possible through virtual methods. The chapter argued that childrens' lack of understanding could result in them becoming detached and unresponsive in terms of their input at hearings, effectively denying their right to be heard.

While it has been suggested that the use of technology could increase service user engagement with practitioners and frontline workers, the reverse can also be true. Chapter 4 noted that remote methods of communication made it more difficult for practitioners to achieve the engagement required to bring about compliance with COVID-19 regulations. The introduction of virtual visits in prisons (Chapter 5), albeit a welcome introduction, was fraught with technological difficulties and delayed implementation, which impacted levels of engagement among residents in the beginning. Chapter 6 identified examples of good practice utilizing technology to promote continued engagement among children, but also recognized that the move to digital contact made it more difficult to contact some children. Further still, it was argued that the use of digital technologies in these cases had the potential to reduce the child's opportunity to disclose abuse, particularly if their contacts were in earshot of an abusive adult.

Finally, the chapters in this collection also raised issues around digital poverty and access to resources which would allow continued engagement with services. While practitioners and frontline staff had to navigate new systems and developing online infrastructures at the same time as trying to do their jobs, service users also needed access to and an understanding of these new methods of contacting key services. All of this had the potential to cause considerable anxiety and also a range of safeguarding issues. For probation officers in training (Chapter 10), there was considerable anxiety around not only the use of online infrastructures but also learning in a digital environment. Such anxieties potentially hindered the levels of learning that could otherwise have been achieved. For the service users discussed in Chapter 8, it was noted that there has been an increase in online modalities of sex work due to poverty and (in this instance) the pandemic was seen to push more women into sex work due to their financial difficulties. This, however, was only a viable source of income for those who had the particular skill sets, resources and experience to earn money sustainably and, importantly, safely. It is argued in the chapter that 'those who do not have access to technology, permanent Wi-Fi, and an address and bank account for a mobile phone contract, for instance, are prevented from using safer ways of selling sexual services'. The issue of digital poverty was also noted in this chapter as problematic for practitioners, as street-based workers often did not have phones, making contact difficult.

While the increased use of digital technologies has proven to be beneficial in allowing agencies to continue working with service users during the pandemic, there is cause for caution as we begin to recover. The switch to digital technology is not a panacea to an inability to engage in person. Not only are there issues with regards to procedural inequalities, engagement and safeguarding, but also the fundamental nature and operation of justice is changed. As such, there are a few things that need to be considered if technology is to be implemented in work on crime and justice as we being to emerge from the COVID-19 pandemic, and in preparation for any future pandemics. We now know that:

4. Greater investment in infrastructures is needed to ensure technology can be utilized reliably.
5. Virtual justice is not applicable in all cases. More thinking needs to be done around when and for whom such technologies are utilized.
6. More investment in relation to digital poverty, providing service users with access to technology and training on how to use it safely, will allow for greater engagement with services and more effective safeguarding for service users.

It is important to note here that in-person interaction remains the priority, and criminal justice agencies and services should seek to maintain this wherever possible. As we begin to recover from the COVID-19 pandemic, and with a thought to future pandemic preparedness, investment in digital infrastructures in the ways outlined in this chapter will allow for continued engagement moving forward.

Moving on from COVID-19: some key concerns

At the time of writing, it seems as though we are beginning to emerge from the COVID-19 pandemic. The majority of public services are returning to their version of pre-pandemic normality, though they remain bruised from the pandemic experience. As this emergent recovery continues, we need to start thinking about the legacy of COVID-19 and what this teaches us not only about how we can be better prepared for the next pandemic, but also about the nature of crime and justice more generally.

When the pandemic first hit, the majority of the criminal justice agencies discussed in the first part of this collection resorted to a base-level risk management approach. This was largely due to the limited infrastructure for remote engagement at the time and the reduction in available support services. While this is understandable to a degree, with the notion of risk management being pervasive throughout criminal justice, such an approach will leave a lasting legacy that must be considered. It is unclear at this point what long-term impact the pandemic will have had on service users, but it is clear that there needs to be a concerted focus on rehabilitation and service user engagement and support moving forward in order to mitigate against the deleterious effects of two years of restrictive COVID-19 regulations. Broader concerns around resources and resilience remain. A recent report by the Criminal Justice Joint Inspection (2022: 25) notes that 'the system is getting by because of an artificially supressed level of activity and reduced performance management and quality expectations'. Unfortunately, it would appear that the more punitive arm of criminal justice is once again gaining strength. The prison population has topped 80,000 for the first time in two years, and the Conservative government has launched an expansive programme of prison building, which is expected to increase capacity by 20,000 places by 2025. In March 2022, it was also announced that 30 Nightingale courtrooms will be extended into 2023 in order to tackle the backlog of cases going through the court system, a move that, alongside an increase in police numbers, will certainly see more individuals pass through court, prison and probation systems which are yet to fully recover, if full recovery is even possible.

If we are to avoid negative long-term impacts on the COVID-19 generation of criminal justice-experienced people, recover from this pandemic and prepare for any that come in the future, there needs to be a system-wide effort to promote successful engagement and rehabilitation for people with convictions. Yet, as it stands, such an approach does not seem to be forthcoming. Instead, we can see each agency within the overarching criminal justice system working towards their own recovery. The Criminal Justice Joint Inspection report shares these concerns, noting that 'without a coordinated whole-system plan, progress is likely to be disjointed. Given the nature of the Criminal Justice System, as one service recovers, that is likely to push issues into the next, and that service may not have recovered sufficiently to cope' (2022: 25). This collection demonstrates the need for a more holistic understanding of criminal justice if we are to work successfully towards COVID-19 pandemic recovery and future pandemic preparedness.

References

Criminal Justice Joint Inspection (2021) *Impact of the Pandemic on the Criminal Justice System: A Joint View of the Criminal Justice Chief Inspectors on the Criminal Justice System's Response to Covid-19*, [online] Available from: www.justiceinspectorates.gov.uk/hmicfrs/wp-content/uploads/2021-01-13-State-of-nation.pdf

Criminal Justice Joint Inspection (2022) *The Impact of the COVID-19 Pandemic on the Criminal Justice System – a Progress Report*, [online] Available from: www.justiceinspectorates.gov.uk/cjji/wp-content/uploads/sites/2/2022/05/CJ-Covid-19-recovery-progress-report-web-2022.pdf

Davies, N., Atkins, G., Guerin, B. and Sodhi, S. (2020) *How Fit Were Public Services for Coronavirus?* London: Institute for Government.

Lord Chief Justice (2018) *The Lord Chief Justice's Report 2018*, London: Judicial Office.

McKay, C. (2022) 'Digital justice and video links: connecting and conflating courtroom and carceral space', in K. Duncanson and E. Henderson (eds) *Courthouse Architecture, Design and Social Justice*, Abingdon: Routledge, pp 191–221.

United Nations (1989) *United Nations Convention on the Rights of the Child*, [online] Available from: www.ohchr.org/sites/default/files/crc.pdf

Ward, J. and McMurray, R. (2020) *The Dark Side of Emotional Labour*, Abingdon: Routledge.

Index

References to tables appear in **bold** type.
References to endnotes show both the
page number and the note number (127n7).

A
adult entertainment platforms 154
adverse childhood experiences 110
alcohol 180–2
All-Wales Youth Offending Strategy 109
anti-'lockdown' protests 2
Article 3 of the UNCRC 114
arts-based interventions 217
attention deficit hyperactivity disorder (ADHD) 114, 116
audiovisual technology 46

B
basic command unit (BCU) 15
Basis Yorkshire 160
Black Lives Matter (BLM) 2, 138, 141, 220
Black Swan, The (Taleb) 30n2
blended learning approach 192, 207
Box Project at HMP Parc 219–41
British Crime Survey (BCS) 168
broadcast justice 42–5
broader sex work community 159
Buckland, Robert 94
'business as usual' approach 202

C
Capability Maturity Model (CMM) 13
Capability Maturity Model Integration (CMMI) 14
case fatality rates (CFRs) 80
Certificate in Qualification of Social Work (CQSW) 192
charitable organizations 258
'child criminalization' 116
Child First
 approach 109
 justice **110**
 thinking 119
child poverty 110
Coates, S. 96
Coker, R. 80

collective in sensemaking 18–20
common law jurisdictions 41
'communities of coping' 200
community-based peer sex worker organizations 151
Conservative Party 94, 95
'constructive innovations' 116
Contagious Diseases Act 1864 153
convenience sampling 194
Coronavirus Act 33, 41, 137, 139
coronavirus disease 19 (COVID-19) 1
Coronavirus (COVID-19): The impact on probation systems 190
counterterrorism legislation 50
court-based technology 37
Couzens, Wayne 2
COVID-19 11–12
 crime, justice and 4–7
 and drug trends (*see* drug trends)
 emergence 15
 enduring pains and gains of 124–6
 maturity 13–15
 pains and gains of 111–23
 pandemic on criminal courts 33–42
 police response during pandemic 24–9
 policing during 15
 Professional Qualification in Probation (PQiP) and (*see* Professional Qualification in Probation (PQiP))
 restrictions affecting, initial 110–11
 themes relating to emergence 16–24
COVID-19 National Framework for Prison Regimes and Services 5
CPS 43
'creeping abolitionism' 150
Crime and Disorder Act 1998 108
Crime Survey for England and Wales (CSEW) 168–70, 172
criminal justice
 pandemics in 2–4, 254–6

INDEX

policy 5, 99
system 2, 3, 32, 37, 41, 44, 92, 93, 97, 154, 158–9, 162, 163, 191, 210
Criminal Justice Act 2003 52
Criminal Justice Joint Inspection 38, 262, 263
Crown Prosecution Service 38
custody, COVID-19 in 86–7
  cohorting strategy 84–5
  delaying sentencing and release 92–3
  Exceptional Regime Management Plan (ERMP) 81–2
  pandemics in prison 76–80
  plugging 'epidemiological pump' 80–1
  population management strategy 82–3
  populist politics vs public health 93–5
  successes and areas for improvement 87–91
  supporting rehabilitation for 95–8

D

Dark Net trade 177
desistance-focused probation practice 60
'desistance paradigm' 60
digital poverty 117
  and communication 156–7
digital resource poverty 157
digital technologies 117, 259–62
Diploma in Probation Studies (DipPS) 192
Diploma in Social Work (DipSW) 192
distance-learning coordinator 244
domestic violence situations 155, 259
drug availability 173–6
drug distribution and enforcement responses 176–8
drug harms 182–4
drug indicators, relative stability of 172
drug-related poisonings 182
Drugs in the time of COVID 166
drug supply system 178
drug trends 166
  alcohol 180–2
  county lines 178–80
  drug availability 173–6
  drug distribution and enforcement responses 176–8
  drug harms 182–4
  national prevalence trends and other proxy measures 168–73

E

easy-to-manage learning materials 209
'emotional dirty work' 63, 258
emotional labour 60, 61
emotional literacy 60
end-to-end case management system 37, 45
'enforcement-driven mentality' 192
English Collective of Prostitutes (ECP) 153
'epidemiological pumps' 78, 81

Equality and Human Rights Commission 39
exceptional delivery model (EDM) 50, 52, 56, 59–61, 64, 69, 70, 190
Exceptional Regime Management Plan (ERMP) 5, 81–2, 86, 88, 90, 95, 96, 98, 255

F

face-to-face learning 192
face-to-face meetings 50
face-to-face teaching 193, 208
family life and tensions 16–18
Family-Work-Conflict 196
Floyd, George 138
formal youth justice system 4
frontline workers, importance of 257–9

G

gender-and trauma-informed accommodation 161
Global Drugs Survey 175
grounded theory 15

H

Health Protection Agency 77
Health Protection (Coronavirus) Regulations 2020 137, 139
higher education institutions 208
Higher Education Policy Institute 169
HM Courts & Tribunals Service (HMCTS) 35, 37, 38, 40, 43
HM Crown Prosecution Service Inspectorate (HMCPSI) 35
HM Inspectorate of Probation (HMIP) 90, 91, 96
HMP Manchester 242–6
  COVID-19 diary 246–53
HMP Parc 219–41
HMPPS National Research Committee 52
HM Prison & Probation Service (HMPPS) 79, 84–6, 90, 98, 191, 202
Howard, Michael 192

I

illicit drug market 172
Independent Sexual Violence Adviser (ISVA) 159
instrumental learning 212
International Committee on the Rights of Sex Workers in Europe (2021) 151
international jurisdictions 94
inter-prison transfers (IPTs) 82

J

Judicial Review and Courts Bill 2021 44
Justice Select Committee 190
juvenile sentencing options 113

K

Knife Crime Prevention Orders 126

L

Law Society Gazette, The 40
Legal Aid, Sentencing and Punishment of Offenders Act 2012 52, 127n7
lockdown legislation 53

M

mature organization 12
maturity models 14
mental health cases 248
mental health issues 162
mental health support 159
Misuse of Drugs Act 1971 184
moral rehabilitation 59

N

National Audit Office (NAO) 33, 35, 36
National Framework for Prison Regimes and Services 88
National Health Service 141
National Offender Management Service 192
National Preventive Mechanism 54
National Probation Service (NPS) 50–2, 64, 66, 191
National Ugly Mugs (NUM) 152, 155, 157–9
National Vocational Qualifications (NVQs) 192
National Wellness Institute 204

O

Office for National Statistics (ONS) 169, 171, 172, 179, 181, 182
online child–family visitation 121

P

'pains of imprisonment' thesis 107
personal protective equipment (PPE) 19, 141, 244, 246
personal rehabilitation 59
Police, Crime, Sentencing and Courts Act 2022 145
Police, Crime, Sentencing and Courts Bill 2021 2
police encounters, navigating and managing 142–5
population management strategy 82–3
populist politics vs public health 93–5
portal justice 42–5
post-pandemic justice 42–5
post-pandemic society 23
Prisoners' Education Trust (PET) 243
Prison Governors Association 83, 95
Prison Reform Trust (PRT) 77, 90
prison service 81, 257
Prisons Strategy White Paper 98
Probation Qualification Framework (PQF) 192, 193
Probation Roadmap to Recovery 51

Probation Service 4, 191
process maturity 14
Professional Qualification in Probation (PQiP) 7, 190, 196–206, 258
  approaches to learning 206–10
  method 194–5
  probation training 192–4
  transforming rehabilitation, reunification of probation and probation training 191–2
professional socialization 207
'promotion of diversion' 126
Protective Isolation Units (PIUs) 85
public health safety 163n2

Q

quasi-criminalized laws 150

R

racism 6, 140
'radical socialist model' 70
recreational drug market 177
Referral Order 118
regime management policies 257
rehabilitation 59–62
remote communication 56, 67, 69
remote supervision 65, 66
resilience and preparedness 256–7
'resource based view' 14
Reverse Cohort Unit (RCU) 89
reverse transcription–polymerase chain reaction (RT-PCR) 85
risk and public protection, managing 57–9
risk management service 11

S

Sage EMG Transmission Group 79, 99
scientific community 12
Section 60 of the Criminal Justice and Public Order Act 1994 176–7
Secure Children's Homes (SCHs) 121, 122, 125, 127n10
Secure Training Centres (STCs) 122, 127n10
self-isolation 2
senior probation officers (SPOs) 64
sensemaking, collective in 18–20
severe acute respiratory syndrome coronavirus 2 (SARS-CoV-2) 1
sexual health clinics 156
sexual violence 157
sex work community 163
sex worker client group 158
sex worker peer-led organizations 159
sex worker peer-led responses 159–60
single justice procedure (SJP) 43, 44
social distancing 86
specialist sex work organizations and multiagency partnerships 160–1
spillover theory 196
substitute drugs 184

INDEX

'sustained innovation' 37
SWARM 159
synthetic cannabinoid receptor agonists (SCRAs) 175
synthetic cathinones 175

T
Taleb, Nassim Nicholas
  Black Swan, The 30n2
Target Operating Model 51
'temporary prison accommodation' 87

U
UK Health Security Agency 77
UK justice system 159
UK Network of Sex Work Projects 152
United Nations Convention on the Rights of the Child (UNCRC) 260
unpaid work (UPW) 50, 53, 57, 67, 68

V
virtual hearings 260
virtual justice 259–62
virtual learning environment 208
vulnerability 167

W
work-based competency assessment 192
'work-based distance learning model' 192
Work-Family-Conflict 196
World Health Organization (WHO) 1

Y
Young Offender Institutions (YOIs) 111, 113, 115–19, 121, 122, 126, 127n10, 258
Youth Caution and the Youth Conditional Caution 127n7
Youth Conditional Caution 118
Youth Custody Service (YCS) 127n1, 127n10
youth justice
  engagement in 5
  system 5
Youth Justice Board (YJB) 108–11, 113, 114, 119, 120, 127n1, 127n4, 127n8
youth justice system (YJS) 107, 112, 117, 118, 126
  after initial lockdown 123–4
  child first justice 109–10
  enduring pains and gains of COVID-19 124–6
  in England and Wales 108–9
  initial COVID-19 restrictions affecting 110–11
  pains and gains of COVID-19 111–23
youth unemployment rate 125

www.ingramcontent.com/pod-product-compliance
Lightning Source LLC
Chambersburg PA
CBHW051532020426
42333CB00016B/1888